Faith and Reason

Faith and Reason

The Possibility of a Christian Philosophy

Neil Ormerod

Fortress Press
Minneapolis

FAITH AND REASON
The Possibility of a Christian Philosophy

Cover image: Abstract oil painting on canvas, OttoKrause. iStock item number
476578752.
Cover design: Joe Reinke

Hardcover ISBN: 978-1-5064-3264-9
eBook ISBN: 978-1-5064-0590-2

The paper used in this publication meets the minimum requirements of American
National Standard for Information Sciences — Permanence of Paper for Printed
Library Materials, ANSI Z329.48-1984.

Manufactured in the U.S.A.

Contents

Introduction   1

1. The Debate over a "Christian Philosophy"   3

2. Étienne Gilson and the Possibility of a Christian   35
    Philosophy

3. Bernard Lonergan and the Possibility of a Christian   75
    Philosophy

4. Lonergan and Gilson in Dialogue   119

5. Contemporary Debates on Faith and Reason   147

    Bibliography   177
    Permissions Granted   185
    Index   187

Introduction

The genesis of this project lay in a collaborative research venture between myself and one of my colleagues at the Australian Catholic University on the possibility of a Christian philosophy. Initially, the plan had been to work on a three-way dialogue between Étienne Gilson, Bernard Lonergan and Joseph Ratzinger. While I had expertise in Lonergan, my colleague had the needed expertise in Ratzinger. For us both, the work of Gilson would be a new field to plough. As matters transpired, my colleague departed the university and the academy, leaving me with the option of dropping the project, or doing what I could with the writings of Gilson and Lonergan. In the end this was the more congenial choice, extending my reading into a new and interesting area, while allowing me to bring my own expertise in the work of Lonergan to bear in an explicit and concerted manner.

The plan of the book is simple. I begin by placing the debate over the possibility of a Christian philosophy into its twentieth century context. It was a time of significant renewal of the Thomist tradition, and Gilson and Lonergan both played a significant role in that renewal. Still they took that renewal in different and to some extent opposed directions. In fact Gilson was a harsh critic of so-called transcendental Thomism, while Lonergan is often placed within that movement.

In the second chapter I spell out in some detail Gilson's position on the possibility of a Christian philosophy with attention to his concern with being, and the contribution of Aquinas. Gilson was a strong proponent of the possibility of a Christian philosophy and wrote some significant works on this theme. He brings to philosophy a strong sense of history, so that the history of philosophy becomes a laboratory wherein philosophical experiments succeed or fail. It is a bold position and I hope I have done it justice. His critique of the transcendental approach—once you start with subjectivity you cannot get out—has become a relatively standard criticism of the type of approach Lonergan adopts. I would especially like to thank Daniel De Hann for his strong critique of my first efforts in writing this chapter. He saved me from some misreadings of the Gilsonian texts. Nonetheless, I of course take responsibility for the final version.

Chapter 3 turns to the work of Lonergan, focusing on his early Thomistic works and his philosophical masterpiece, *Insight*. Lonergan is a profound and original thinker who has brought the Thomist tradition into dialogue with modern philosophy, science, and historical method. As with my account of Gilson I have had to keep my focus on questions of faith and reason, and the possibility of a Christian philosophy. This is not a term Lonergan himself adopts, preferring the term "Christian realism," but I argue that in many ways his work exemplifies the sort of thing Gilson had in mind.

In the fourth chapter I bring these two thinkers into dialogue, trying to highlight the similarities, while also locating their specific differences. Overall, I argue that Lonergan both survives the Gilsonian critique and provides a better response particularly in light of the rise of modern science than Gilson is able to do. In MacIntyre's terms, I would say Lonergan's account is rationally superior to that of Gilson.

Finally, in chapter 5, I bring resources from both Gilson and Lonergan to bear on some contemporary debates on three fronts: the rise of the new atheists; the question of religious violence; and the challenges of the Radical Orthodoxy movement. Our two thinkers still have something significant to contribute, I believe, on each of these fronts.

As I noted at the beginning of this introduction, the project had its origin in a larger project. But as I undertook it on my own, another more personal motivation helped push me to its completion. Over the full span of my career I have had friendly but persistent jibes from my friend and colleague Gerald (Gerry) Gleeson that Lonergan is a transcendental idealist. I have come to recognize this jibe as coming out of Gilson's critique of the transcendental turn to the subject. As the project progressed I saw it at least in part as my response to Gerry's comments. So to you, Gerry, if not actually dedicated, at least motivated, this work is offered.

Neil Ormerod

1

The Debate over a "Christian Philosophy"

The debate over the relationship between Christian faith and worldly wisdom has been part of Christianity from its very beginnings. In his first letter to the Corinthians Paul offers only Christ crucified to the Jews who seek miracles and the Greeks seeking wisdom (1 Cor 1:21–23). Yet in the same breath Paul can speak of Jesus as the "power and wisdom of God" (v24) so those who seek wisdom must ultimately be seeking Christ. Faith too has its wisdom to offer and the early Christian Apologists were not slow to compare Jesus with the leading lights of Greek philosophy.[1] A similar tension exists in relation to the power of reason to know the existence of God. In the letter to the Romans Paul initially seems to allow that reason may know of God's existence: "Ever since the creation of the world his eternal power and divine nature, invisible though they are, have been understood and seen through the things he has made" (Rom 1:20). Yet immediately Paul will add: "for though they knew God, they did not honor him as God or give thanks to him, but they became futile in their thinking, and their senseless minds were darkened" (Rom 1:21). Sin has perverted human reasoning making it futile and senseless.

As we move beyond the immediate apostolic era and find the cultural range of those converting to Christianity increasing, we begin to

------

1. Some of the earliest artistic depictions of Jesus by the early church present him as Greek philosopher.

identify persons who bring to their Christian faith a deeper level of learning in the philosophies of the day. Justin Martyr (c. 100–160 CE), for example, was well versed in the various philosophical schools of the day, and used his learning to provide a defense, or apology, for Christian faith. Drawing on the Logos-Christology of John's Gospel, he was able to connect the Christian narrative with philosophical speculations within Stoicism and Platonism, both of which referred to *logos* as divine reason. This allowed him to claim that Christianity is the "true philosophy" since it alone knows the true Logos which enlightens all peoples. Indeed wherever we find true human wisdom it is because the "seeds of the Logos" (*sperma tou logou*) had been sowed in their minds.[2]

We find a more dialectic attitude in the work of Tertullian (160–220 CE) who posed the question, "What has Athens (Greek philosophy) to do with Jerusalem (Christian faith)?"[3] Despite this more polemic stance, Tertullian, who was well versed in Roman law and had absorbed Stoic thought prior to his conversion to Christianity, provided us with some of our more enduring philosophical categories in relation to Trinitarian theology. To him we owe the first use of the terminology of substance (*substantia*) and person (*persona*) which were to become enshrined in Christian doctrine. Yet even here, his dependence on Stoic thought-forms misled him into a subordinationist stance because he could only conceive of substance in a materialist sense. For Tertullian, the Son was extruded from the substance of the Father and so has a beginning in time; moreover angels, and even God, all have bodies, composed of "spiritual" substance.[4]

This ongoing dance of faith and reason, theology and philosophy, divine and human wisdom, has been a crucial feature of Christian thought since Christianity's inception. At times it has been a close embrace; at others a more stand-offish posture has been adopted. In some writers, faith clearly takes the lead, setting the parameters, rhythm, and tempo of the dance, perhaps overwhelming reason to the point of absorption; in other writers, reason seems to lead the dance and faith may be led in directions it would rather not go. For all his evangelical adherence to Christian faith, Tertullian was misled by his

2. See the treatment of Justin's work in John Behr, *The Way to Nicaea*, The Formation of Christian Theology; v. 1 (Crestwood, NY: St. Vladimir's Seminary Press, 2001).
3. Tertullian, *De praescriptione*, vii.
4. Bernard J. F. Lonergan, *The Way to Nicea: The Dialectical Development of Trinitarian Theology*, trans. Conn O'Donovan (London: Darton, Longman & Todd, 1976). This is available now in new translation in *The Triune God: Doctrines*, ed. Robert M. Doran and H. Daniel Monsour, trans. Michael Shields, Collected Works of Bernard Lonergan (Toronto: University of Toronto Press, 2009), 29–255.

philosophical commitments and was judged harshly by future gen-
erations, as was Origen (184/185–253/254 CE), whose middle Platonism also eventuated in subordinationism.[5] If we scroll forward to more
recent times, the dance between faith and reason has grown even more
complex to encompass questions in relation to the natural sciences,
historical reason, and now the social sciences. Within such an expand-
ing frame, it is not just theology that struggles to find its proper place,
but also philosophy which must labor to identify its specific set of concerns to justify its place within the academy.[6]

The Basic Question

Against this backdrop we can ask the question, "Is a Christian philosophy possible?" However, in asking the question in this form we should
note how the ground has shifted over the centuries. For Justin and Tertullian philosophy could refer to a way of life characterized by a love of
or search for wisdom. It was not so much a "profession" as a calling or
vocation to follow the divine impulse of reason within. In these terms a
"Christian philosophy" was possible because Christ is nothing less than
divine Wisdom itself. One could easily push the argument further to
claim that "Christianity is the only *true* philosophy" because it alone
knows true Wisdom. However, over time, and certainly in our own era,
philosophy has become an autonomous academic discipline with various schools and approaches, not all on good terms with one another.[7]
In the present context the notion of a "Christian philosophy" can be
viewed as an affront to the autonomy of the discipline, an attempt to
reimpose dogmatic strictures on what can and cannot be claimed as
true, not on the basis of reason "alone" but on traditional religious
authority. Christian philosophy is then oxymoronic, a self-contradic-
tion, not to be tolerated in intelligent company.

The question may then need to be reframed to ask about the relationship between faith and reason. Faith is both a gift from God and
a call to obedience to what God has revealed. Not just an inner con-

---

5. Lonergan, *Way to Nicea*, 56–67.
6. Of course the term "philosophy" used to encompass the natural sciences, political thought, ethics, and so on. With the scientific revolution science separated itself from philosophy while the human sciences hived off into social, economic, and political thought. What then is the proper "object" of philosophical enquiry? In the Anglo-American sphere philosophy has retreated into the analysis of ordinary language through conceptual clarification and the use of logic, referred to as analytic philosophy.
7. One might think, for example, of the dividing line between Anglo-American analytic philosophy and European approaches which are more phenomenological.

viction, it has cognitive contents, beliefs which a believer is called to uphold as true regardless of the apparent demands of reason or circumstances of moral pressure. Christians may be willing to die for their beliefs, or perhaps misguided enough to even kill for them. Even apart from the debate over faith and reason, there has been a long history of dispute over the precise boundaries of what is to be believed as revealed by God as true. For the early church it concerned issues of Trinitarian and Christological doctrine; now the battle ground has shifted to questions about evolution, homosexuality and women in ministry. Is the Bible sufficient? What role has tradition? What about ecclesial authority? These are all debates internal to belief. They do not exclude the use of reason, but in the dance of faith and reason, faith is clearly the leading indeed dominant partner.

On the other hand, the notion of reason is also not that clear cut or univocal. In a broad and general sense what people consider reasonable has varied from one place and time, one culture, to another. In the United States it is considered reasonable for citizens to carry arms, while in many countries carrying arms may cause one to be arrested. In ancient times, gladiatorial battles to the death in stadiums packed with cheering crowds were considered normal; now we seek to protect our star athletes from sustaining any life-threatening injury, and rightly so. In many societies over human history an appeal to tradition ("this is the way we have always done things"), religious or not, was considered sufficient warrant to continue along the same path. In fact it is difficult to conceive of a society where some such appeal is never invoked as a way to hold onto certain procedures or processes that have worked in the past.[8] If by reason we mean an appeal to such general plausibility structures or background beliefs constitutive of a society or particular community, then reason is very fluid and relative to one's time and place. Here the distinction between faith and reason begins to blur, as faith becomes just another plausibility structure to be invoked by some communities but not others.

However, we might mean reason in a very precise and exact sense of particular cognitive activities and processes; or a particular method which is reason *par excellence* against which other claims to being reason simply pale into insignificance. Certainly logic will play a role, but so will creative insight, careful judgment, sifting of evidence and so on. If we are to discuss the relationship between faith and reason at

8. Most nations hold on to symbols and traditions (flags, constitutions, rituals of taking office) of the past to enact the present authorization of political authority.

this more critical level we must begin with a relatively precise account of reason itself, its activities, processes and procedures, to see exactly how and why it differs from faith and how the two may or may not relate to one another. Yet here we strike real problems, and particularly philosophical problems. Despite all their efforts, philosophers have produced not one account of reason, but several, each seeking to provide the "real" account of how reason operates. Broadly we may identify *empiricist* accounts of knowing which focus on the operation of the senses and their material objects. There are *idealists* who highlight the creative role of the knowing subject but differ as to its significance. And so there are Kantian, Platonic and Hegelian idealists all of whom give different accounts of knowing and its relationship to reality. And finally there are *realists* who acknowledge the role of intelligence in the subject while asserting knowledge of reality, but these too may be naïve, dogmatic or critical realists, each affirming something different in the operations of reason and their relationship to what is real.[9] On what basis do we adopt one over the other?

At this stage, moreover, the modern debate has been largely hijacked by the dogmatic assertion that scientific knowing and its methodology are the only valid ways of conceiving reason.[10] This is particularly evident in the arguments of the new atheists and their followers who assert a hegemonic dominance of modern science to the exclusion of theological, philosophical, and other forms of knowing which do not conform to their particular conception of science. This is often joined with an extra-scientific, in fact metaphysical, account of reality in reductionist terms. Behind these claims one can often identify relatively naïve accounts of the knowing process, often an odd mix of overconfidence in logic and an empiricist/materialist account of knowing and reality.[11]

And so the question of the relationship between faith and reason throws up many difficulties on both sides of the equation. Not only whose faith, but whose account of reason and rationality will we take as normative and why? Which definition of philosophy and whose brand of Christianity do we adopt to answer the question of the possibility of a "Christian philosophy"? In order to keep some level of con-

9. Of course apart from these cognitional concerns there are philosophies which focus on ethical/moral issues, existential philosophies, political philosophies, and so on.
10. This is particularly evident in the writing of the "new atheists" such as Richard Dawkins, Christopher Hitchens and others.
11. See for example Neil Ormerod, "Bernard Lonergan and the Recovery of a Metaphysical Frame," in *Theological Studies* 74 (2013): 960–82.

trol over these issues I shall focus on a particular religious and philosophical tradition, that of Western Christianity. Within that Christian tradition I shall narrow the focus onto the contributions of two key figures, Augustine of Hippo (354–430) and Thomas Aquinas (1225–1274), giants of the Western Christian intellectual tradition. The impact of their contributions continues to echo within contemporary debates on these issues. The focus shall tighten to the ways these debates have been formulated within Catholic Christianity in the twentieth century, where both ecclesial authorities, theologians and philosophers, have all made sophisticated contributions. Within the confines of the present study the focus shall grow tighter onto the work of two outstanding Christian thinkers of the twentieth century, Étienne Gilson and Bernard Lonergan, both inheritors of the Thomistic tradition, though both have received that tradition in significantly different ways.

Augustine and the Platonic Turn

Together Augustine and Aquinas have shaped every aspect of Catholic theological thought and impacted significantly debates on the relationship between grace and nature, faith and reason, theology and philosophy. To raise questions about the possibility of a Christian philosophy is to engage of necessity with these two thinkers. Yet both are so vast in their outputs as to defy easy summary or characterization. Without seeking to do justice to the wealth of literature each of these figures has produced and the commentaries their work has generated, I shall focus on particular aspects which are relevant to the present discussion.

The first and most significant issue to raise is the impact of Platonic (or more precisely neo-Platonic) thought on Augustine. It is not clear whether Augustine read directly the work of Plato, but he is very clear that he read the work of unnamed "Platonists."[12] This is directly indicated in the *Confessions*, Book 7, where he explains how his reading of these authors assisted in his own "intellectual conversion" away from thinking of reality as "out there" in space and time and began to think of reality in terms of "truth." As he narrates: "I was still forced to imagine something corporeal spread out in space, whether infused into the world or even diffused through the infinity outside it . . . because any-

---

12. The exact identity of Augustine's Platonic influences has been open to debate. For a discussion see Brian Dobell, *Augustine's Intellectual Conversion: the Journey from Platonism to Christianity* (Cambridge: Cambridge University Press, 2009).

thing to which I denied these spatial dimensions seemed to me to be nothing at all" (7,1,1).[13] However with the assistance of these Platonic authors he begins to view reality differently: "Is truth then a nothing, simply because it is not spread out through space, either finite or infinite?" The reality of truth is now as real to Augustine as his own existence: "no possibility of doubt remained in me; I could more easily have doubted that I was alive than that truth exists, truth that is seen and understood through things that are made" (7,10,16).[14] Nonetheless, while these authors helped eliminate a hindrance to Augustine's full conversion to Christian faith, of themselves they are insufficient to get him over the line. While he acknowledges the fact that they introduced him to the Logos/Word ("not the same words were used, but precisely the same doctrine was taught, buttressed by many and various arguments" [7.9.13]),[15]

> But that he came to his own home, and his own people did not receive him; but to those who did receive him he gave the power to become children of God; to those, that is, who believe in his name—none of this did I read there. (7.9.13)[16]

Clearly Augustine recognizes here both continuity and discontinuity between faith and reason. Reason, mediated through his reading of the Platonists, could lead him to acknowledge the divine reason as creator and sustainer of the world, but not lead him to recognize that this divine reason had become incarnate in human history. For that revelation and faith are needed.

The second issue is Augustine's understanding of human cognition and the role of divine illumination in knowing. This is part of his Platonic heritage and suffers from the issues that commonly arise therein.[17] Most notably there is a problem of how to relate Platonic "ideals" to our human knowledge of the world we live in. The ideals are in the mind of God, unchanging and unchangeable, whereas the human mind is inconstant and mutable. For Augustine, following the neo-Platonist, Plotinus, held that in order for the mind to know the ideals, it requires an illumination from outside itself, from God: "The mind needs to be enlightened by light from outside itself, so that it can

---

13. Augustine, *The Confessions*, trans. Maria Boulding (New York: Vintage Books, 1998), 159.
14. Ibid., 173.
15. Ibid., 170.
16. Ibid.
17. See Alasdair MacIntyre, *Three Rival Versions of Moral Enquiry: Encyclopaedia, Genealogy, and Tradition* (Notre Dame, IN: University of Notre Dame Press, 1990), 100–101.

participate in truth, because it is not itself the nature of truth. You will light my lamp, Lord" (*Confessions*, IV.xv.25).[18] There is some ambiguity in relation to the nature of this illumination, whether it be direct content infused into the mind by God, or a divine light which enables us to know the ideals. However, what appears clear is that human knowing is dependent on our relationship to God. Where this relationship is broken through sin, then it would seem to imply that we can no longer know anything. This was a conclusion Augustine was willing to draw, though one he would later regret: "I do not approve having said in the prayer, O God, Who dost wish the sinless alone to know the truth; for it may be answered that many who are not sinless know many truths."[19] However, this retraction does not resolve the issue of the role of illumination; it merely highlights the difficulty of the position.

A third issue, not unrelated to his illuminationism, is raised by Augustine's repeated reference to the text of Isaiah 7:9 (LXX) in its Latin translation: "Unless you believe, you will not understand."[20] This text has particular significance with regard to the relationship between faith and reason, precisely because it appears to prioritize faith as necessary in order that reason achieves its goal of understanding. This may give some credence to those who would argue that for Augustine faith not only trumps reason, but it is only within the realm of faith that reason is truly reasonable. Christian philosophy would then be the only true philosophy. However, it is important to attend to the contexts within which Augustine uses this text. A couple of examples will suffice. In *De Libero Arbitrio* (On Free Will) he refers to the text twice. In the first instance the problem he is dealing with is how to avoid laying blame for sin back to God, if "everything which exists is created by one God."[21] This is indeed a profound and difficult theological question. In the second instance the context is also clearly one of theological understanding: "unless we ought to start by believing any important question of theology which we wish to understand."[22] Similarly in *De Trinitate* (On the Trinity), the first use of the text occurs at

---

18. Also see Augustine, *The City of God*, trans. Marcus Dods, Book 10, ch. 2: "Plotinus, commenting on Plato, repeatedly and strongly asserts that not even the soul which they believe to be the soul of the world, derives its blessedness from any other source than we do, viz, from that Light which is distinct from it and created it, and by whose intelligible illumination it enjoys light in things intelligible." Available at http://www.newadvent.org/fathers/120110.htm.

19. Retact i. 4. Quoted in *STh* I–II q109 a1.

20. He references this text in various works including *De Trinitate, De Libero Arbitrio, Contra Faustum Manichaeum, De Fide et Symbolo*, to name a few.

21. *De Libero Arbitrio*, Book 1, 2.4.

22. *De Libero Arbitrio*, Book 2, 3.5.

the end of Book 7 where Augustine is seeking to transition the reader from his account of the inner Trinitarian relations to Book 8 where he will seek to understand those relations through an analogy with certain psychological operations. Though the text from Isaiah is clearly a favorite text for Augustine, its applicability is often directly in relation to understanding the mysteries of faith. It would be difficult to extend it to a general epistemological principle.

The Augustinian synthesis of Christian faith with neo-Platonic philosophy provided a robust intellectual framework for theological reflection throughout the early Middle Ages. However, as can be seen from the few comments above, part of that legacy included problems and dilemmas that needed to be resolved. If one accepts at face value the theory of divine illumination and a general priority of faith over reason and understanding, then one may well conclude that only a Christian philosophy can be a true philosophy. But even Augustine could recognize the difficulties of his account of illumination while his putative priority of faith over reason may only be applicable within a theological context of faith seeking understanding.

Aquinas and the Aristotelian Revival

There is a well-established and almost traditional narrative concerning the impact of the discovery of Aristotelian texts on the Middle Ages in general and upon the work of Thomas Aquinas in particular.[23] While there has more recently been an attempt to move him more towards a Platonic position, particularly in the writings of John Milbank,[24] and a growing appreciation of the Platonic structure of exodus and return in the basic architecture of the *Summa Theologiae*,[25] there remain more than substantial grounds to keep Aquinas well within the Aristotelian camp, particularly in relation to his metaphysics, his account of cognition, and his ethics.[26]

However, prior to taking up this issue, we need to attend to another context within which Aquinas was operating. Just prior to Aquinas, the high Middle Ages had made an important theological breakthrough that was to shape all future theological development. Philip, Chancel-

---

23. See for example Aidan Nichols, *Discovering Aquinas: An Introduction to his Life, Work, and Influence* (Grand Rapids, MI: Eerdmans, 2003); Marie-Dominique Chenu, *Aquinas and his Role in Theology* (Collegeville, MN: Liturgical Press, 2002).
24. John Milbank and Catherine Pickstock, *Truth in Aquinas* (New York: Routledge, 2001).
25. Chenu, *Aquinas and his Role in Theology*, 98.
26. Aquinas's ethics are overwhelmingly influenced by Aristotle's *Nichomachean Ethics*.

lor of the University of Paris (1218–1230), introduced into theology "the theory of two orders, entitatively disproportionate: not only was there the familiar series of grace, faith, charity, and merit, but also nature, reason, and the natural love of God."[27] The ability to make such a distinction was itself built upon an Aristotelian understanding of natures as the metaphysical determinant of the activities of a being. This breakthrough allowed for the resolution of unresolved tensions in the earlier Augustinian framework on grace that tended to view human nature as empirically given, and hence more fluid and changeable (for example, human nature was different prior to the fall, after the fall, and redeemed in Christ) than the metaphysically stable notion of human nature that emerges in Aristotelian metaphysics. The significant word here is two "orders." Often we find this distinction shifting to a separation producing a two-layered account of human existence, whereas the term order should evoke a sense of relative ordering and structure within a whole.[28] What this ordering and structure are remain to be discovered. As Lonergan has noted, the distinction made it possible, for example, "(1) to discuss the nature of grace without discussing liberty, (2) to discuss the nature of liberty without discussing grace, and (3) to work out the relations between grace and liberty."[29] In our context it will lead to a discussion of faith and reason, each in their proper turn, and then an attempt to work out the relations between them without collapsing either into the other. Aquinas's theology represents the most comprehensive incorporation of this theoretical breakthrough that has been bequeathed to us by the tradition.

We can witness the power and significance of this breakthrough in relation to questions of faith and reason as Aquinas is working out the implications of the introduction of the grace-nature distinction in the *Summa Theologiae*. In *STh* I–II q109 a1 Aquinas begins his account of grace by focusing on a very precise point of tension in the illuminationist position of Augustine: Whether a man can know any truth without grace? After noting objections to the position, drawn from the writings of Augustine, and then noting Augustine's own retraction of those objections Aquinas seeks his own response. He acknowledges that to

27. Bernard J. F. Lonergan, *Grace and Freedom: Operative Grace in the Thought of St. Thomas Aquinas*, ed. Frederick E. Crowe and Robert M. Doran, Collected Works of Bernard Lonergan (Toronto: University of Toronto Press, 2000), 17.
28. We see this shift when the term "order" is replaced by terms such as "sphere" or "realm." In modern parlance we might speak of dimensions rather than orders, which though less precise than orders is better than spheres or realms.
29. Bernard J. F. Lonergan, *Method in Theology* (London: Darton, Longman & Todd, 1972), 310.

know anything at all requires God's help (*divinum auxilium*), but such help should not be equated with a grace which brings salvation:

> We must therefore say that, if a man is to know any truth whatsoever, he needs divine help in order that his intellect may be moved to its act by God. But he does not need a new light added to his natural light in order to know the truth in all things, but only in such things as transcend his natural knowledge.[30]

Thus there is a "natural light" of intellect proportionate to natural human knowledge, but there is also the possibility of a revealed knowledge which requires something added to this natural light, that is, the light of faith. While he will acknowledge that this natural light is a created participation in the divine light, it remains proper to human nature as such, a participation in, not a sharing of, the divine intellect. Here the grace-nature distinction impinges directly onto our question of the faith-reason debate.

The respect Aquinas has for Aristotle is further evident in his repeated references to him as "the Philosopher." For Aquinas, Aristotle is the philosopher *par excellence*. This respect does not equate with a slavish following of Aristotle in all aspects, but it does indicate the basic orientation of Aquinas's thought. In his earliest major work, *De Esse et Essentia*, we find an extensive engagement with the metaphysics of Aristotle, who is present simply as "the philosopher." Aquinas finds himself in repeated agreement with Aristotle (often noting, "as the philosopher says . . ."). On the other hand, the Platonic position (as Aquinas understood it) which separated the ideal from the real—"the notion of the genus, or of the species, belongs to an essence as to some real thing existing outside singular things"—is simply rejected out of hand. The text is replete with references to Aristotelian terminology of potency and act, matter and form, whereas the characteristic Platonic notion of participation is not to be found. Of course, Thomas will depart from Aristotle in arguing that form is not the cause of act, and that a distinct cause for act or the act of existence must be found. Classically, this is expressed as the real distinction between essence and existence, a position already present in this early work.[31] Only in God is

---

30. Throughout this book all quotations from Aquinas's *Summa Theologiae* are from Benziger Bros. edition, translated by Fathers of the English Dominican Province (1947).
31. Thomas Aquinas, *De Esse et Essentia*, 77: "Now, every essence or quiddity can be understood without anything being understood about its existence. For I can understand what a man is, or what a phoenix is, and yet not know whether they have existence in the real world. It is clear, therefore,

existence identical to essence. Of course in his later works Aquinas will speak of the relationship between the existence of God and the creature in terms of the Platonic term, participation, but the underlying structure remains Aristotelian. Also one may claim that the source of the insight that essence and existence are distinct may be traced back to the revelation of the divine name in Exodus—"I am who I am"—but nonetheless Aquinas's handling of the question here is clearly philosophical, not theological.[32]

This preference for an Aristotelian stance over and against a Platonic one is further evidenced in Aquinas's account of cognition or reasoning. In the *Summa Contra Gentiles*, Book 2, ch. 98, 12–20, Aquinas notes that there are two distinct, even opposed, views of knowing. For Aristotle, knowing is by identity: "Accordingly, the intellect, the thing understood, and the act of understanding are the same." In an act of understanding the intellect in some sense ("intentionally") *becomes* the thing understood. This he contrasts with the Platonic approach in which "understanding is effected through the contact of the intellect with the intelligible thing." This position prioritizes or highlights the duality of knowing, of knower and known, not their identity.[33] It is clear from the whole tenor of the *SCG* that Aquinas adopts the Aristotelian position over the Platonic one on just about everything.[34]

While this specifies one aspect of Aquinas's cognitional approach— identity versus confrontation—and its epistemological implications, it can hardly claim to be a full account of his approach to the question of knowing. However, it is difficult at this stage to say more, in part because of the complexities of the issue, and in part because the diversity of understanding of Aquinas on this point will become evident as we consider the distinctive approaches of Gilson and Lonergan on the question. I will note, though, Lonergan's reference to the work of Georges van Riet who "needed over six hundred pages to outline the various types of Thomist epistemology that have been put forward in the last century and a half."[35] Aquinas's position on cognitional

that existence is other than essence or quiddity, unless perhaps there exists a thing whose quiddity is its existence." Available at http://dhspriory.org/thomas/english/DeEnte&Essentia.htm.

32. Significantly the Exodus text only appears a handful of times in the *Summa Theologiae*, more as a theological prop than a proof text.

33. Lonergan will refer to this as knowing through "confrontation." Bernard J. F. Lonergan, *Verbum: Word and Idea in Aquinas*, ed. Frederick E. Crowe and Robert M. Doran, Collected Works of Bernard Lonergan (Toronto: University of Toronto Press, 1997), 192.

34. As Aquinas notes in relation to Plato's account of the soul in relation to the body, "But this doctrine seems not to fit the facts," *SCG* Book 2, ch. 57, 3. Plato's positions are regularly mentioned only to be repudiated.

and epistemological questions must be rescontructed from a variety of sources, and the process of reconstruction is inevitably influenced by the horizon of the interpreter, which may include presuppositions already aligned to viewing knowing in terms of identity or of confrontation.

Given the stature of Aquinas he will inevitably be enlisted by each side of the discussion on the possibility of a Christian philosophy. On the one hand there will be those who invoke his name to argue for the impossibility of a "Christian philosophy," on the grounds of a strict separation of faith and reason, theology, and philosophy. For these Aquinas is a Christian philosopher only in the sense that he is a Christian undertaking philosophy. On the other hand, and less plausibly, there are those who read Aquinas as thoroughly Platonic-Augustinian leading to the conclusion that only a Christian philosophy is a true philosophy. Finally, there will be those somewhere in the broad middle of this divide who find in Aquinas the paradigm of what it means to be a Christian philosopher, one who consistently maintains the distinction between faith and reason, but whose faith position has helped shape his philosophy, not necessarily through the content of faith, but in the ways in which the demands of faith have brought about a refinement and deepening of various philosophical topics.

Aeterni Patris and the Intellectual Recovery of Aquinas

The pontificate of Leo XIII witnessed the production of some seventy-seven encyclicals during his twenty-five year reign. The two most significant offerings of this vast output were his best known encyclical, *Rerum Novarum* (1891), which addressed the "new things" of industrialization, the plight of the worker, and the nascent labor union movement; and *Aeterni Patris* (1879), an attempt to counter the intellectual decadence into which Catholic theology and philosophy had fallen during the eighteenth and nineteenth centuries, by holding forth the work of Thomas Aquinas as the gold standard of Catholic thought. He called on Catholic scholars to once again turn to the medieval genius through a reading of his original text, in order to reform their disciplines. Significantly for our current project, the subtitle of the encyclical was "On the restoration of Christian Philosophy," though the term "Christian

---

35. Bernard J. F. Lonergan, *Insight: A Study of Human Understanding*, ed. Crowe Frederick E. and Robert M. Doran, Collected Works of Bernard Lonergan (Toronto: University of Toronto Press, 1992), 433. The work referred to is G. van Riet, *L'Épistémologie Thomiste. Recherches Sur Le Problème de la Connaissance Dans L'école Thomiste Contemporaine* (1946).

philosophy" does not appear in the body of the text. While Leo recapitulates the contributions of various Christian thinkers over the centuries to the issue at hand, with special mention of Augustine, once he begins to talk about Aquinas (for the first time in n. 14), his work dominates the discussion. Thomas is the "chief and master of all towers . . . rightly and deservedly esteemed the special bulwark and glory of the Catholic faith" (AP n. 17); indeed "faith could scarcely expect more or stronger aids from reason than those which she has already obtained through Thomas" (AP n. 18). In the end Leo gives Aquinas a ringing endorsement:

> While, therefore, We hold that every word of wisdom, every useful thing by whomsoever discovered or planned, ought to be received with a willing and grateful mind, We exhort you, venerable brethren, in all earnestness to restore the golden wisdom of St. Thomas, and to spread it far and wide for the defense and beauty of the Catholic faith, for the good of society, and for the advantage of all the sciences. (AP n. 31)

Given this ringing papal endorsement, Catholic philosophers and theologians could not but respond by returning to the thought of Aquinas. Nonetheless this return did not produce a single outcome but produced at least three broad approaches to Thomas in response to the emerging cultural forces of the day.

Neo-Thomism

One form of Thomism sought to continue within the wake of the great commentators of Aquinas, who had forged the identity of Scholasticism. In the first instance theological issues could be settled by an appeal to a text from the master. Where there was some doubt or apparent contradiction within the texts of the master, one would appeal to the great commentators of the master to settle the matter; and if no resolution was to be found one would attempt to resolve the matter oneself. A good resolution would be found in making a proper distinction and so establishing both the meaning of the text and eliminating the apparent contradiction. This approach also tended to take a hostile stance to modernity. Other philosophical positions were so many adversaries to be vanquished, not dialogue partners with whom one might engage in mutual fruitful dialogue. The development of modern science generally passed them by as it was not viewed as relevant to their own positions. And critical history, a major cultural advance of the eighteenth and nineteenth centuries, made little impact on their methodology. Authors were generally not considered as products of their eras within a particular social and cultural context, but as texts that spoke equally to every age.

At its best this approach produced impressive intellectual constructs which consolidated Christian belief within a single overarching perspective. At its worst it produced an a-historical conceptualism, more interested in words and concepts than the questions and insights that generated them or the realities they intended.[36] Their systems were indeed impressive, once one accepted their basic premises, but a growing number of Catholic intellectuals found the price of accepting them far too high.[37] As the Catholic Church turned toward a less hostile and more open stance in relation to the "world" after Vatican II, it began adopting critical historical methods in reading Scripture and other historical texts, and took modern sciences, both natural and social, into consideration. Inevitably the approach of the Neo-Thomists began to look more and more dated. While it still survives in some quarters, with its own journals and some teaching institutions, it is unlikely to experience the dominance it once had in Catholic intellectual thought during the early twentieth-century.

Historical Thomism

With their initial development, the methods of critical history applied to a reading of the Bible often resulted in less than happy outcomes. The first quest for the historical Jesus deployed the method as a way of separating Jesus from the Church, seeking to get behind the ecclesially constructed "Christ of faith" to discover the "Jesus of history." This caused rightful alarm among ecclesial authorities reaching its climax with the Modernist crisis towards the end of the nineteenth century and the beginning of the twentieth century. Catholic scholars were required to take an oath against Modernism which precluded the use of critical historical methods to interpret the Bible. However, it did not preclude their use in other settings, such as patristic sources or in the history of philosophy. Catholic scholars began to use the methods of critical history in producing critical editions of ancient texts, in grasp-

---

36. On the sources of this conceptualism see Nick Olkovich, "Conceptualism, Classicism and Bernard Lonergan's Retrieval of Aquinas," *Pacifica* 26, no. 1 (2013): 37–58.

37. Among those who turned against the scholastic Neo-Thomism of the day is a who's who of twentieth century Catholic intellectuals: Yves Congar, Henri de Lubac, Karl Rahner, Hans Urs von Balthasar, Bernard Lonergan, Edward Schillebeeckx, and Joseph Ratzinger.

ing their historical ordering, and in filling out the social and cultural context of their thought forms.

Still it is perhaps not surprising that some of the outstanding proponents of this approach came from outside normal (clerical) Catholic intellectual life, their training gained in "secular" environments. Étienne Gilson (1884–1978) studied philosophy at the Sorbonne, immersing himself in the history of philosophy. His output was prodigious and he was a tireless proponent of the work of Thomas Aquinas, read as Gilson read him. Gilson was able to locate Aquinas within the dynamic flow of philosophical ideas in the medieval era. In particular Gilson championed the idea of there being a "Christian philosophy" with the work of Thomas Aquinas being the prime exemplar.[38] Jacques Maritain (1882–1973) was born to Protestant parents, became agnostic, but converted to Catholicism at the age of twenty-four. He too studied at the Sorbonne, but in the natural sciences, taking up philosophy at a later stage of life. In some ways he was closer to the Neo-Thomists than Gilson, but he sought to bring Thomism into dialogue with modern science and political thought, being a key player in the development of the United Nations Universal Declaration on Human Rights. A more recent thinker in the same mold is Alasdair MacIntyre (1929–), another convert to Catholicism while in his fifties. MacIntyre was a philosophical prodigy, initially drawn to Marxism, but seems to have reasoned himself into Catholicism on the basis of its intellectual coherence, at least in its Thomistic form. The influence of Aquinas on his thought comes through all the stronger in his later works, but it is always an Aquinas read historically, as part of an intellectual tradition MacIntyre wants to make historically self-conscious through his notion of a tradition of rationality.[39] I shall appeal to this notion as a way of reading the construction of a Christian philosophy later in this work.

This approach of historical Thomism helped alleviate the risk of intellectual stagnation within Thomism more broadly. It was more willing to locate Aquinas within his world, to delineate more clearly where his work fit within the history of ideas, and bring him into a more fruitful dialogue with contemporary thought. It gave Thomism a

38. Étienne Gilson, *The Christian Philosophy of St. Thomas Aquinas*, trans. I. T. Eschmann (New York: Random House, 1956).

39. One can trace the growing influence of Aquinas from Alasdair MacIntyre, *After Virtue: A Study in Moral Theory*, 2nd ed. (Notre Dame, IN: University of Notre Dame Press, 1984); *Whose Justice? Which Rationality?* (Notre Dame, IN: University of Notre Dame Press, 1988); *Three Rival Versions*. This is the decade of his conversion. On the relationship between MacIntyre and Gilson see Peter Mango, "MacIntyre's Gilsonian Preference," *Studia Gilsoniana* 2 (2013): 21–32.

broader intellectual standing as the standing of figures such as Gilson, Maritain and MacIntyre transcended the boundaries of Catholicism or even Christianity.[40]

Transcendental Thomism

A third approach has been labelled, rightly or wrongly, "transcendental Thomism."[41] It began with various philosophers in Leuven who wanted to bring Thomas into dialogue with streams in contemporary philosophy, in particular with the approaches of René Descartes and Immanuel Kant. These two figures were representative of the modern "turn to the subject," a shift away from the more classical metaphysical approach of Aquinas and scholasticism, towards questions of cognition and epistemology. For Kant this shift was a Copernican revolution in philosophy. Just as Copernicus had shifted our view of the cosmos from a geocentric model to heliocentric, so the turn to the subject shifted the priority of philosophy from metaphysics, the study of being, from which all other issues were secondary and derivative, to a priority of cognition and knowledge, from which other issues would then be dealt with. Descartes's famous "Cogito ergo sum," "I think and so I am," was indicative of such a shift, though Kant's implementation was far more radical and influential. The position of the Leuven Thomists, notably Joseph Maréchal (1887–1944), was that the turn to the subject as found in Kant could be brought into alignment with Thomistic cognitional and epistemological theories and lead eventually to a Thomistic metaphysics.[42]

The two most famous names associated with this approach are Karl Rahner (1904–1984) and Bernard Lonergan (1904–1984). Rahner's initial doctorate in philosophy, on Thomistic questions of knowledge, later published as *Spirit in the World*, was rejected as too Kantian.[43] Still Hegel and Heidegger had more influence in the long run on Rahner than Kant. Certainly his work is representative of the "transcendental turn to the subject" as he himself would acknowledge.[44] It is difficult to overestimate the impact on Catholic theology of Rahner's work dur-

---

40. This is very evident in the widespread interest in and discussion of the work of MacIntyre in contemporary moral philosophy.
41. Otto Muck, *The Transcendental Method* (New York: Herder and Herder, 1968).
42. Joseph Donceel, ed. and trans., *A Maréchal Reader* (New York: Herder & Herder, 1970).
43. Karl Rahner, *Spirit in the World* (New York: Bloomsbury, 1994). Given this knockback Rahner went on to quickly complete a doctorate in theology. The rest, as they say, is history.
44. This is very evident in his classical work *Foundations of Christian Faith: An Introduction to the Idea of Christianity* (New York: Crossroad, 1982).

ing the twentieth century. He was a prolific writer on a wide range of topics, though on his own admission he was not a systematic thinker and his contributions were often more ad hoc and pastoral.[45] Though his reputation tended to wane in the later part of the twentieth century—many for ecclesially political reasons—he remains a theological giant.

As prolific as Rahner was, Lonergan's output was more measured, almost circumspect.[46] His main outputs were two major books, *Insight: A Study of Human Understanding*, and *Method in Theology*.[47] Prior to this he wrote in article and thesis format major studies on Aquinas that were subsequently published as books,[48] and three collections of essays, papers published or presented in various settings.[49] Since his death there has been a major publishing project to produce his collected works, which includes course material from his stints teaching,[50] and personal projects such as two volumes on economics.[51] As Lonergan is a focus of a later chapter, I shall say more on the nature of his work then.

Despite the association with such significant figures, this approach to reading Thomas has not been without its philosophical critics, perhaps most vocal of all being Gilson. Gilson argued that the turn to the subject present within this approach inevitably ended up with a self-enclosed subject unable to break out to make contact with reality. By conceding the idealist starting point, the inevitable outcome was idealism, not the realism inherent in Thomism. Gilson prosecuted his case

45. The twenty-plus volumes of his *Theological Investigations* represent only a fraction of his output, which included theological encyclopedias and dictionaries, books, meditations, prayers, and so on.

46. In this regard, Lonergan is more reminiscent of the mathematical genius, Carl Friedrich Gauss whose personal motto was "Few but Ripe." Gauss published little because he judged his work not up to the absolute standard of perfection he held to. It is claimed his unpublished notebooks could have advanced mathematics by fifty years or more.

47. First published as Bernard J. F. Lonergan, *Insight: A Study of Human Understanding* (London: Darton, Longman & Todd, 1958). A critical edition has now appeared in the Collected Works of Bernard Lonergan.

48. Lonergan, *Grace and Freedom*; Lonergan, *Verbum*.

49. Unimaginatively called *Collection*, ed. Frederick E. Crowe and Robert M. Doran, 2nd ed, Collected Works of Bernard Lonergan (Toronto: Toronto University Press, 1988); *A Second Collection*, ed. William F. Ryan and Bernard Tyrrell (Philadelphia: Westminster, 1974); *A Third Collection*, ed. Frederick E. Crowe (New York: Paulist Press, 1985).

50. For example, works on the Trinity and Christology: *The Triune God: Systematics*, ed. Robert M. Doran and H. Daniel Monsour, trans. Michael Shields, Collected Works of Bernard Lonergan (Toronto: Toronto University Press, 2007); *The Triune God: Doctrines*; *The Ontological and Psychological Constitution of Christ*, ed. Frederick E. Crowe and Robert M. Doran, trans. Michael G. Shields, Collected Works of Bernard Lonergan (Toronto: University of Toronto Press, 2002).

51. Bernard J. F. Lonergan, *For a New Political Economy*, ed. Philip McShane, Collected works of Bernard Lonergan (Toronto: University of Toronto Press, 1998); *Macroeconomic Dynamics: an Essay in Circulation Analysis*, ed. Frederick G. Lawrence, Patrick Hugh Byrne, and Charles C. Hefling, Collected works of Bernard Lonergan (Toronto: University of Toronto Press, 1999).

with vigor in two works.[52] We shall take this up in more detail in a later chapter. Of particular interest will be whether Lonergan's position stands condemned under the Gilsonian critique or survives it.[53]

The Debate over the Possibility of a Christian Philosophy[54]

In the wake of *Aeterni Patris*, the 1930s witnessed a furious debate between various strands of Thomism on the possibility of a Christian philosophy. Indeed the contributors read like a who's who of largely French intellectual life at the time (Gilson, Maritain, Maurice Blondel, Gabriel Marcel, Henri de Lubac, to name a few). Broadly the responses fell within three types:[55]

- a neo-Thomist response that argued for a strict separation of theology and philosophy and so denied the possibility of a Christian philosophy as negating the autonomy of the discipline. One such response is that of Pierre Mandonnet who argued that "Certainly Christianity has transformed the world, but it has not transformed philosophy." The notion of a Christian philosophy can then only mean "the philosophical activity of philosophers who happen to be Christian." However, "progress in the philosophical order does not take place by Scripture, but by reason."[56] More accommodating was the position of Fernand Van Steenberghen who preferred to speak of "Christian wisdom" rather than "Christian philosophy." However, to speak of "'Christian philosophy' [as] a genre of speculation intermediate between philosophy *tout court* and theology" runs the risk of confusing the two. He finds it more an exercise in apologetics rather than genuine philosophy which must remain true to its own methods.[57]

- a more historical approach, exemplified by Gilson, that Christian

---

52. Étienne Gilson, *Thomist Realism and the Critique of Knowledge* (San Francisco: Ignatius Press, 2012); *Methodical Realism: A Handbook for Beginning Realist*, trans. Philip Trower (Front Royal, VA: Christendom Press, 2011).

53. Certainly it was the opinion of Eric Mascall that Lonergan's position survived the charge of Kantian idealism. See Eric Mascall, *The Openness of Being: Natural Theology Today* (London: Darton, Longman and Todd, 1971), 90.

54. Here I draw on the excellent work of Sadler, *Reason Fulfilled by Revelation: The 1930s Christian Philosophy Debates in France*, ed. Gregory B. Sadler, trans. Gregory B. Sadler (Washington, D.C.: Catholic University of America, 2011).

55. I only consider those participants who had some relationship to Thomism here. As Sadler's work makes clear there were other contributors

56. Quoted in *Reason Fulfilled by Revelation*, 81.

57. Ibid., 81–83.

revelation impacted significantly the development of philosophical thought and the philosophy so impacted could in some sense be called Christian. Gilson sought a path between those who would exclude the incorporation of philosophy into questions of faith ("theologism"/fideism) on the one hand, and those who would exclude faith from any contribution to philosophy ("rationalism"), on the other. His response to these two extremes is to be found in the actual interaction between faith and reason within the history of philosophical thought. To this end he argued that there are "philosophies, i.e, systems of rational truths, whose existence cannot be explained historically without taking account of Christianity's existence."[58] We shall spell this out more fully in the next chapter where we consider in more detail Gilson's contribution to the debate on the possibility of a Christian philosophy.

- finally those who wanted the push the matter further, to incorporate Christian belief in some way into the content of philosophy. Some of these operated in a more transcendental mode, finding in the human ordering to the truth an orientation to a supernatural end. This would culminate in a rather heated debate over whether or not Thomas Aquinas held that human beings had a *natural* desire to see God."[59] In this context we have philosophers such as Blondel and Marcel who bring questions of grace and nature, and in particular our paradoxical state of being a finite nature oriented to a supernatural end, into the heart of philosophy. Blondel considers the two previous approaches to suffer from "conceptualism" and "historicism" and so are unable to provide an adequate solution to the question of a "Christian philosophy."[60] Drawing on Aquinas, Blondel describes his stance as a "philosophy of insufficiency": "the desire of vision, of possession of the divine, of beatitude, a desire that every intellect is belabored by in its essence, but that, at the same time, remains inevitably 'inefficacious' without the gratuitous aid of the supernatural gift."[61] In a similar vein Marcel views this paradox as an essential element in Christian philosophy: "there is

58. Ibid., 53–56.
59. This debate lay at the heart of the *nouvelle théologie* movement. In some sense the debate over the possibility of a Christian philosophy was a precursor for this latter debate. On the debate over the "natural desire to see God" see Stephen Duffy, *The Graced Horizon: Nature and Grace in Modern Catholic Thought* (Collegeville, MN: Liturgical Press, 1992); Steven Long, *Natura Pura: On the Recovery of Nature in the Doctrine of Grace* (Bronx, NY: Fordham University Press, 2010).
60. *Reason Fulfilled by Revelation*, 69, 73.
61. Ibid., 71.

Christian philosophy only there where this paradox, this scandal is not only admitted or even accepted, but embraced with a passionate and unrestricted gratitude."[62]

One of the tensions operating in this debate is that between abstract and more concrete modes of thought. If one abstracts one's notion of reason from any particular historical or personal context, then it is possible to bracket faith from the discussion. Reason so conceived is then viewed as autonomous and independent of faith and revelation. If one moves to a more historical conception of reason, as suggested by the writings of Gilson and MacIntyre, then one can begin to find a role for faith in shaping the development of philosophy. This shaping may well be attainable without faith, but with difficulty and more obscurely; however, given the light of faith some matters, such as the existence of human freedom, the immortality of the soul, and the existence of God, become clearer to reason itself.[63] Finally, if we immerse ourselves in the context of the existential and historical subject, as loved and graced by God, in which the Incarnation is given as an historical event, then the supernatural becomes one component of the "real" world to which one may attend. Once you take this step the boundary between theology and philosophy begins to blur, as philosophers struggle with the given-ness of the supernatural within human experience. Here we find the third type of approach identified above.

Fides et ratio and an Appeal to Metaphysics

While *Aeterni Patris* was the first encyclical to address the issue of the role of philosophy and reason in relation to Christian faith, it was not the last. In 1998, over a century after Leo's encyclical, John Paul II issued *Fides et ratio* (*Faith and reason*), to turn Catholic philosophers' and theologians' attention once more to the debate over the mutual relationship of faith and reason. The backdrop to this encyclical was not one of the scholastic decadence that had spurred Leo, but the emergence of philosophical positions which undermined the possibility of reaching truth:

---

62. Ibid., 79. This embrace of "paradox" is evident in the Radical Orthodoxy movement.
63. This position is essentially that of Vatican I, *Dei Filius*, chapter 2.

different forms of agnosticism and relativism . . . have led philosophical research to lose its way in the shifting sands of widespread skepticism. Recent times have seen the rise to prominence of various doctrines which tend to devalue even the truths which had been judged certain. A legitimate plurality of positions has yielded to an undifferentiated pluralism, based upon the assumption that all positions are equally valid, which is one of today's most widespread symptoms of the lack of confidence in truth. (FR n. 5)

Given a Catholic concern for the intimate relationship between faith and reason, and the dependence of good Catholic theology upon sound philosophy, such a growing "lack of confidence in truth" must be viewed with alarm by the Church. What is striking for those outside the Church is the willingness of the Church to dabble in matters of purely philosophical provenance in a way which would appear to undermine the rightful autonomy of the discipline. Yet for John Paul II faith and reason are not separable, but are "two wings on which the human spirit rises to the contemplation of truth" (FR intro). Both need one another in the restless search for truth. In terms of our current discussion on the possibility of a Christian philosophy *Fides et ratio* goes well beyond the position of *Aeterni Patris*, and adds some significant elements.

While the term "Christian philosophy" appears only in the subtitle of *Aeterni Patris*, *Fides et ratio* has a specific section dealing with the term itself (FR n. 76). The encyclical acknowledges the validity of the term, "but it should not be misunderstood." The Church has no "official" philosophy but there is "a Christian way of philosophizing, a philosophical speculation conceived in dynamic union with faith." It claims that there have been "important developments of philosophical thinking which would not have happened without the direct or indirect contribution of Christian faith." Such developments shape the notion of a Christian philosophy. The encyclical distinguished two aspects of a Christian philosophy. There is a "subjective" aspect, "in the sense that faith purifies reason. As a theological virtue, faith liberates reason from presumption, the typical temptation of the philosopher." Then there is an objective aspect, "in the sense that it concerns content." Christian philosophy focuses its attention on "certain truths which might never have been discovered by reason unaided, although they are not of themselves inaccessible to reason" such as the existence of a creator God, "a truth which has been so crucial for the development of philosophical thinking, especially the philosophy of being," the reality of sin and evil, the spiritual nature of human existence, human dignity, equality and freedom, and so on. Significantly the encyclical stretches this list of objective content to "the need to explore the rationality of certain truths expressed in Sacred Scripture, such as the possibility of man's supernatural vocation and original sin itself." Still this extension does not turn philosophers into theologians since they are to explore such topics with "their own purely rational method."

Another significant aspect of the encyclical is the way it presents an almost historicist account of reason. In ways that echo Gilson's historical approach and MacIntyre's notion of a tradition of rationality, it speaks of a dynamic interplay of revelation and philosophical reflection over the centuries.

> Revelation therefore introduces into our history a universal and ultimate truth which stirs the human mind to ceaseless effort; indeed it impels reason continually to extend the range of its knowledge until it sense that it has done all in its power, leaving no stone unturned. (FR n. 14)

Indeed much of Chapter 4 of the encyclical reads like an unfolding narrative of the ways in which faith has stirred the human minds in developing and sustaining an ongoing tradition of rationality, culminating in the contribution of Aquinas:

> It is therefore minimizing and mistaken to restrict their work simply to the transposition of the truths of faith into philosophical categories. They did much more. In fact they succeeded in disclosing completely all that remained implicit and preliminary in the thinking of the great philosophers of antiquity. (FR n. 41)

One outcome of this position is a privileging of the Greco-Latin tradition of philosophy: "the Church cannot abandon what she has gained from her inculturation in the world of Greco-Latin thought. To reject this heritage would be to deny the providential plan of God who guides his Church down the paths of time and history" (FR n. 72). It is within this tradition of philosophical development that revelation has had its greatest impact.

A further significant aspect for this current project is the emphasis the encyclical places on a return to metaphysics and a criticism of approaches based on the turn to the subject. *Fides et ratio* questions the modern "one-sided concern to investigate human subjectivity." It notes of modern philosophical research that "abandoning the investigation of being [it] has concentrated instead upon human knowing," accentuating "the ways in which this capacity is limited and conditioned," leading to agnosticism, relativism and skepticism (FR n. 9). It rejects any restriction of philosophy to the "fields of human knowing or its structures," preferring that philosophy begins with a metaphysical philosophy of being (FR n. 55).

Yet even in this general sense of suspicion regarding the turn to the subject, the encyclical itself appeals in a number of instances to the data of human interiority. It begins with an appeal to the "quest for meaning which has always compelled the human heart" (FR n. 1). It appeals to the "wonder" awakened in us by the contemplation of creation and the primacy of "philosophical *enquiry*," which grounds an "*implicit philosophy*" (FR n. 4). It quotes approvingly of Augustine— "Deep within the human person there dwells the truth" (FR n. 15). Finally it speaks of our great desire for knowledge "which works in such a way that the human heart, despite its experience of insurmountable limitation, yearns for the infinite riches which lie beyond, knowing there is to be found the satisfying answer to every question as yet unanswered" (FR n. 17). There are certainly elements here from which a philosophy of human knowing could be built, based on human interiority. However, the explicit message of the encyclical is to view such a move with suspicion.

The final significant aspect is, as we might expect, a ringing endorsement of the work of Thomas Aquinas. There is a subsection of the encyclical entitled "The enduring originality of the thought of Saint Thomas Aquinas" which spells out the nature of his contribution to Catholic thought, both philosophical and theological. In Thomas we find the "harmony that exists between faith and reason" (FR n. 43). Since both come from God there can be no contradiction between them. Philosophically Aquinas "passed therefore into the history of Christian thought as a pioneer of the new path of philosophy and universal culture" while also being "a model of the right way to do theology" (FR n. 43). As with *Aeterni Patris*, so too for *Fides et ratio*, Aquinas is the model for the Catholic intellectual life.

While some may read the encyclical as a defensive document, seeking to shore up the achievements of the past, far more importantly it is a plea for philosophers (and to theologians where necessary) to trust in the power of reasoning to know reality. To not so trust in the end is a counsel of despair, a dead end of skepticism and relativism. In that sense it sides with some of the more vocal atheist critics of religious belief in trusting in the power of reason to come to the truth. Where it differs from these critics is in its confidence that faith, particularly Christian faith, is an ally not an enemy to reason.

In terms of the forms of Thomism we considered above it might be fairest to say that *Fides et ratio* comes closest to the more historical forms. There are certainly echoes of the positions of Gilson, with the assertion of the priority of metaphysics over the turn to the subject, and a family resemblance to MacIntyre's notion of a tradition of rationality in the privileging of the Greco-Latin tradition of philosophizing embedded in the encyclical.[64] The more traditional stance of the Neo-Thomist is neither affirmed nor negated, while the turn to the subject present in the transcendental approach is criticized, though it may take heart with some aspects where an appeal to interiority is present.

Contemporary Debates and Issues

In philosophical and theological matters nothing stands still for long and while *Fides et ratio* provided an important contribution to the debate over the possibility of a Christian philosophy, other movements and events were to shift the focus of the debate in new and at times opposed directions. In this current work I shall consider three of these, without seeking to be comprehensive. I shall return to these three in the final chapter of the book where I shall respond to them through the outcomes of the dialogue between Gilson and Lonergan.

Radical Orthodoxy

While Radical Orthodoxy has been a predominantly Anglo-Catholic movement, it has had an impact within Roman Catholic thought through Catholic theologians such as William Cavanaugh.[65] It is perhaps best described an as attempt to revive a neo-Platonic Augustinianism within philosophy and theology, one that presupposes or prioritizes certain religious commitments as intrinsic to reason itself. Drawing on modern notions of reason as historically constituted (as found in MacIntyre), Radical Orthodoxy proposes that different "narratives" of reason are basically incommensurable and incompatible. In particular, the narrative of reason present within secular society is

---

64. For a three-way comparison between the encyclical, MacIntyre, and Lonergan, see Neil Ormerod, "Faith and Reason: Perspectives from MacIntyre and Lonergan," *Heythrop Journal* 46 (2005): 11–22.
65. See for example William T. Cavanaugh, *Torture and Eucharist: Theology, Politics, and the Body of Christ* (Oxford: Blackwell Publishers, 1998); *The Myth of Religious Violence: Secular Ideology and the Roots of Modern Conflict* (New York: Oxford University Press, 2009).

simply a heterodox version of Christianity, and is incompatible with true Christian belief.[66] As a key proponent of the movement, John Milbank provocatively states in the opening pages of his seminal study, *Theology and Social Theory*, "once there was no secular."[67] Our social world is a construction, not "natural." The present construction of a "secular" social order and "secular" reason is "made" and can be unmade; indeed for Christians they should be unmade because they are incompatible with Christian life and practice. The target of this particular work is the social sciences, whose various forms Milbank deconstructs, while claiming that in the end only ecclesiology, a Christian theology of the church, is the true sociology.[68] This has clear parallels to earlier debates about the nature of Christian philosophy and the position of some that only Christian philosophy can be a "true" philosophy. As we saw above, de Lubac was a contributor to that position, and the Radical Orthodoxy movement has adopted him as a precursor to their own position.[69] The movement has also enlisted Aquinas to their cause, reading him through Augustinian eyes as adopting an illuminationist account of reason.[70]

While the movement is in many ways sympathetic to Catholic orthodoxy, its commitment to an historicist account of reason would appear to run afoul of the call in *Fides et ratio* for philosophers of all persuasions to be confident in the use of reason. *Fides et ratio* does adopt an historical account of reason's unfolding potentialities, but it is a far cry from adopting a relativist historicism of the type we find in Radical Orthodoxy.

66. In this sense it shares characteristics with the thought of Karl Barth. See Gregory Baum, *Essays in Critical Theology* (Kansas City, MO: Sheed & Ward, 1994), 52.
67. John Milbank, *Theology and Social Theory: Beyond Secular Reason* (Cambridge, MA: Blackwell, 1991), 9.
68. Ibid.
69. Milbank, *The Suspended Middle: Henri de Lubac and the Debate Concerning the Supernatural* (William B. Eerdmans, 2005). Also Milbank, *Theology and Social Theory*, 219–28.
70. Milbank and Pickstock, *Truth in Aquinas*. See the comments of Paul J. DeHart, *Aquinas and Radical Orthodoxy: A Critical Inquiry* (New York: Routledge, 2012), esp. 29: "One finds there the same insistence upon the fundamentally Augustinian and illuminationist character of Aquinas's theory of knowledge, the same suggestion that the ontology of created spirit forbids its confinement to the 'merely natural' sphere." Many have questioned the accuracy of radical orthodoxy's reading of Aquinas. See Mark D. Jordan, "Truth in Aquinas by John Milbank, Catherine Pickstock," *The Journal of Religion* 83, no. 2 (2003): 304–5; Bruce Marshall, "Truth in Aquinas," *Thomist* 66, no. 4 (2002): 632–37.

The New Atheism

The events of 9/11 (September 11, 2001) injected a new energy into the debate over faith and reason through an almost unbreakable connection forged in some minds between religious faith and terrorist violence. Far from being a private option that could be confined to the church, synagogue or mosque, faith was exposed, at least to the satisfaction is its critics, as an irrational force turned against the rational world of secular democracy. In this way the rise of terrorism, as perpetrated by "religious" fanatics, gave enormous impetus to what has been called the "new atheism."[71] Leading figures of the movement, Richard Dawkins,[72] Sam Harris,[73] Christopher Hitchens[74] and more recently Lawrence Krauss,[75] became celebrity atheists, not just discussing atheistic positions, but denigrating religious belief, ridiculing believers, and demanding the elimination of religion from society. As Hitchens's famous work claimed in its subtitle, "Religion poisons everything."

For these thinkers, religion and reason are implacably opposed to one another. However, while they despise theologians, they have only marginally more respect for or understanding of the work of philosophy. Only science and its empirical method are the way to truth. As I have already noted, behind such a stance often lies quite a naïve account of scientific reason and an implicit metaphysical reductionism that is not a necessary consequence of that form of reasoning properly understood. Nonetheless, the emergence of modern science does raise questions for any project claiming to be a Christian philosophy. It must be able to give a credible account of science as not only compatible with Christian beliefs, but may also argue that through its own intellectual dynamism scientific method points radically to God as a source of scientific intelligibility in the universe.

The other challenge that the new atheism throws up is that of the connection between religious belief and violence. If religious belief has divine authority it trumps reason at every turn. It is all too easy to slide into a position where such religious belief brooks no opposition and will turn against any opposition with a "divine" wrath. As Charles

71. As distinct from the "old atheism" which was largely confined to academic philosophers who debated passionately but politely with their religious opponents.
72. Richard Dawkins, *The God Delusion* (London: Bantam, 2006).
73. Sam Harris, *The End of Faith: Religion, Terror, and the Future of Reason* (New York: Norton, 2004).
74. Christopher Hitchens, *God is not Great: How Religion Poisons Everything*, 1st ed. (New York: Twelve, 2007).
75. Lawrence Krauss, *A Universe from Nothing: Why there is Something rather than Nothing* (New York: Free Press, 2012).

Taylor (hardly an atheist critic of religion) notes, "the great spiritual visions of human history have also been poisoned chalices, the causes of untold misery and even savagery."[76] As *Fides et ratio* acknowledges, reason has had a role in purifying belief: "One of the major concerns of classical philosophy was to purify human notions of God of mythological elements" (FR n. 36). There are many aspects of religious belief that require such purification, from fundamentalist readings of the Bible to anthropomorphic notions of God as an old man in the sky (or fairy at the bottom of the garden!). Both philosophy and science have a role to play in such a process of purification. And where religion makes demands on reason to act against itself, under the threat of violence, then religion has been perverted into the demonic, of "untold misery and even savagery." In the dance of faith and reason, reason itself can draw a line in the sand beyond which faith must not go.

Benedict XVI's Regensburg Address[77]

It is in this context, close to the fifth anniversary of 9/11, that Pope Benedict XVI gave what was to become a controversial talk at the University of Regensburg. He prefaced the main point of his paper with a reference to a dialogue between "the erudite Byzantine emperor Manuel II Paleologus and an educated Persian on the subject of Christianity and Islam." The point of his paper was "the central question about the relationship between religion and violence" and "why spreading the faith through violence is something unreasonable." In the context of "Islamic" terrorism even to frame the questions through this particular historical reference was going to be controversial. However, behind the controversy he generated, Benedict was seeking to stress the connection between faith and reason: "not to act in accordance with reason is contrary to God's nature." In particular he was attempting to rule out any voluntarist account of divine action which would place God even above the strictures of reason, that God "is not bound up with any of our categories, even that of rationality." Such a sundering of faith from reason can be used to justify any and all forms of religious violence in the name of God's unfathomable will.[78]

76. Charles Taylor, *Sources of the Self: The Making of the Modern Identity* (Cambridge, MA: Harvard University Press, 1989), 519. Significantly this was written well before religious violence exploded into the popular imagination. The theme is much more fully explored in his *A Secular Age* (Cambridge, MA: Belknap Press, 2007).
77. Text available at http://w2.vatican.va/content/benedict-xvi/en/speeches/2006/september/documents/hf_ben-xvi_spe_20060912_university-regensburg.html.

Again as in *Fides et ratio*, Benedict argues for the providential nature of the conjunction of Biblical revelation with Greek philosophy: "The encounter between the Biblical message and Greek thought did not happen by chance." Indeed the encounter was "mutually enriching" with a "profound harmony between what is Greek in the best sense of the word and the biblical understanding of faith in God." This position stands in some contrast to the program of "dehellenization" which Benedict argues began with the Reformers who found in the conjunction of faith and philosophy an "articulation of the faith based on an alien system of thought"; it was then given extra impetus by liberal Protestantism, particularly Adolf von Harnack (1851–1930), who sought to "return simply to the man Jesus and to his simple message, underneath the accretions of theology and indeed of Hellenization" in order to "bring Christianity back into harmony with modern reason, liberating it, that is to say, from seemingly philosophical and theological elements, such as faith in Christ's divinity and the triune God."

This neglect of philosophical reason and metaphysics in particular leaves the field open to those who then claim that only scientific reason is valid: "In the Western world it is widely held that only positivistic reason and the forms of philosophy based on it are universally valid." Such a stance "would end up reducing Christianity to a mere fragment of its former self." Yet without a metaphysics of creation, science is incapable of explaining its own success: "Modern scientific reason quite simply has to accept the rational structure of matter and the correspondence between our spirit and the prevailing rational structures of nature as a given, on which its methodology has to be based."

We can grasp in this address Benedict's intention to reject both options posed by the split between faith and reason. On the one hand he rejects any appeal to faith which would unilaterally trump reason and in doing so may sanction violence. To reject the constraints of reason is to act against the divine nature which is the source of all reason. To split faith and reason is to play into the hands of religious extremism. On the other hand he is equally rejecting of those who would pit reason against faith in the name of reason. By reducing reason to sci-

---

78. Benedict singles out Duns Scotus for introducing into the Christian intellectual tradition this split between intellect and will. Again we find the same charge, more anonymously stated in *Fides at ratio* FR n. 45 -though Scotus is not mentioned by name he is clearly identifiable—"From the late Medieval period onwards, however, the legitimate distinction between the two forms of learning became more and more a fateful separation. As a result of the exaggerated rationalism of certain thinkers, positions grew more radical and there emerged eventually a philosophy which was separate from and absolutely independent of the contents of faith."

entific and technological reason they reduce humanity and in fact constrain reason to unreasonable limits. In what might be considered a swipe in the direction of Richard Dawkins, Benedict notes, "Attempts to construct an ethic from the rules of evolution . . . end up being simply inadequate." Nonetheless, while Benedict and Catholic theology more generally seek to hold this middle ground, a balance between the demands of faith and reason, even within this ground there are various nuances of position that allow for the development of different stances on the questions we are seeking to study.

Conclusion

As noted earlier in this introductory chapter, the present work will focus on the contribution of two thinkers in the Thomist tradition, Étienne Gilson and Bernard Lonergan. Both occupied a Catholic "middle ground" seeking to balance out the competing demands of faith and reason. Both rejected the complete separation of theology and philosophy evident in the neo-Thomist revival of St Thomas, and both equally rejected a position that would see philosophy subsumed within or even "evacuated" by theology.[79] Both also understood their work as a response to the earlier call by Pope Leo XIII in *Aeterni Patris* to restore Aquinas to a position of eminence within Catholic thought. Yet on some key issues their positions diverged significantly. Indeed Gilson was particularly critical of the general direction of transcendental Thomism, while Lonergan for his part has made limited but critical comments on the work of Gilson.[80]

In bringing these two thinkers into conversation I cannot pretend to be a neutral observer. My engagement with and knowledge of the work of Lonergan goes well beyond what I can claim to know of Gilson's. While appreciative of the latter's work, the argument of the book (such as it is) will be that Lonergan's project both survives the Gilsonian critique of the turn to the subject, and is "rationally superior" (in the sense given by MacIntyre) to the position of Gilson inasmuch as Lonergan can address questions raised by modern science more effectively than Gilson. Further that the work of Lonergan exemplifies that envis-

79. The term "evacuated" comes from the radical orthodoxy of Milbank. See DeHart, *Aquinas and Radical Orthodoxy*, 50.
80. See his comments in Bernard J. F. Lonergan, "Metaphysics as Horizon," in *Collection*, ed. Frederick E. Crowe and Robert M. Doran, Collected Works of Bernard Lonergan (Toronto: University of Toronto, 1993), at 193–97, where Lonergan refers to Gilson as a "dogmatic realist." I shall indicate other references to Gilson's work by Lonergan in Chapter 3.

aged by Gilson in relation to the notion of a Christian philosophy, doing for the present age what Aquinas did for his, in providing a critical balance between faith and reason within our contemporary world.

2

Étienne Gilson and the Possibility of a Christian Philosophy

Étienne Gilson was one of the most influential Catholic philosophers of the twentieth century.[1] He brought Thomism out of the confines of Catholic Neo-Scholasticism and into dialogue with a larger stream of thought, enabled by his keen sense of the whole sweep of the history of philosophy. For Gilson, history is a laboratory within which philosophical ideas and their consequences are worked out, indeed "the history of philosophy is to the philosopher what his laboratory is to the scientist."[2] One reason for the strength of his contribution was his prolific output and the scope of his writings. During his career he wrote over forty books and countless articles. He penned historical surveys of philosophy, specialized works on Augustine, Aquinas, Bernard of Clairvaux, John Duns Scotus, Abelard, Dante and Descartes, as well as works with a more contemporary focus, on aesthetics, democracy,

---

1. His status was acknowledged when he was one of five recent Western philosophers named by Pope John Paul II in the encyclical *Fides et ratio*.
2. Étienne Gilson, *The Unity of Philosophical Experience* (San Francisco, CA: Ignatius Press, 1999), 95. Lonergan refers favorably to this aspect of Gilson's work. See Bernard J. F. Lonergan, *Verbum: Word and Idea in Aquinas*, ed. Frederick E. Crowe and Robert M. Doran, Collected Works of Bernard Lonergan (Toronto: University of Toronto Press, 1997), 39, n. 126. Also *Insight: A Study of Human Understanding*, ed. Crowe Frederick E. and Robert M. Doran, Collected Works of Bernard Lonergan (Toronto: University of Toronto Press, 1992), 15.

atheism, and linguistics. All acknowledge Gilson's strength as a historian of philosophy (he held a chair at the history of medieval philosophy at the Sorbonne from 1921 to 1932), though some have questioned
his method of integrating history into philosophy.[3] One of the great
institutional achievements of his long career was the establishment of
the Pontifical Institute for Medieval Studies (PIMS) at St Michael's College, University of Toronto.

Given the breadth of his writings I cannot hope to do justice to their
full range and scope.[4] I shall focus on the question of the possibility and nature of a Christian philosophy as Gilson understood it. Here
Gilson was a leading exponent of the notion, and a major participant in
debates within France on this topic in the 1930s and 1940s.[5] I shall also
consider his very forceful rejection of the approach of the transcendental Thomists, as he encountered them in the Leuven school. A key
question concerns Gilson's handling of the question of knowing, since
as I indicated in the previous chapter, if you want to talk about the
relationship between faith and reason, you need to articulate a sound
understanding of reason itself.

One final caveat is needed. Anyone who has written over the span of
sixty or more years (from 1913–1979) will undergo some development
in his or her thought. Gilson himself was aware that his position on
Thomas Aquinas shifted over that time. The works I shall focus on are
those written in the 30s to 50s, when both Gilson was engaged in the
debate on the possibility of a Christian philosophy, and writing some of
his most significant works. To that extent I shall not be examining possible development in his thought except in those instances where I can
grasp elements that might be significant to the topic of this work. Here
the task is also made more difficult as some of his works went through
various editions and revisions, making the task of tracking develop-

3. See Wayne John Hankey, "From Metaphysics to History, from Exodus to Neoplatonism, from
Scholasticism to Pluralism: the Fate of Gilsonian Thomism in English-speaking North America,"
Dionysius 16 (1998): 157–88.
4. The main works of Gilson's I shall draw upon are: *Being and Some Philosophers*, 2nd ed. (Toronto:
Pontifical Institute of Mediaeval Studies, 1952); *The Christian Philosophy of St. Thomas Aquinas*, trans.
I. T. Eschmann (New York: Random House, 1956); *The Unity of Philosophical Experience*; *God and Phi-
losophy*, 2nd ed. (New Haven, CT: Yale University Press, 2002); *Methodical Realism: A Handbook for
Beginning Realist*, trans. Philip Trower (Front Royal, VA: Christendom Press, 2011); *Thomist Real-
ism and the Critique of Knowledge* (San Francisco: Ignatius Press, 2012); *The Philosopher and Theology*
(New York: Random House, 1962); *From Aristotle to Darwin and Back Again: A Journey in Final Causality,
Species, and Evolution* (San Francisco: Ignatius Press, 2009).
5. See his contribution to the collection, *Reason Fulfilled by Revelation: The 1930s Christian Philosophy
Debates in France*, ed. Gregory B. Sadler, trans. Gregory B. Sadler (Washington, DC: Catholic University of America, 2011).

ments in his thought more difficult. Overall I cannot claim full mastery of all of Gilson's thought.

Critique of the Leuven Thomists (c. 1930s)

We begin our account of Gilson's work, not with the question of a Christian philosophy, but with a question concerning philosophical method. Writing in the 1930s Gilson was responding to a movement among some Thomists to take as their starting point, not being, but knowing, and seeking a critical justification for that knowing. In particular, he had in his sights the work of the Leuven Thomists, Fr. L. Noël and Cardinal Mercier and their followers who adopted a Cartesian methodology; and Joseph Maréchal who adopted a Kantian approach.[6] Maréchal is now perhaps the best known of the Leuven Thomists, for his association with a movement known, rightly or wrongly as "transcendental Thomism."[7] This debate is important for the overall concerns of the present work, because Gilson's stance has been taken by some as a major criticism of the work of our other leading thinker, Bernard Lonergan.[8] It is important then to consider Gilson's work in this regard to uncover both his position and its relevance to the approach taken by Lonergan.

At this time Gilson published two works, one a collection of occasional essays, *Methodical Realism: A Handbook for Beginning Realists*, and a later more comprehensive handling of the topic, *Thomist Realism and the Critique of Knowledge*. As justification for writing a second volume on the topic, he notes that the response of some to his first efforts had revealed "just how profoundly classical metaphysics had been contaminated by Kant's Critique."[9] In this present overview I shall focus on the latter work, bringing in material from his earlier collection where helpful.

The problem that Gilson is addressing is that of idealism, either in its Cartesian or Kantian form. Both take as their starting point a doubt about the validity of knowing, and both seek to provide some form of justification for knowing itself, as the foundation for all philosophy.

---

6. Maréchal is not mentioned in the first work, but receives a chapter in the second.
7. This included two major figures, Karl Rahner and Bernard Lonergan.
8. Anecdotally this seems to be the case. When a friend and I were first beginning to read Lonergan, our university was visited by the eminent scientist Stanley Jaki SJ, who was a keen follower of Gilson—he wrote the introduction to Gilson, *Christian Philosophy of St. Thomas Aquinas*. When my friend mentioned an interest in Lonergan Jaki became very agitated, strongly stating something along the lines of "once you start with knowing, you never get out."
9. Gilson, *Thomist Realism and the Critique of Knowledge*, 24–25.

This stands in contrast with the received Thomistic view of beginning with being, or metaphysics, as the foundation for philosophy. Towards the end of his work, Gilson sums up his response to both approaches: "There is no middle ground. You must either begin as a realist with being, in which case you will have a knowledge of being, or begin as a critical idealist with knowledge, in which case you will never come in contact with being."[10] While his opponents seek to develop a "critical realism"—critical in the sense of beginning with epistemological questions—the positive position that Gilson seeks to develop is one of "dogmatic realism." This position he describes thus:

> If realism has the wherewithal to justify and conduct all the necessary critiques, it cannot itself be based upon any of them. A starting point for all of them, it is the product of none. In short . . . any aspect of a realist philosophy may be subjected to criticism except its very realism. This is the true position of dogmatic realism which we defend.[11]

From this perspective, claims to be a "critical realism" are self-contradictory or self-undermining.

The first four chapters of this work are concerned with those Thomists who adopted a Cartesian method of universal doubt to philosophy. Descartes began with a universal doubt and a search for an indubitable basis for knowledge. All knowledge, philosophical, scientific, mathematical, and so on, was then to be reconstructed on this indubitable basis. This starting point leads to an attempt to provide a critical basis for realism, that is, one which can "satisfy the requirement laid down by modern thought since Descartes which seeks to ground philosophy upon an indisputable certainty."[12] What Descartes achieved through his method is to make the reality of the external world problematic, in need of demonstration rather than being self-evident. He regarded "as insufficient our natural feeling that the existence of the beings apprehended in virtue of the union of body and soul is self-evident. Instead, it relies upon a special operation of the understanding to confer an intellectual certitude upon our natural feeling, guaranteeing it by means of the principle of causality."[13] This creates the problem of the "bridge," a bridge "from thoughts to things by

10. Ibid., 149.
11. Ibid., 152.
12. Ibid., 55. Gilson is here quoting L. Noël, "La Méthode du réalisme" in *Revue néoscolastique de philosophie* (1931): 437.
13. Gilson, *Thomist Realism and the Critique of Knowledge*, 30–31.

relying on the principle of causality."[14] In order to provide a bridge, Descartes invokes God, whose veracity "guarantees the reliability of our sensations, the existence of the external world" for this existence "is no longer self-evidently certain and can in turn only be guaranteed by the existence of God."[15] Yet how can we know with certitude the existence of God without knowing the existence of the external world? As Gilson notes, "There is no escape from this dead end."[16] In his earlier work, he refers to this position as "mediate realism."[17]

Next Gilson takes aim at those who would claim an "immediate realism" while claiming still to hold onto the critical stance of Descartes. Gilson has great difficulty reconciling these two claims, that of a critical and immediate realism.

> It is not hard to see that a realism based upon a critique that is distinct from realism itself, far from being immediate, will have only a conditional validity, dependent in the last analysis upon the critique that justifies it. In other words, we will be sure of apprehending immediately a reality independent of our thought, but we will not be immediately certain.[18]

Of any claim to be a critical immediate realism, Gilson asks, "is this realism of the external world sufficient without its critique?"[19] If the answer is yes, then what exactly is the need for the critique? If no, how can one avoid the problems of idealism? "Immediate realism spontaneously becomes self-contradictory."[20] Gilson is particularly disapproving of those who would seek to read such a position into the writings of Aristotle and Aquinas. For both Aristotle and Aquinas the first principle of philosophy, being, not only needs no critical justification, but cannot receive one because any such justification would presume it. All branches of human knowledge emerge from this principle. "A Thomist would never doubt the validity of mathematics simply because he had not yet constructed a metaphysics. For him, every rational being is naturally in possession of the first principle and makes valid use of it in all branches of learning, even though he may be ignorant of the correct metaphysical formula or even of the very existence

---

14. Gilson, *Methodical Realism*, 14.
15. Gilson, *Thomist Realism and the Critique of Knowledge*, 48.
16. Ibid., 48.
17. Gilson, *Methodical Realism*, 31: "To begin with an internally experienced feeling, and then to infer the external reality of its object by means of the principle of causality, is manifestly to introduce between the psychological experience and its object an intermediary, which is itself the proof."
18. Gilson, *Thomist Realism and the Critique of Knowledge*, 59.
19. Ibid., 60.
20. Ibid., 61.

of the first principle." Metaphysics is then not the basis of knowledge, but "the peak of human knowledge."[21]

In two chapters Gilson considers attempts to integrate Descartes', "Cogito ergo sum" ["I think therefore I am"] into Thomism. As he notes, though Aquinas had no problem asserting the "cogito" of Descartes, he would just not have made it foundational for our certitude of the external world.[22] However, it does raise the question of our source of knowledge of our own interiority. In other words, how do we understand the nature of consciousness itself? Is the knowing subject present to itself simply as "an object of knowledge" or does "the knowing subject grasps itself, by means of knowledge, as a subject distinct from knowledge itself"?[23] The subject is present to itself—grasps itself—in the act of knowing something else, as a subject distinct from that knowledge itself. Gilson's concern here is to break the claimed privilege of epistemology, based on the priority of self-knowledge abstracted from knowledge of external reality, over metaphysics. "It is certainly true that if man were not endowed with the power of knowledge there would be no object of knowledge, but it is equally true that if no object were given there would be no knowledge."[24] We must choose between conceiving of human beings as beings capable of knowledge among other beings, or abstract them from their concrete existence, while conferring on this abstraction "extraordinary privilege of questioning both the existence of the subject whose function it is and the existence of the other beings without which the function could not be exercised."[25] This second option leads inevitably to idealism and the inversion of the hierarchy of the sciences.

> When every question starts with being, the highest science is the science of being as being. Therefore, every true realism recognizes the unconditional primacy of metaphysics. But when every question starts with knowledge, metaphysics loses its absolute dominance and must delegate some of its powers to the critique. Let us proceed further. No matter how much one may hate to admit it, the idealist position implies the unconditional primacy of the critique over metaphysics, at least as far as method is concerned.[26]

---

21. Ibid., 74–75.
22. Ibid., 100–101.
23. Ibid., 107.
24. Ibid., 107. As we shall see in the next chapter, this position of Gilson is very similar to that of Lonergan. In particular see Lonergan, *Insight*, ch. 11.
25. Gilson, *Thomist Realism and the Critique of Knowledge*, 107–8.

This question of the relative priority of metaphysics and the theory of knowledge will recur when we consider Lonergan's handling of the same set of concerns raised here. Certainly taken at face value, Gilson's stance here can be read as a serious criticism of Lonergan's approach: "If you start with thought alone, you will never get beyond it, but if you do not start with thought alone, you will not have to do anything further in order to grasp existing beings since you will already be in contact with them."[27] However, I do not think the criticism holds for Lonergan's approach.

Gilson then turns his attention to the more Kantian approach adopted by Maréchal. Here, the focus is not so much on the subject of knowing, but the object known, on a critique of metaphysics *per se*. In fact Maréchal sought to distinguish between a metaphysical critique and the "transcendental" critique offered by Kant. Rather than a radical questioning of the object, the metaphysical critique presupposes not only the existence of beings, but also the positive orientation of knowledge towards being. "Once this has been accepted the critique begins. It consists of returning to these initial affirmations by means of the reflexive method in order to criticize them."[28] He distinguishes this from the transcendental critique which consists of "suspending the primitive, absolute affirmation of being in order to examine the contents of consciousness in themselves and to analyze the conditions which constitute them as objects of knowledge."[29] Maréchal seeks to develop a critical realism wherein these two critiques can be shown to coincide.

Gilson has no particular difficulty with Maréchal's notion of the metaphysical critique; his difficulty (and incredulity) is with the possibility of aligning this with the transcendental critique. For Maréchal has "retained a fully developed metaphysical realism which was explicitly exempted from all criticism" while "the transcendental critique halts the movement of the intellect toward its object 'and isolates the apparent content of consciousness in order to consider it in itself'."[30] These two stances are not just in tension for Gilson, but contradictory. Maréchal on the other hand seeks a way out of the "prison" of subjectivity by an appeal to the dynamism or finality of the subject in relation

26. Ibid., 109.
27. Ibid., 126.
28. Ibid., 131.
29. Ibid., 132.
30. Ibid., 134.

to its object. However, Gilson argues that this finality is itself a consequence of the reality of the object.

> When thought turns toward an object, the object has already taken the first step. It is because the object has first come up against the subject that thought is then able to turn toward it. Moreover, this is why, unlike the transcendental critique, the so-called metaphysical critique has no need to postulate its object; if it had not already grasped this object, neither it nor its finality would exist.[31]

Indeed for Gilson there is a fundamental contradiction between the two approaches. The metaphysical critique renders the transcendental critique unnecessary, while the transcendental critique renders the metaphysical one impossible. "Now, the transcendental critique does not simply disagree with such contact; it rejects and excludes it as contrary to the very nature of the critique."[32] This conclusion holds not only for Maréchal's approach but for all forms of a so-called critical realism: "Every critical realism involves similar impossibilities, and, although each variety has its own favorites, their cause is the same."[33]

If the previous Cartesian and Kantian forms of idealism represent failed attempts to begin philosophy through an examination of the role of the subject, there nonetheless remains the task of giving an account of the subject as both knowing and apprehending being. This Gilson undertakes in the final two chapters of his book. What then is the relationship between intellect and being as Gilson (and Aquinas) present it? The problem we face is that existence is particular (this or that existent) while intellect grasps the universal. On the other hand, the senses also pertain to the particular. So how do sense and intellect combine to provide knowledge of being? The solution for Gilson lies in the concrete unity of the human subject: "Properly speaking, neither the senses nor the intellect knows; it is the individual man who knows by means of the senses and the intellect. There are several actions but only one subject, one being who possesses distinct yet harmonious powers and produces these diverse actions."[34] A major problem with idealist approaches is that they sunder this unity, splitting thought from sense to create a false problem of the "bridge." For Gilson, on the other hand, one must uphold "the fundamental positions

31. Ibid., 140.
32. Ibid., 143.
33. Ibid., 144.
34. Ibid., 173. Properly speaking this is a quote from Domet de Vorges, but one which Gilson describes as providing "exquisite exactitude."

of classical realism in which the knowing subject is, and can only be, the substance Man, the union of soul and body."[35] Once we forget this unity we are forced to provide some sort of mediation between thought and sense, what he refers to as a mediatism or mediate realism.[36] There then results not a physical realism but a "metaphysical realism which only comes to grips with being as it is conceived abstractly, rather than grasping concrete acts of existence."[37] Still this is only a partial realism which contains the seeds of idealism. To overcome this idealism one must hold to the self-evidence of the reality of the external world as a principle, not a postulate. The difficulties of such a stance "begin only when the philosopher undertakes to transform this sensible certitude into a demonstrative certitude of the intellect."[38]

> Let us hold fast to this precious formula. It is impossible to demonstrate sensation because it is itself a principle. In order to understand the realist position and accept it in its purity, it is necessary to recall that, in the order of existential judgments, sensible perception has the nature and value of a principle of knowledge . . . there is in Aristotelianism, in addition to the first principle which regulates all judgments, a first source of all knowledge, and that is sensation.[39]

As a principle, it cannot be deduced or argued for. Its acceptance is foundational to the project as Gilson envisages it.

Still there is a question of how such existential judgments (i.e. judgment of existence) are to be made. Here Gilson argues that "our judgments are made between two extremes: sensation and the intuition of intellectual principles."[40]

> If we view the whole problem of the existential judgment as it should henceforth be presented to us, it is in fact reduced to describing the complex act by which man apprehends the existence which his mind conceives but does not perceive and which his senses perceive but do not conceive.[41]

---

35. Ibid., 176.
36. Ibid., 176–77. See also Gilson, *Methodical Realism*, 31.
37. Gilson, *Thomist Realism and the Critique of Knowledge*, 177–78.
38. Ibid., 181.
39. Ibid., 183.
40. Ibid., 185. The language here is reminiscent of Lonergan's notion of a particular form of realism as a half-way house between idealist and empiricism. See Lonergan, *Insight*, 22.
41. Gilson, *Thomist Realism and the Critique of Knowledge*, 187.

Following Aquinas, Gilson finds some analogy between the existential judgment and the problem of the apprehension of particulars, something which is grounded in sensation, though there is still a problem in identifying how the apprehension of existence differs from other apprehensions of singulars. The guiding principle here is the oft repeated formula, "that being is the first thing encountered by the intellect."[42] Further there is nothing in the intellect which is not first in the senses, so that "This much is certain, then, from the beginning of this new inquiry: the apprehension of being by the intellect consists of directly seeing the concept of being in some sensible datum."[43] Certainly Gilson distinguishes with Aquinas the first and second acts of intellect: the first is simple and conceives the essences of things; the second is complex, affirming or denying these essences of one another, which is judgment. However, this second act depends on the principle of contradiction which according to Aquinas presupposes the principle of being, so being is already grasped within or prior to the order of essences. "Here we discover the true realist meaning of the formula: *ens est quod primum cadit in intellectu*. With its first thrust the intellect apprehends what is most profound in its object: the *actus essendi*."[44] Being is in fact the first object "of all human understanding without exception."[45]

Gilson has certainly provided a thoroughgoing analysis and criticism of the idealist positions as present in the Leuven Thomists. Their sundering of the unity of the human subject by splitting thought from sensation, either through radical doubt (Descartes) or through the transcendental critique (Kant), leads philosophy as Gilson argues into a dead end. Nonetheless his own more positive account of the subject and their relationship to being remain unsatisfying, particularly in relation to what he calls existential judgments. For example, following Aquinas he refers to the second act of intellect as a judgment, presumably an existential judgment, which comes after the first act of conception, yet existence is already apprehended as the first object of intellect. To quote Gilson more fully:

> Existence escapes the senses, for they are only able to perceive certain sensible qualities and group them into stable associations. What the senses perceive exists, and existence is included in what the senses per-

42. Ibid., 196.
43. Ibid., 197.
44. Ibid., 205.
45. Ibid., 207.

ceive, but the senses are only the bearers of a message which they are incapable of reading, for only the intellect can decipher it. However, the intellect alone cannot decipher it completely. What it is able to read in the sensible datum is the answer to the question: what is this?[46]

What is missing in this account is precisely the role of judgment, the second act of intellect, coming after the conception of essence (what is this?), intellect's first act. If existence is already determined through the interplay of sense and the first act of intellect, then the role of judgment as second act would appear to be redundant. We shall find some of this same ambiguity present in some of his later writings as well.[47]

History as a Philosophical Laboratory (1937–1950)

Two of Gilson's works, *The Unity of Philosophical Experience* and *Being and Some Philosophers,* are clear examples of his thesis that history is the laboratory of philosophical ideas. Both provide a historical overview of streams of philosophical thought, not for the sake of undertaking a history of philosophy, but from the perspective of philosophy itself, as a catalogue of largely failed philosophical experiments, leading us to the position Gilson seeks to promote, that of the centrality of being and a realism that grasps being as its proper object. I shall focus on *Being and Some Philosophers* as his later more developed work, with some cross-referencing to the second.[48]

In the preface to *Being and Some Philosophers*, Gilson spells out the nature of his project. He begins with a reference to the definition of philosophy provided by the pragmatist, William James, which Gilson finds actually re-enacts "the whole history of that definition from the time of the Greeks up to our own day."[49] In particular he notes a shift that occurs from philosophy as concerned with what is first in things to becoming more concerned with a certain "broadness of mind," an intellectual attitude which seeks to steer clear of dogmatism and almost suspends questions of reality and truth. These two distinct

---

46. Ibid., 197. We find a similar difficulty in Gilson's earlier work, *Methodical Realism*, 77–78, where he argue for "the direct and concrete evidence of a sensory intuition, which translates itself abstractly and directly into a judgment."

47. John Knasas, a strong defender of Gilson acknowledges that Gilson's account of judgment needs further filling out. See John F. X. Knasas, "A Heideggerian critique of Aquinas and a Gilsonian reply," *The Thomist* 58, no. 3 (1994): 415–39, at 438–39.

48. The later work provides, to my mind, a much sharper focus on the status of *being* within the different philosophies involved.

49. Gilson, *Being and Some Philosophers*, viii.

starting points, with things or thoughts becomes one's basic philosophical principle and:

> Nothing is more important for a philosopher than the choice he makes of his own philosophical principles. The principle of principles is that a philosopher should always put first in his mind what is first in reality. What is first in reality need not be what is the most easily accessible to human understanding; it is that whose presence or absence entails the present or absence of all the rest in reality.[50]

And for Gilson this principle of principles is being. This first principle is obvious to everyone as knowers, but problems arise once we need to give an account of it: "what [we] so infallibly know *qua* men, [we] so often overlook *qua* philosophers."[51]

Nonetheless, there is something intrinsically puzzling about being. The givenness of being is in some sense self-evident but also something easily missed: "the truth about [being] cannot be proved, it can only be seen—or overlooked."[52] The book is then an invitation to see what is most obvious, to not overlook the importance of being; and so Gilson describes it as a "dogmatic book."[53] This claim is indeed puzzling and we can inquire as to it status. What can we say to someone who has overlooked the truth of being? It is almost as if Gilson precludes arguments for the position he is proposing. But the book itself is a type of argument, on the basis of the deleterious consequences of a failure to advert to being.[54] So he does allow for some type of dialectic approach to being.[55] Alternatively we may view his appeal to the puzzling status of being as an appeal to some type of conversion experience, what Lonergan will later call an "intellectual" conversion. Once such a conver-

50. Ibid., ix.
51. Ibid.
52. Ibid., x.
53. Ibid. In his other writings he refers to his position as one of "dogmatic realism." See Gilson, *Thomist Realism and the Critique of Knowledge*, 152: "If realism has the wherewithal to justify and conduct all the necessary critiques, it cannot itself be based upon any of them. A starting point for all of them, it is the product of none. In short, unlike critical idealism, which is critical to the extent that it is an idealism, any aspect of a realist philosophy may be subjected to criticism except its very realism. This is the true position of dogmatic realism which we defend."
54. This would be akin to the Sherlock Holmes principle: eliminate all the alternatives and whatever is left must be true. This could be viewed as the principle of Gilson's historical experimentation.
55. Indeed Lonergan refers to it as an "extraordinarily erudite application of the method Aristotle names 'dialectic'." See Bernard J. F. Lonergan, "Review of Etienne Gilson, Being and Some Philosophers," in *Shorter Papers*, ed. Robert Croken, Robert M. Doran, and H. Daniel Monsour (Toronto: University of Torontw, 2007), 185. Also see the Introduction to Lonergan, *Insight*, 15, where Lonergan refers positively to Gilson's approach to history in philosophy.

sion occurs, everything falls into place, but apart from that conversion, everything remains obscure.[56]

These issues aside, the book unfolds as a series of chapters which focus on the various strategies philosophers have adopted that in one way or another overlook the primacy of being, focusing instead on various components of being such as matter, substance or essence. Plato overlooks an ambiguity in the word "being." "It may mean either *that* which is, or the fact that it *is*. Of these two meanings, Plato resolutely ignores the second."[57] Further since being in the first of these two senses required explanation outside itself to explain its existence, this must come from some further principle beyond being, which Plato calls "the One." For Plato, "the One, then, is an immensely powerful principle, which is able to beget everything, and which, in point of fact, does beget everything" but which itself has no being, since it is beyond being.[58] In fact "the One is nothing, because it is much too good to be something."[59] Gilson of course recognizes the significance of Platonic and Neo-platonic thought within the Christian theological tradition, especially in the thought of St Augustine, but in the end "logically speaking, one cannot think at one and the same time, as a Neoplatonist and as a Christian."[60] Nonetheless this has not stopped any number of Christian thinkers from adopting Neo-platonic thought within their theologies. Gilson identifies any number, starting with Augustine and ending with Meister Eckhart (1260–1328).[61] All such attempts to find a principle beyond being "sooner or later lead to mysticism. Now mysticism in itself is excellent, but not *in* philosophy."[62]

If Plato represents an attempt to find a principle beyond being, Aristotle's difficulty lies in a reduction of being to substance. According to Gilson, "the metaphysics of Aristotle is the normal philosophy of

---

56. Gilson makes a similar comment when he notes that "Even his most faithful interpreters have themselves sometimes overlooked the Thomistic notion of being, because it is difficult to grasp and because, even after it has been grasped, it is still more difficult to hold." (Gilson, *Christian Philosophy of St. Thomas Aquinas*, 29). Lonergan makes similar comments about intellectual conversion, its difficulty and tenuous nature. See Bernard J. F. Lonergan, *Method in Theology* (London: Darton, Longman & Todd, 1972), 238–39.

57. Gilson, *Being and Some Philosophers*, 15.

58. Ibid., 21.

59. Ibid., 22.

60. Ibid., 31.

61. Gilson also deals with Eckhart in *The Unity of Philosophical Experience*, 87–89. "The God of Meister Eckhart is not posited as simply beyond the reach of human knowledge, but, in true neoplatonic manner, as escaping all knowledge, including His very own" (87).

62. Gilson, *Being and Some Philosophers*, 40. One might wonder what Gilson would make of the contemporary resurgence of Platonism and attempts to read Aquinas through a Platonic lens. Undoubtedly he would view it as another failed philosophical experiment.

all those whose natural trend of mind or social vocation is to deal in a concrete way, with concrete reality."[63] However, it is this very concreteness in Aristotle that leads him astray, reducing being to the concreteness of substance. For Aristotle, "the *is* of the thing is the *what* of the thing, not the fact that it exists, but that which the thing is and which makes it to be a substance."[64] What distinguishes one individual thing from another is then the matter which individuates them, so that beings as substance are constituted by matter and form (or intelligibility). Thus Aristotle fails to distinguish between individuation and individuality; however, to make such a distinction "one must have realized that, no less necessarily and perhaps more deeply than essence, existence enters into the structure of actual being."[65] This Aristotelian oversight leads in its turn to various historical failed experiments, which Gilson illustrates through reference to two Aristotelian commentators, the Muslim scholar Averroes (1126–1198) and the Christian author, Siger of Brabant (1240–1284). Where these two authors face difficulties is that through their respective faith context, each acknowledges the existence of a creator God. "In short the distinction between creatures and their Creator entails, in creatures themselves, a distinction between their existence and the essence of their being."[66]

However, there remains the question of the relationship between this faith context and philosophy. As Gilson notes, this theologically based distinction is altogether different from the philosophical problem: "It is a purely philosophical problem, which consists in determining whether or not, within a created being, after it has been created and during the very time when it is, there is any reason to ascribe to it a distinct act in virtue of which it *is*."[67] As he notes, all Scholastic philosophers and theologians ascribed to the first theological distinction between essence and existence, but many lived without the second, including Duns Scotus (1266–1308) and Suarez (1548–1617). Gilson quotes Scotus to the effect that the distinction "is simply false"[68]; existence is then simply a determination of essence, an accident, not a distinct metaphysical principle. The universe of being is then a graded hierarchy of essences with God at the top of the hierarchy. As Gilson

63. Ibid., 42.
64. Ibid., 46.
65. Ibid., 50.
66. Ibid., 63.
67. Ibid., 63.
68. Ibid., 89.

notes, "Clearly enough, we are here in a metaphysical world in which essence is identical to being."[69]

Similarly Gilson provides a thorough analysis of the essentialism of Suarez, noting that he "begins by identifying being with essence."[70] However, what is of as much interest is Gilson's own puzzlement as the debate over the distinction between essence and existence between Suarez and the "Thomists." While it has the "appearance of a purely dialectical game" what is really at stake "here is the notion of being" present in both sides.[71] Here we are reaching at "absolutely primitive positions and, so to speak, primitive philosophical options."[72] In ways which echo Lonergan's account of being as a puzzling notion (see the next chapter), Gilson almost despairs at the cross-purposes of the debate. "There would be no point in protracting a discussion which is obviously marking time. It now resembles one of those conversations in which one man says to another: 'Don't you see it?' 'No.' 'Well, have a better look. Do you see it now?' Then what? All that is left to do is for the man who thinks he sees to account for the fact that the other does not."[73] How does one determine one's basic philosophical options in such matters? Gilson finally pins it down to a basic question: "What he [Suarez] would like to know is *quid existentia sit*: what is existence, as if existence could be a *what*."[74] If existence is a *what*, then essentialism follows. If not, then we can begin to conceive of existence as a distinct metaphysical constituent of real things. Essence and existence are then distinct, on purely philosophical grounds.

Gilson then follows up the Suarezian legacy into the birth of modern philosophy in the idealism of Descartes, Kant and Hegel. Each of these philosophers represents different outcomes in the failure to properly recognize the distinction between essence and existence. Descartes directly follows Suarez in rejecting the distinction between essence and existence, to such an extent that for Descartes, concepts are everything and since "there is no definable concept of existence, then existence is nothing."[75] For Kant the Suarezian position was mediated by

69. Ibid., 91. Lonergan is likewise critical of Scotus's notion of being: "Duns Scotus contended that, besides the unity of the name, there is also a unity of content. If no part or aspect of you is by identity a part or aspect of me, still neither of us is nothing. There is, then, some minimal conceptual content that positively constitutes what is expressed negatively by the negation of nothing." For Scotus, "The concept of being is the concept with least connotation and greatest denotation." Lonergan, *Insight*, 392.
70. Gilson, *Being and Some Philosophers*, 101.
71. Ibid., 100.
72. Ibid., 103.
73. Ibid., 104.
74. Ibid., 105.

the work of Christian Wolff. For Wolff, existence becomes removed from his metaphysics. "In the philosophy of Wolff, existence is completely excluded from the field of ontology. . . . Strictly speaking, an ontology is a metaphysics without natural theology, because it is a metaphysics without existence."[76] However, Kant also had to contend with the radical givenness of existence present in the writings of David Hume. "What are we to do with existence, if all our perceptions are distinct existences, and if the mind never perceives any real connection between them? To this question [Kant's] own answer was finally to be: The mind does not perceive such connections, it *prescribes* them."[77] Gilson finds in this empirical turn a "standing legacy from Hume," and argues that the critical idealism of Kant "includes a realism of existence."[78] However, it comes at the price of separating the question of existence from philosophy altogether. "The whole effort of Kant's philosophy, in so far at least as existence is concerned, has been to keep it out of philosophy. Human knowledge needs it in order to have something to know, but that is all. The sole business of existence is to be, after which it has nothing more to say. That things are is a fact to be accepted as such, but what they are is something for which the human understanding alone is responsible."[79] This was Kant's Copernican revolution, to place the human mind at the center of philosophy, displacing being and metaphysics as central. From Kant onwards epistemology reigns and metaphysics declines. If Kant seeks to at least anchor his project in the empirical givenness of being, Hegel's absolute idealism severs any connection to the empirical, in a grand attempt to create the world through thought alone: "Hegel sees nothing fundamentally wrong in assuming that, from the very fact that something is being thought, it is being known in itself."[80] What then is being? Nothing but "the most poverty stricken of all concepts, and it is so because of its supreme abstractness. . . . Being is what is left of the concreteness of an essence after all that which it is has been removed from it"[81] For Gilson, Hegel's absolute idealism represents the end of the centuries old struggles between essence and existence. Existence

75. Ibid., 110.
76. Ibid., 119.
77. Ibid., 122.
78. Ibid., 127.
79. Ibid., 128.
80. Ibid., 133. See also Lonergan on Hegel: "Hegel's range of vision is enormous; indeed, it is unrestricted in extent. But it is always restricted in content, for it views everything as it would be if there were no facts." Lonergan, *Insight*, 398.
81. Gilson, *Being and Some Philosophers*, 136.

has been completely marginalized. If it is to reappear, it will do so as a religious protest against the sterility of philosophy. And so Hegel begets Kierkegaard who turns from the abstract logic of Hegel's essentialism to the concrete subjectivity of the Christian believer struggling with his or her Christian identity. For Kierkegaard, systems are inherently closed whereas existence is always open. However, for Gilson Kierkegaard's "existentialism" is devoid of a metaphysics; it lacks "any speculative metaphysics of being."[82] In its place we find "the truth of ethico-religious knowledge [which] lies in its very appropriation by the knowing subject."[83] Still Gilson fears that what is left is the solipsistic subject unable "to reach another existence than his own."[84]

This sequence of failed historical experiments does not lead Gilson to some evolutionary philosophical scheme, to some new and improved philosophical account of being and existence. Rather, it leads to the recovery of a position whose implications have long been forgotten. "It may seem strange, and almost preposterous, to look back to the thirteenth century for a complete metaphysical interpretation of being, according to which neither essence nor existence is considered irrelevant to it . . . paradoxically enough, what was perhaps deepest in the philosophical message of Thomas Aquinas seems to have remained practically forgotten since the very time of his death."[85] Gilson proceeds to spell out the familiar metaphysical elements of potency, form, act, matter, substance, essence, and existence that are the staples of Aquinas's account of being.

While there would be some benefit in detailing some of this account, I would like to focus on one aspect of Gilson's account of Aquinas's metaphysics in its relationship to that of Aristotle. This is a significant discussion because it highlights the relationship between faith and reason operative in Aquinas's thought, and illustrates something of Gilson's conception of what a Christian philosophy might mean in practice. Gilson focuses our attention on Aristotle's account of matter and its place within the constitution of material beings.[86] For Aristotle,

---

82. Ibid., 146.
83. Ibid., 149.
84. Ibid.
85. Ibid., 154. Also Gilson, *God and Philosophy*, 78: "One might have expected at least this, that once in possession of so fundamental a truth, men would carefully preserve it. But they did not. Its loss almost immediately followed."
86. It is easy for a contemporary reader to be misled at this juncture. For Aristotle and Aquinas, matter does not mean what most modern readers think it means. We tend to think of matter in terms of stuff made up of atoms, or elementary particles of various types. This is not what is meant here. All such things (subatomic particles and the like) are existing substances composed like every material being of "matter," form and act. Matter in the Aristotelian and Thomistic sense is not a

"matter is a first cause ... because it enters the structure of material substances as one of their irreducible constituent elements." However, since matter is a first cause in its own right, "there remains in the Aristotelian domain of being something which the God of Aristotle does not account for, which is matter, and for this reason the metaphysics of Aristotle cannot be reduced to unqualified unity."[87] This is not a position Aquinas can maintain, because as a Christian theologian he holds that God is the Creator of all things *ex nihilo*. The Christian doctrine of creation thus requires a transformation of metaphysics. "Metaphysics, then, necessarily becomes that science which is the science of being both in itself and in its first cause, because it is the science of God as knowable to natural reason. This inner reordering of metaphysics by the final causality of its ultimate object confers upon the diversity of its aspects an organic unity," a unity not present in Aristotelian metaphysics.[88]

There remains however the question of being and substance. Aristotle identifies substance with being, and as Gilson notes, Aquinas often seems to do so as well. However, here too, Aquinas's commitment to a metaphysics of creation requires something more than Aristotle's conception of being as substance. As Gilson notes, "Aristotelian substance cannot enter the world of St Thomas Aquinas without as the same time entering a Christian world; and this means it must undergo many inner transformations in order to become a created substance."[89] At the heart of this discussion lies the question of the real distinction between essence and existence, and hence the radical contingency of all finite essences. Still, this distinction is a "purely" philosophical position, even if it was given birth by its Christian context.

> Because the acme of reality is substance and, in substance itself, essence, Aristotelian being is one with its own necessity. Such as its philosopher has conceived it, *it cannot possibly not exist.* On the contrary, the created world of Thomistic substances is radically contingent in its very existence,

thing but a principle of a thing. A more accurate word in our setting might be materiality rather than matter.

87. Gilson, *Being and Some Philosophers*, 156. There are clear parallels between the Aristotelian account of matter and that of Process Philosophy where again materiality appears as a cause independent of divine creative activity. See Neil Ormerod, "Chance and Necessity, Providence and God," *Irish Theological Quarterly* 70 (2005): 263–78.

88. Gilson, *Being and Some Philosophers*, 157. See also Gilson, *Christian Philosophy of St. Thomas Aquinas*, 43: "In turning the ontology and logic of Aristotle to his own account, St. Thomas transposed them from their original tone, that of essence, to his own tone, that of existence. Whence this first conclusion which is to affect our whole interpretation of Thomism: in entering the doctrine of St. Thomas, the metaphysics of Aristotle has received an entirely new existential meaning."

89. Gilson, *Being and Some Philosophers,* 160.

because it might never have existed. And it is not only radically contingent, but it is totally so.[90]

We can witness here the interaction of revealed content (doctrine of creation) and philosophical reason, leading to a new metaphysical account of being, while remaining within the framework of reason itself (natural theology).

What then do we learn from Gilson's historical laboratory of philosophical ideas? Both the centrality and elusiveness of being. As he says in the book's introduction, "the truth about [being] cannot be proved, it can only be seen—or overlooked."[91] While we can point to the consequences of failing to advert to the truth about being through a consideration of the various philosophical positions he presents, in the end we are dealing with fundamental philosophical options which "can only be seen—or overlooked." The truth about being can then only be asserted, so that with Gilson we can identify his position as one of dogmatic realism, based on the author's personal appropriation, a "wandering quest for truth." The book thus has the form of a personal and public confession: "It is and it can be nothing more than an invitation to look and see."[92] There remains one further question for Gilson to deal with: How do we know being? To this we now turn.

Gilson refers to the Thomistic axiom that "being is the first principle of human knowledge" in the initial pages of his work *Being and Some Philosophers*.[93] Yet it is only at the conclusion of this work, in the final chapter, that he turns his attention to the question of knowledge rather than the question of being. As we saw in his account of the Leuven Thomists, Gilson held that starting with knowing leads inevitably to the problem of idealism. For Gilson, being leads to thought rather than thought leading to being. Still some account of human knowledge is necessary if we are to enter into debates about the relationship between faith and reason. Unless we have a fairly precise account of reason itself, any such debate will be futile. And so in the final chapter of *Being and Some Philosophers*, Gilson presents an account of the connection between knowing and being.

---

90. Ibid. Here indeed the position of Aquinas is more closely aligned to the method of modern science. The need to empirically verify scientific hypothesis through the data indicates the absolute contingency of scientific theories. Scientific hypotheses are not necessary accounts but contingent upon empirical verification. See Neil Ormerod, *A Public God: Natural Theology Reconsidered* (Minneapolis: Fortress, 2015), 53–69.
91. Gilson, *Being and Some Philosophers*, x.
92. Ibid.
93. Gilson, *Being and Some Philosophers*, 2.

Gilson begins with a paragraph drawn heavily from Thomas Aquinas. "To know is to *conceive* knowledge" and what is conceived is a "*conceptio*" expressed in words. This intellectual conception is twofold. It may be simple "when our intellect forms the quiddity of a thing" or it may be complex "as happens when our intellect compounds or divides (*componit et dividit*) such quiddities." The first of these occurs when we form a concept (*conceptus*), the second when we come to a judgment (*judicium*).[94] He provides no further analysis of or justification for these assertions apart from a footnote to the work of Aquinas.[95]

Rather than exploring the meaning of this dense paragraph, Gilson immediately turns his attention to the second of these two, the judgment, not in itself, but in its expression in propositions. "Propositions are usually defined as enunciations which affirm or deny one concept of another concept."[96] This move allows Gilson to shift attention from the operations of the knowing subject stated in his first paragraph, to a linguistic, grammatical, logical and eventually metaphysical analysis of the significance of the "copula" ("is") as it is used in propositions. The outcome of this lengthy analysis is to argue that the intention of the judgment enunciated in a proposition is to assert existence.

> The two prerequisites to the possibility of existential judgments are that reality should include an existential act over and above its essence, and that the human mind be naturally able to grasp it. That there is such an existential act in reality has been established by showing that all the philosophical attempts to do without it have resulted in philosophical failures. That the human mind is naturally able to grasp it is a fact, and if so many philosophers seem to doubt it, it is because they fail to grasp the cognitive power of judgment. Because it lies beyond essence, existence lies beyond abstract representation, but not beyond the scope of intellectual knowledge; for judgment itself is the most perfect form of intellectual knowledge, and existence is its proper object.[97]

This paragraph illustrates a number of important themes. The first is the laboratory nature of the history of philosophy, so amply illustrated in the previous chapters of the book. The second is the importance of the metaphysical distinction between essence and existence ("an exis-

94. Ibid., 190.
95. That this was the cause of some problems is evident in his need to provide further clarification in an appendix to the second edition in response to two critical reactions to his work from Thomists who sought to push him back into an essentialist stance. See ibid., 216–32.
96. Ibid.
97. Ibid., 202.

tential act over and above its essence"), as illustrated by that history. The third is the epistemological conjunction of knowing and being that Gilson establishes. As existence is beyond and above essence, so judgment is more than concept ("abstract representation"), and constitutes the "most perfect form of intellectual knowledge." He is able to achieve this analysis without resort to a turn to the subject of knowing in whom these operations take place.

All this is relatively clear. The first operation of intellect provides us with a concept which corresponds to the essence of the thing; the second operation of intellect, the judgment, grasps the existence of the thing. However, there remain questions about the actual cognitive process of the subject. In particular, what role does sensory input have in this process? Here matters become a little less clear. Gilson wants to maintain the Thomistic dictum that "being is what falls first into the mind."[98] This dictum provides him with the significance of the senses. "What comes first is a sensible perception whose object is immediately known by our intellect as 'being.'"[99] On the other hand this "immediately known" is directly followed by a more detailed stance:

> First, the knowing subject apprehends *what* the given object is, next it judges *that* the object is, and this instantaneous recomposition of the existence of given object with the essences merely acknowledges the actual structure of these objects. The only difference is that, instead of being simply experienced, such objects are now intellectually known.[100]

This direct sensible perception immediately releases the two operations of conception and judgment. All this occurs within the concrete unity of the human knowing subject:

> In short, true realism is neither the realism of essence nor a realism of *thing*; it is the realism of being, and this is why it is both an immediate and natural realism. Being is neither intuited by a sensibility nor understood by an intellect; it is known by a man. An organic chain of mental operations links the sense perception of what is known as being to the abstraction and to the judgment through which man knows it as being . . . it is sensible concreteness itself which is known as a being. . . . We directly know perceived data as beings, so that our direct knowledge of them includes an intuitive experience of their very acts of existing.[101]

98. Ibid., 204.
99. Ibid.
100. Ibid.
101. Ibid., 206–7.

Here we find the same emphasis we found in his earlier works on the unity of the knowing subject. However, we should also note the terminological shift, for here Gilson speaks of an "immediate and natural realism" where in his earlier works he rejects the notion of an "immediate realism" (and a "mediated realism") in favor of his Thomistic realism. Still there is a lack of clarity here. On the one hand, judgment grasps being, on the other we "directly know perceived data as beings, so that our direct knowledge of them includes an intuitive experience of their very acts of existing." As Gilson scholar John F. X Knasas notes, in reference to precisely this section of *Being and Some Philosophers*, Gilson's thought here has "the appearance of an undeveloped notion of the intellectual act of judgment."[102] What is evident, however, is the close connection here between the metaphysical issues and the cognitional ones. Gilson aligns the two acts of intellect, conceiving and judging, with the metaphysical notions of essence and the act of existence. To keep these two distinct is in fact necessary in order to distinguish his existential understanding of Aquinas from that of the essentialist position he rejects.[103]

The Nature and Possibility of a Christian Philosophy

As Gilson admits, the term Christian philosophy is contentious.[104] On the one hand there are those who seek to keep philosophy purely distinct from religious or theological input, keeping faith and reason completely separate. Such input would undermine the nature of philosophy as based on reason alone. On the other hand there are those who find no need for philosophy since theology is itself self-sufficient with its sources in revelation: "They proceeded from faith to faith, by faith."[105] If there is to be a Christian philosophy, it will be subsumed within theology and Christian philosophy will then be the only true philosophy. Gilson himself provides a defence of the term, tracing its antecedents to nineteenth century works, and its usage in the encycli-

---

102. Knasas, "A Heideggerian Critique of Aquinas and a Gilsonian Reply," 138.
103. This is particularly evident in the Appendix where Gilson is forced to defend the distinction in the face of two critics who are promoting a more essentialist understanding of Aquinas.
104. Étienne Gilson, *Medieval Essays*, trans. James G. Colbert (Eugene, OR: Cascade Books, 2011), 73, n. 63, notes the rather strong debates over the use of the term. Also Gilson, *Christianity and Philosophy*, trans. Ralph MacDonald (London/New York: Sheed & Ward, 1939), 93: "The notion of Christian philosophy, which had cost me so much trouble to justify from the facts and E. Bréhier's denying its existence had been imposed on me at the end of long research, from which a little attention to the teaching of the church could have spared me."
105. Gilson, *Christian Philosophy of St. Thomas Aquinas*, 10. There are parallels here of both purely secular approaches to philosophy and to the claims of Radical Orthodoxy.

cal *Aeterni Patris* (whose full title includes the phrase "On the restoration of Christian Philosophy"). Significantly for the current analysis, Gilson's argument is to some extent a historical one. Christianity has developed its own distinctive philosophical approach to various questions, particularly in metaphysics, and though these positions are arguable in their own right, their inspiration or motivation can be found in the efforts of Christian thinkers to provide an account of revelation.

> Thus I call Christian, every philosophy which, although keeping the two orders formally distinct, nevertheless considers the Christian revelation as an indispensable auxiliary to reason. For who ever understands it thus, the concept does not correspond to any simple essence susceptible of abstract definition; but corresponds much rather to a concrete historical reality (practice) as something calling for description.[106]

In terms that MacIntyre would use, for Gilson Christian philosophy is a particular historical practice or tradition of reasoning. The two sides of the opposition to the term noted above arise from reading the nature of philosophy in an essentialist, a-historical manner whereas Gilson is focused on the historical practice of philosophy. "Christian philosophy arose at the juncture of Greek philosophy and of the Jewish-Christian religious revelation, Greek philosophy providing the technique for rational explanation of the world, and Jewish-Christian revelation providing religious beliefs of incalculable philosophical import."[107]

How then does Gilson conceive of the relationship between revelation and philosophy? Two commentators, Hugh Williams and Richard Farara, both describe it in the following terms:

> A Christian philosophy then, for Gilson, is more than one that is simply open to the supernatural, rather the supernatural is a *constitutive element* but *not of its texture*. This means that the two orders of faith and reason are kept formally distinct, yet Christian philosophy considers Christian faith and revelation as an indispensable aide to reason.[108]

---

106. Gilson, *The Spirit of Mediaeval Philosophy*, trans. A. H. C. Downes (Notre Dame: University of Notre Dame Press, 1991), 37. See also Gilson, *Christian Philosophy of St. Thomas Aquinas*, 84: "The history of Christian philosophy is in large measure that of a religion becoming progressively conscious of philosophical notions which as a religion it could, strictly speaking, do without. But she recognized more and more clearly that these notions were capable of defining the philosophy of those faithful who wished to have one."

107. Gilson, *God and Philosophy*, 48.

108. Hugh Williams, "The Continuing Relevance of Étienne Gilson's Christian Philosophy: A Review of Étienne Gilson's, Three Quests in Philosophy," *Science et Esprit* 63, no. 1 (2011): 85–100, at 87, n. 4 [emphasis added]. Farara uses a similar phrase, "Christianity may be a *constitutive element* of a phi-

Revelation does not provide the content in the sense that, for example, belief in the Trinity becomes a component of philosophical enquiry. However, other matters—the distinction between essence and existence, the immortality of the soul, the nature and existence of God—are all matters which naturally arise for the practice of Christian philosophy. As Farara notes:

> The paradigm for Christian philosophy is a demonstration of a saving truth revealed by God and accessible to the light of natural reason. God's existence is the most basic of such truths. It constitutes the "field par excellence for Christian philosophy, for here it may show itself as at once fully philosophic and fully Christian."[109]

Of course the paradigmatic example of a Christian philosopher for Gilson is Thomas Aquinas. Gilson's book entitled *Elements of Christian Philosophy* is basically an exposition of the philosophy of Aquinas.[110] However, he is equally clear that one can be a Christian as well as a philosopher, but not qualify as a Christian philosopher in the way he uses the term. And so for Gilson, as venerable a figure as St. Anselm is not counted as a Christian philosopher, for his method is too rationalist, trying to prove strictly revealed truths by reason alone.[111] As Gilson argues:

> This is why the thinkers with whom we are dealing here, and St. Anselm in particular, although very important for the history of philosophy and especially of Christian philosophy, cannot simply be classified as "Christian philosophers." The purely rational nature of their methods of demonstration allows many of their conclusions to be incorporated without modification into philosophy, and that is why they are part of its history, but the object of "Christian philosophy" is very different from what St. Anselm proposes. A Christian philosopher knows that he can rationally "demonstrate" nothing regarding the Trinity or the Incarnation.[112]

losophy, but *not in its texture*, not in its reasoning processes" [emphasis added]. See Richard Fafara, "Gilson and Gouhier: Framing 'Christian Philosophy'," *Heythrop Journal* 49, no. 6 (2008): 995–1014, at 1009. The notion of "texture" is fairly imprecise and given both authors use it, it is likely its origins are in Gilson himself, but I have not found an exact reference in his writings.

109. Fafara, "Gilson and Gouhier: Framing 'Christian Philosophy'." 998. The inner quote is from Gilson, *The Spirit of Mediaeval Philosophy*, 485. Also on the same page: "Since Christian revelation teaches us only truths necessary for salvation, Gilson maintained that 'its influence could extend only to those parts of philosophy that concern the existence and nature of God, and the origin, nature, and destiny of the soul'." The inner quote here is not clearly referenced.

110. Gilson, *Elements of Christian Philosophy* (Garden City, NY: Doubleday, 1960).

111. There are those who would dispute this as an accurate account of Anselm, but it is a not uncommon position to hold.

112. Gilson, *Medieval Essays*, 76, n. 64. Perhaps more recent evaluations of Anslem's approach would be more sympathetic.

The Debate on the Possibility of a Christian Philosophy

As we noted in the opening chapter of this work, Gilson's conception of the nature of Christian philosophy was born within a rather heated debate within largely French intellectual circles in the 1930s and 40s. The debate drew contributions from leading Catholic intellectuals, such as Maurice Blondel, Gabriel Marcel, Marie-Dominic Chenu and Jacques Maritain, to name a few.[113] I shall focus on one contribution to this debate from Gilson as a succinct statement of his understanding of the possibility of a Christian philosophy, together with a consideration of some of the responses that Gilson's essay provoked.

In 1931, Gilson presented a paper to the *Société française de Philosophie* entitled "The Notion of Christian Philosophy."[114] This paper was itself a response to an earlier paper by Emile Bréhier who had questioned the validity of Gilson's use of the term "Christian philosophy" in his study on Augustine.[115] Gilson begins by noting different stances that can be held in relation to the term. There are those for whom Christian philosophy cannot be, because philosophy is undermined by fallen human reason, and should be replaced by attending to revelation alone, a position he refers to as theologism or fideism. Others present the opposed view that philosophy must remain aloof from any claims of revelation in order to maintain its own proper autonomy, a position he refers to as rationalism. For these people, "There can be Christians who would be philosophers, but no Christian philosophers. There cannot be a Christian philosophy because philosophy dispenses with revelation, just as reason dispenses with prejudice."[116] This group includes neo-Thomists who hold for a strict separation of theology and philosophy.

He contrasts the abstractness of both these positions with the Augustinian emphasis on the concrete subject. For Augustine, any philosophy that "faithfully translates the Christian man's experience is necessarily Christian."[117] This approach also runs into difficulties because it breaks down the formal distinction between the natural and

113. Key contributions to the debate, together with a lengthy introductory analysis by the editor can be found in *Reason Fulfilled by Revelation*.
114. Gilson, "The Notion of Christian Philosophy," in *Reason Fulfilled by Revelation: The 1930s Christian Philosophy Debates in France*, ed. Gregory B. Sadler (Washington DC: CUA Press, 2011). Gilson comments further on this debate in his later work, *The Philosopher and Theology*, 64–66.
115. See Emile Bréhier, "Is There a Christian Philosophy?," in *Reason Fulfilled by Revelation: The 1930s Christian Philosophy Debates in France*, ed. Gregory B. Sadler (Washington DC: CUA Press, 2011), 99.
116. Étienne Gilson, "The Notion of Christian Philosophy," in *Reason Fulfilled by Revelation: The 1930s Christian Philosophy Debates in France*, ed. Gregory B. Sadler (Washington DC: CUA Press, 2011), 129.
117. Ibid., 129.

supernatural orders. In responding to these various options, Gilson presents a fairly comprehensive account of what he means by a Christian philosophy, which I now quote at length:

> It is a matter of knowing whether Christianity has played an observable role in the constitution of certain philosophies. If philosophical systems exist, purely rational in their principles and their methods, whose existence would not be explained without the existence of the Christian religion, the philosophies that they define merit the name Christian philosophies. The notion does not correspond to a concept of a pure essence, that of the philosopher or that of the Christian, but to the possibility of a complex historical reality: that of a revelation generative of reason. The two orders remain distinct, even if the relation that unites them be intrinsic.[118]

Here we find Gilson seeking a middle path between the abstract and ahistorical conceptualism of both the fideists and the rationalists, and the concrete historicism of Augustine. In a move which will be taken up by MacIntyre's notion of a tradition of rationality,[119] and by *Fides et ratio*'s analysis of the impact of Christian revelation upon the history of philosophical reflection, Gilson asks us to consider the possibility of "a revelation generative of reason." Revelation then drives reason to be more true to its own internal demands, clearing away false leads, freeing reason from self-imposed restraints, and demanding ever greater precision *through its efforts as reason* to understand what God has revealed. Gilson expands on this later in his essay:

> What is peculiar to the Christian is being convinced of the rational fertility of his faith and being sure that this fertility is inexhaustible. If we pay attention, that is the true meaning of St. Augustine's *credo ut intelligam* [believe so that you may understand] and St. Anselm's *fides quaerens intellectum* [faith seeking understanding]: a Christian's efforts to draw some of reason's knowledge from faith in revelation. That is why these two formulas are the true definition of Christian philosophy.[120]

While his historical turn clearly distinguishes Gilson from his conceptualist opponents, he needs to work more forcefully to distinguish his approach from those thinkers such as Bergson and Blondel, whose names appear during his discussion of the more concrete Augustinian

---

118. Ibid., 130.
119. Notably in Alasdair MacIntyre, *Whose Justice? Which Rationality?* (Notre Dame, IN: University of Notre Dame Press, 1988), and *Three Rival Versions of Moral Enquiry: Encyclopaedia, Genealogy, and Tradition* (Notre Dame, IN: University of Notre Dame Press, 1990).
120. Gilson, "The Notion of Christian Philosophy," 138–39.

position. From the Augustinian position "the notion of Christian phi-losophy offers no particular difficulty." Because of the profound unity of the human subject, "a man's faith and a man's reason are not two uncoordinated accidents of the same substance."[121] However, the dan-ger is then that because the Christian views God as wisdom and phi-losophy as the love of wisdom, the Christian philosopher "is the only true philosopher."[122] How then does Aquinas avoid this end-point? "St. Augustine always seeks notions comprehensive enough to embrace the concrete in its complexity. St. Thomas always seeks notions precise enough to define the elements that constitute the concrete. In a word, the former *expresses* the concrete, the latter *analyses* it."[123] While the conceptualists (rationalist, neo-Thomists) forget the concrete unity of the subject, Gilson argues that the Augustinians note the unity with-out analysing it into concepts. He agrees that "concepts are born from the concrete unity of the real. But if it is necessary for us to return there, it is equally necessary that we do not remain there."[124] Gilson clearly is trying to find a mid-point between the two positions, one which neglects the concreteness of existence, and the other which fails to rise above it!

Gilson's strength lies in his attention to the historical realm, arguing not from abstract essences of either philosophy or Christianity but from the concrete embodied beings who both are Christian and philos-ophize. This turn to the historical certainly resonates with contempo-rary thought. Still one may ask just how convincing are his efforts to distinguish his position from that of the Augustinians? In his response to Gilson, Maurice Blondel clearly thinks Gilson fails in this regard. He finds it difficult to distinguish Gilson's stated position with that "attrib-uted to certain Augustinians while refusing them a properly philo-sophical value."[125] Not surprisingly he finds Gilson's accounts of both Thomist and Augustinian positions as bit of a caricature, while distanc-ing himself from Gilson's account of the Augustinian.[126] Blondel is con-

---

121. Ibid., 135.
122. Ibid., 134.
123. Ibid., 135.
124. Ibid., 137.
125. Maurice Blondel, "Does Christian Philosophy Exist as Philosophy?," in *Reason Fulillled by Revelation: The 1930s Christian Philosophy Debate in France*, ed. Gregory B. Sadler (Washington DC: CUA Press, 2011), 145.
126. Since Bergson and Blondel are the only names Gilson mentions in relation to the Augustinian account, without actually calling them as such, one gets the impression that Blondel's response reflects a certain amount of annoyance at Gilson for what he feels is a misrepresentation of his position. "This use of Augustinianism Mr. Gilson attributes anonymously to some recent Augus-tinians does not fit (it goes without saying the true attitude, implicit or explicit, of) Augustine

cerned that Gilson's approach runs the risk of "forcibly stripping the data [of revelation] of their supernatural originality. . . . One seems to use them as they give themselves to be, but really this revealed, this supernatural, is transubstantiated into human ideas and moral experiences."[127] Blondel clearly raises an interesting point, but part of the difficulty for both authors is the question of the scope of revelation. Blondel is concerned that the philosophical use of revelation will reduce revelation to the purely natural plane. However, it may well be that within the event of revelation there are elements which, while of supernatural origin, are themselves naturally knowable, though with some difficulty and perhaps given our fallen nature a difficulty verging on impossibility with some divine prompt. Is the existence of God an element of supernatural revelation or naturally knowable? Or God as creator? In both Gilson's appeal and Blondel's rebuttal the discussion remains relatively abstract. To some extent this abstraction is overcome in Gilson's more developed account on his writings on Thomas Aquinas, who more than anyone exemplifies Gilson's notion of a Christian philosopher.

Gilson in *Christian Philosophy of Thomas Aquinas*

We can find a relatively succinct and more developed presentation of what Gilson means by the term "Christian philosophy" in his introduction to his major work, *The Christian Philosophy of Thomas Aquinas.*[128] I should note of course that the word Christian does not appear in the original French title on this book, nor does the phrase appear except incidentally in the text itself. What is clear, however, is that Thomas Aquinas remained for Gilson the exemplar of what is meant by a Christian philosopher, and that Gilson has assimilated his own philosophical stance to his reading of Aquinas. The introduction to this work then represents Gilson's account of how faith and reason work in harmony to produce a genuinely Christian philosophy.

Gilson begins by noting the close connection between Aquinas's philosophy and theology. While noting Aquinas's extensive commentaries on Aristotle, he argues that "if they had all perished, the two *Summae* would still preserve all that is most personal and most profound in his

himself, and is equally foreign to the philosophical and religious work I have attempted on my part." Blondel, "Does Christian Philosophy Exist as Philosophy?," 142–43.
127. Ibid., 146.
128. Gilson, *Christian Philosophy of St. Thomas Aquinas.* This is an English translation of *Le Thomisme. Introduction à la philosophie de saint Thomas d'Aquin*, 5th ed., Paris, 1948.

philosophical thought, whereas, if the theological works of St. Thomas had been lost, we should be deprived of his most important contributions to the common treasure of metaphysical knowledge."[129] It is in his engagement with theological issues that Aquinas is at his most creative as a philosopher. The two aspects of his work are intertwined: "The theology of St. Thomas is a philosopher's theology; his philosophy is a theologian's."[130] Despite this, Aquinas is not blurring the distinction between faith and reason, giving either side of the distinction improper say in relation to the other. "If it were impossible to present the philosophy of St. Thomas after the order of his theology without, by the same token, confusing reason with faith, it would be much better to renounce this order."[131] In words which will later find an echo in the encyclical of Pope John Paul II, *Fides et ratio*, Gilson speaks of the ways in which faith and reason work together:

> Faith in revelation does not destroy the rationality of our knowledge but rather permits it to develop more fully. Even as, indeed, grace does not destroy nature but heals and perfects it, so faith, through the influence it wields from above over reason as reason, permits the development of a far more true and fruitful rational activity.[132]

Gilson notes particularly the distinction in Aquinas between the *revelatum* and the *revelabilia*. The former refers to "that whose very essence it is to be revealed, because we can only come to know it by way of revelation."[133] As noted above, central examples of this would be the doctrines of the Trinity and the Incarnation. The latter, the *revelabilia* (translated as the revealable), "designates the status of the philosophical elements that have been integrated with a theological synthesis"[134] that are "drawn, so to speak, into the orbit of theology as included in revelation which assumes it in view of its own end." [135] Such an element in revelation is needed because:

129. Ibid., 8.
130. Ibid.
131. Ibid., 9.
132. Ibid., 18. In relation to *Fides et ratio*: "Revelation therefore introduces into our history a universal and ultimate truth which stirs the human mind to ceaseless effort; indeed it impels reason continually to extend the range of its knowledge until it senses that it has done all in its power, leaving no stone unturned" (FR n. 14).
133. Gilson, *The Christian Philosophy of Thomas Aquinas*, 11.
134. Ibid., 9. I find it a bit odd that his notion of the revealable is simply philosophical. One could also argue that there are moral precepts that are revealable, not just metaphysical ones. It should be noted that the *Dogmatic Constitution on the Catholic Faith* of Vatican I makes basically the same claims regarding the revealable, though its focus is more on moral questions.
135. Ibid., 14.

Disagreement over the same questions, even among reputedly wise men, completely baffles [many a person]. It was then most helpful that Providence should propound as truths of faith a number of truths accessible to reason, so that everyone might easily share in the knowledge of God without fear of doubt or error.[136]

Here the most significant example of a revealable for Gilson is the distinction between essence and existence, or as he rephrases it, the distinction between "essence (*essentia*) and the act-of-being (*esse*)."[137]

Let us ask Thomistic theologians whether the distinction between essence and existence is a truth deriving from natural knowledge or a revealed truth, and most of them will reply that it is from natural knowledge and pertains directly to philosophy. They are right. Nevertheless, St. Thomas is of the opinion that God revealed this philosophic truth.[138]

The location of this philosophical revelation is given in Exodus 3:13–14 where God reveals to Moses the divine name, "Thus will you reply to the children of Israel: He Who Is sends me to you."[139] As Gilson comments: "Let us note well that for St. Thomas this revelation of the identity of essence and existence in God was the equivalent of a revelation of the distinction between essence and existence in creatures."[140]

This is an instructive example because it highlights the constitutive role of history in the practice that Gilson speaks of in relation to Christian philosophy. While claiming that the distinction between essence and existence is part of the revealable, it is also clear that he credits Aquinas with introducing the distinction into philosophical and theological discourse. While citing antecedents, particularly in relation to Augustine, still it is Aquinas who introduces it, making it the major characteristic of his position, according to Gilson. That the distinction is an element of the revealable is thus only evident in the history of reception and re-reception of the text of Exodus 3:13–14, within a particular practice of "Christian philosophy."[141] Nonetheless he still maintains that the distinction is "from natural knowledge and pertains directly to philosophy."[142]

136. Ibid., 17.
137. Ibid., 35.
138. Ibid., 11.
139. As translated in ibid., 85. Gilson devotes a whole chapter of his work to this text which, following Aquinas, he refers to as *haec sublimis veritas*.
140. Ibid., 93.
141. Gilson takes this text up repeatedly including his later work, *The Philosopher and Theology*, 24–32.
142. Gilson, *Christian Philosophy of St. Thomas Aquinas*, 11.

Natural Theology

One of the central topics of any proposed Christian philosophy is the question of the existence of God. This question is taken up in Chapter 3 of *The Christian Philosophy of Thomas Aquinas*. However, before entering into this discussion Gilson sets out to first explain why proving the existence of God has become problematic for Aquinas. As long as existence is reduced to an "accident" of essence, rather than a distinct cause of being in its own right, one must "reduce existential being to essential being," so that existence must in some way be deduced from God's essence.[143] We find such an approach in the famous "ontological argument" of Anselm. Anselm begins with a particular conceptual formulation of God, "that which nothing greater can be thought," and then seeks to deduce God's existence from the definition alone. In such cases the "existence" of God is evident, almost too evident, and hence unproblematic. However, once one accepts the real distinction between essence and existence, this pathway is blocked off. God's existence can no longer be deduced from a concept of the divine nature, it must be demonstrated by argumentation with sufficient evidence. As Gilson states the matter:

> Proceeding from essence to existence, we have to look for the proof of God's existence in the notion of God. Proceeding from existence to essence, we have to use proofs for the existence of God to form a notion of His essence. St. Thomas holds this second point of view. After establishing the existence of a first cause, he will establish, through the very proofs of its existence, that this first cause is the being than which none greater can be conceived and which cannot be conceived as not existing. The existence of God will, then, be a demonstrated certitude, and at no time the result of an intuition.[144]

Proving the existence of God then requires moving from a known existent to the unknown existent: "If what we wish to attain is the existence which we think about, then to pass from truths empirically given to their first cause is to pass from one existence to another. This can only be done by an act of faith or through a demonstration."[145] Because Aquinas argues for a real distinction between essence and existence, this is the only path open to him. Interesting to note also here that the

---

143. Ibid.
144. Ibid., 57.
145. Ibid., 56.

existence of God can simultaneously be an act of faith for some, while for others, it can be a demonstrated certitude. The difference lies not in the object believed, God's existence, but in the reasons for holding the truth involved, either through faith or through reason.

He begins his account of argument for God's existence with a detailed explanation of the famous "five ways" of Aquinas: proofs from motion, from efficient cause, from contingency and necessity, from degrees of perfection, and from final cause (or design) (STh I q2 a3). Of these Gilson spends greater attention on the first of these proofs, since it proceeds from what is most empirically obvious, the fact of "motion" or change. The first step is to frame motion not in terms of what we would call "local motion" or movement in space and time, but it terms of a passage from potency to act. Such a metaphysical account is more general than local motion, and includes other forms of change, for example, growth of an organism, or a "change of mind." The argument then moves along familiar lines to argue for a first mover.

> [W]hatever is moved is moved by something else. If, however, that by which a thing is moved is itself moved, it is moved in its turn by some other mover, which mover is moved by another, and so on. But this cannot proceed to infinity, for there would then be no first mover and, consequently, no mover at all, because the second mover only moves because the first moves it, even as the baton only moves because the hand moves it. To explain motion, therefore, it is necessary to go back to a first mover whom nothing moves, that is, to God.[146]

Gilson jumps the gun a little here. The proof arrives at the existence of a first mover. More modestly Aquinas concludes, "and this everyone understands to be God" (STh I q2 a3). There is still some work to do, as Gilson is aware, to establish how such a first mover is identical with the Christian notion of God, whereas Aquinas's conclusion simply appeals to a common notion, "what everyone understands," leaving the technical argument for later. However, Gilson does contribute the important clarification, needed in our present context where there are various disputes about cosmic beginnings:

> The proof does not consist in showing that present motion requires a prime cause in the past, which would be God. It aims simply at establishing that, in the actually given universe, the actually given motion is unintelli-

---

146. Ibid., 60.

ÉTIENNE GILSON AND A CHRISTIAN PHILOSOPHY

gible without a first mover who, in the present, is the source of movement
for all things.[147]

Here we can identify the key to the demonstration. In our encounter
with the world we can identify aspects which are unintelligible in
themselves, that is, while we can know their existence (here for example, motion), a full explanation for their existence is lacking. Motion
is not self-explanatory but requires something else to explain it. Such
a lack of intelligibility demands explanation. Gilson discerns the same
basic pattern at work in all of Aquinas's proofs for God's existence.
"But it is correct to say that the structure of the five proofs of St.
Thomas is identical, even that they form one whole and reciprocally
complete one another." More fulsomely, "We can say, therefore, that
all the Thomistic proofs for the existence of God amount, in the last
analysis, to a search, beyond existences which are not self-sufficient,
for an existence which is self-sufficient and which, because it is so, can
be the first cause of all others."[148] We shall find this same theme—of
the radical insufficiency of the universe, its basic lack of intelligibility
without reference to a primal cause of being—present in the work of
Bernard Lonergan. For Lonergan there is a demand for complete intelligibility which requires God's existence lest the universe collapse into
non-being.

Critiques of Gilson

Anyone with the long-standing career and prolific output of Gilson
will attract their critics. In a major review essay of Gilsonian Thomism
in English-speaking North America, Wayne John Hankey provides an
overview of the impact of Gilson's thought, its reception, and the criticisms it has attracted.[149] Hankey notes the praise that Gilson's work
initially drew from those looking for an alternative to Neo-Thomism,
for example, the comment of Anton Pegis, "More than any other his-

147. Ibid., 64. Despite the theory of the Big Bang, first proposed by the Jesuit physicist George Joseph
Lemaître SJ, some contemporary cosmological accounts do seek to make the starting point more
fuzzy, drawing on hypothetical accounts of quantum gravity. Gilson is right to note the proof
from motion is unaffected by such accounts. They do not depend on the universe having a definite
starting point.
148. Ibid., 81. Similarly, *God and Philosophy*, 71: "Since the nature of none of them [existing things] is
'to be', the most exhaustive scientific knowledge of what they are will not so much suggest the
beginning of an answer to the question: Why are they? . . What [the] sciences cannot teach us is
why this world, taken together with its laws, its order, and its intelligibility, is, or exists."
149. Hankey, "From Metaphysics to History." I take Hankey as a convenient point of reference for the
types of criticisms Gilson's work has attracted, not as endorsement of his critique.

torian, Gilson brought to an end the notion of a scholastic synthesis, medieval or modern."[150] However, Hankey identifies a growing sense of unease about the ways in which Gilson married his historical studies to his philosophical argument: "Still the historical account and the philosophical understanding must be adequate to one another. Above all they must not be confused. Else history will imprison, and indeed prevent, thought, and philosophy will falsify, and hide, history. Gilsonian Thomism seemed finally to North Americans to do both."[151] Quite pointedly, in light of those who attacked both Gilson's historical reconstructions and his level of philosophical argument, "It appeared then already not only that philosophy was impossibly distorted by being tied to history in the Gilsonian manner, but also that history had been falsified by his philosophical use of it."[152]

While such claims could only be addressed by a detailed examination of both Gilson's work and the historical texts he has addressed, a task beyond the expertise of the present author, I would note that the methodological approach adopted by Gilson, his merging of historical account and philosophical understanding, has found a more recent ally in the work of Alasdair MacIntyre, whose dialectical analysis of traditions of rationality, the clashing of different traditions, their merging and development, takes Gilson's historical method to a new level. I would also note that the goal of such a dialectical analysis is not the same as providing a fulsome account of particular authors, but consists precisely in identifying those elements which highlight the dialectic process involved. To those looking for a fulsome account this often appears as a distortion.

The Presence of Neo-Platonism in Thomas

One issue identified as a major weakness is Gilson's treatment of the neo-Platonism present in Aquinas's thought. Some historical scholars have increasingly rejected his sharp separation of Aquinas from the neo-Platonic represented by Augustine, Dionysius and a large number of church fathers. "Thus, it began to be realized that one need not choose between Platonism, on the one hand, and Thomas' doctrine of being, on the other."[153] Hankey identifies key scholars such as George Lindbeck, who "judged that Gilson's blindness to the neoplatonic and

150. Ibid.
151. Ibid.
152. Ibid.
153. Ibid.

participationist character of *esse* in Aquinas made him an unreliable historical guide."[154] Typically this realization has produced an overreaction that now seeks to eliminate or marginalize the contribution of Aristotle to Aquinas's thought. As Hankey notes,

> We know that it makes Gilson's account of the anti-Platonic, anti-essentialist structure of Thomas' metaphysic of *esse* historically untenable. ... Whereas the initial recognition of the essentialist or neoplatonic aspect of Thomas' thought involved appreciating his positive relation to Augustine, and affirming the value of the Augustinian tradition in mediaeval scholasticism, it is now the turn of the Proclean neoplatonism and its Christian extension in the pseudo-Dionysius to have its due.[155]

Now the relationship of Aquinas to his various sources is a complex issue and it is not difficult to focus on particular aspects in support of one's position, while ignoring those that do not.[156] One aspect that is clear is that the neo-Platonic influence of the whole of Christian thought prior to Aquinas, notably through Augustine and Pseudo-Dionysius, was substantial and without doubt held as "in possession." No thinker could afford to ignore or neglect that tradition. Equally clear is the fact that Aquinas transformed key elements of that tradition by bringing it into a profound dialogue with the Aristotelian tradition mediated through the great Muslim commentators of the era.[157] On key questions such as the substantial unity of the human person and on human cognition as through identity rather than confrontation, Aquinas sided with Aristotle over the received Platonism of the day. Finally, his own contemporaries were aware enough of the difference between the received neo-Platonic heritage and the innovations of Aquinas as to condemn a number of the Aristotelian influences present in his work not long after his death. While Gilson may not have appreciated the presence of neo-Platonism on Aquinas's work, his

154. Ibid.
155. Ibid.
156. As a hypothesis I would suggest a better set of categories for understanding the question of sources would be to draw on the categories of Eric Voegelin and further developed by Robert Doran, on the cosmological, anthropological and soteriological cultural types. Rather than the catch-all category of neo-Platonism, we can then view Pseudo-Dionysius as mediating cosmological culture and Augustine soteriological culture into the Christian intellectual tradition. Aristotle is then representative of the anthropological cultural meanings and values. This helps explain why his impact was both so powerful and culturally significant at the time. See Eric Voegelin, *The New Science of Politics: An Introduction* (Chicago: University of Chicago Press, 1952), and Robert M. Doran, *Theology and the Dialectics of History* (Toronto: University of Toronto Press, 1990), for an account of these cultural types.
157. This process of transformation is well brought out in MacIntyre, *Whose Justice? Which Rationality?*, and *Three Rival Versions*.

identification of the impact of Aristotle on this great medieval thinker is not without due cause.[158]

Exodus 3:14 and Metaphysics

Less happy perhaps is the fate of Gilson's reliance on Exodus 3:14 as a key metaphysical text in revelation. For Gilson this is *haec sublimis veritas* buried in the Exodus narrative, a revelation of the divine name pregnant with metaphysical implications that leads slowly and surely to the distinction between essence and existence. As Hankey notes, for a number of Thomist scholars, "The philosophic logic Thomas gave to the metaphysic of Exodus 3:14 could not come out of Scripture itself." To find in this text the particular meaning Gilson ascribed to it was itself dependent on the overall context, largely neo-Platonic, in which Thomas read it. "Not only was Thomas' ontology a philosophical construction related to his situation in history, but further, its particular matrix was primarily neoplatonic and decisively Dionysian."

More corrosively modern biblical criticism is simply unimpressed at the suggestion that a profound metaphysical lies buried in the Exodus text. Several alternate and more likely translations to the text have been provided, such as "I will be who I will be," which relate the meaning of the text to the saving and historical work of God rather than a metaphysical claim about God's existence. As one exegete notes:

> Most critics who comment on this sentence agree that in Hebrew thought the emphasis is not upon pure or abstract being, but rather upon active being and positive manifestations of the Deity in action. Specifically the stress is upon God's presence with Moses and Israel; his "being" is a "being with," a divine presence.[159]

The dominant strand in Biblical exegesis is to place the text within its particular historical and cultural context. While respecting the divine inspiration of the Bible, still the Biblical authors act as true human authors,[160] and there is little evidence of interest among the Old Tes-

---

158. In his much later work (1962) Gilson reasserts this relationship between Aristotle and Aquinas in the strongest terms: "It is beyond dispute that the influence of Aristotle's philosophy on the theology of St. Thomas far outweighs that of other philosophers." Gilson, *The Philosopher and Theology*, 15.

159. J. Philip Hyatt, *Exodus* (Grand Rapids: Eerdmanns, 1980), 76.

160. See the Constitution on Revelation at Vatican II, *Dei Verbum*, n. 11. Gilson himself was less than impressed with the claims of historical criticism: "Above all (and this is our only concern), no philological science could tell us the meaning an inspired author gave to his words, for the sacred

tament authors in metaphysical speculation, at least at the time of the writing of the Pentateuch.

Finally we need also ask, if the meaning attributed to the text by Gilson is so clear and significant *as revelation*, why have so few thinkers in the course of Christian history picked up on it?[161] On Gilson's own account the whole issue of being has been problematic within the history of philosophy, including among Christian philosophers. Indeed some of his most excoriating criticisms are leveled at Christian philosophers and theologians who have neglected the notion of being. If God actually intended this particular revelation through this text, then it has proved relatively ineffectual.

Christian Philosophy

Finally, one may ask whether and to what extent Gilson's call for the development of a Christian philosophy has found continued resonance among Christian thinkers. Here I think he would be disappointed with the sequelae. The changes in Catholicism in the wake of Vatican II deposed Thomism from its once privileged position, despite the exhortations of *Fides et ratio*. Within the resulting philosophic pluralism, even within approaches to Aquinas, the notion of a particular Christian philosophy has been adopted not so much by those in the Thomist school as by a resurgent Augustinianism, with a heavy neo-Platonic influence. Beginning with the work of the *nouvelle théologie*, particularly Henri de Lubac, and the recovery of the neo-Platonism of the early Church Fathers, and culminating in the more recent movement of Radical Orthodoxy, those who proclaim the possibility of a Christian philosophy have increasingly adopted a position Gilson would identify as theologism. Here explicit appeals are made to specifically Christian doctrines such as the Incarnation and the Trinity in order to develop an Incarnational or Trinitarian ontology. Augustine's oft repeated phrase, "unless you believe, you shall not understand" then becomes a general epistemological principle excluding non-believers from understanding the world around us.

---

writer is by definition a person who tries to utter truths beyond human comprehension." Gilson, *The Philosopher and Theology*, 25.

161. Gilson himself reflects some of the tension in relation to this text. In the same breath he can extol Aquinas for his "intellectual boldness" in using the text to move beyond an Aristotelian metaphysics of substance, while claiming that on the basis of the text "the philosopher knows that at the origin and very heart of beings it is necessary to place the pure act of existing." Ibid., 31. If in fact Aquinas was intellectually bold, the resulting metaphysics of existence was clearly not obvious or automatic.

Such approaches eliminate the hard-fought distinction between grace and nature so central to the achievement of Aquinas, and with it any real distinction between faith and reason. Outside the realm of faith there can only be falsehood and confusion. The natural order has been so corrupted by sin that the only solution is God's gracious mercy and love. The only true philosophy properly so called can then be a Christian philosophy, one which incorporates revealed truths into its core. This is precisely the type of solution Gilson sought to avoid. The relative autonomy of philosophy from revelation was for him important; while Christian doctrines may provide a context for philosophical notions to arise—such as the real distinction between essence and existence—it was also essential that such philosophical ideas stood on their own two feet and could find a purely philosophical justification. The taut unity-in-difference between faith and reason could then be maintained, whereas in some of these contemporary approaches the distinction is all but eliminated.

Conclusion

Without doubt Étienne Gilson made a major contribution to Thomistic studies—both historically and philosophically. He helped locate the achievement of Aquinas within a historical context of competing ideas and movements of thought. History becomes the laboratory, or perhaps the battleground, in which philosophical ideas are tested and contested. We can identify some of this legacy and perspective continued in the more recent work of Alasdair MacIntyre.[162] Gilson sought to demonstrate the rational superiority of the Thomism he developed to competing positions, both internally—his attack on the Leuven Thomists—and externally—the ongoing idealist legacy of Descartes and Kant. In particular he resisted any effort to bring Thomism and this idealist legacy into a fruitful dialogue. For many of his generation, his withering attacks on the transcendental Thomists became the gold standard—once you take the turn to the subject you never get out!

This is the context in which we turn to the thought of Bernard Lonergan. In some ways Lonergan exemplified the turn to the subject in modernity. Far from considering it a dead end, for Lonergan, it signified what he would call the emergence of the third stage of meaning, grounded in human interiority. Like Gilson, Lonergan too was thoroughly immersed in the thought of Thomas Aquinas and was sensi-

---

162. Particularly his works: MacIntyre, *Whose Justice? Which Rationality*; *Three Rival Versions*.

tive to a historical reading of his work, but unlike Gilson, he found in Aquinas an initial if unthematized turn to the subject, appeals to interior experience, at crucial points of his thought. Exploiting this perspective Lonergan was able to bring the achievement of Aquinas into dialogue not only with modern philosophical movements, but significantly with modern science. To this we now turn.

3

———

Bernard Lonergan and the Possibility of a Christian Philosophy

Bernard Lonergan was one of the outstanding Catholic intellectuals of the twentieth century. While his published outputs during his lifetime was relatively meagre, mainly his two major works, *Insight: A Study of Human Understanding*,[1] and *Method in Theology*,[2] these were of such depth and originality as to establish his standing among his peers. It is now only after his death, that the full range of his thinking is being made available through the publication of his *Collected Works*.[3] There we can find his thought not only on philosophy and theology but on mathematics and logic, education and art, economics, as well as specialized theological studies on the Trinity, Christology, and grace. Given this range of outputs I cannot hope to cover all aspects of his work. In this chapter I shall focus on three aspects: Lonergan's credentials as a Thomist; his understanding of the relationship between faith and reason, mainly as presented in his book, *Insight* and later writings;

1. Bernard J. F. Lonergan, *Insight: A Study of Human Understanding*, ed. Crowe Frederick E. and Robert M. Doran, Collected Works of Bernard Lonergan (Toronto: University of Toronto Press, 1992).
2. *Method in Theology* (London: Darton, Longman & Todd, 1972).
3. This is a major publishing project under the editorship of Robert Doran and published by University of Toronto Press. There are a projected 24 volumes with some 20 already in print.

and finally how we can view Lonergan as a "Christian philosopher" as envisaged by both Gilson and *Fides et ratio*.

Years Reaching Up to the Mind of Aquinas

In the epilogue to his magnum opus, *Insight*, Lonergan speaks of "spending years reaching up to the mind of Aquinas."[4] The reference here is not just to the years of study of Thomist texts and their commentators during his training for the priesthood but more specifically to the period of his doctoral studies on the question of grace and freedom, published as a series of articles in *Theological Studies*, and his profound engagement with Thomas's cognitional and epistemological theories, all undertaken in the context of the Trinitarian psychological analogy, also published as a series of articles in the journal, *Theological Studies*. Both were published as stand-alone volumes,[5] and both have been republished in the *Collected Works* series published by the University of Toronto Press.[6] The exegetical history of these various texts, which appeared in journal articles, book form, and in the final critical edition, is too complex to unravel here. For simplicity's sake, I shall refer to the *Collected Works* editions as the definitive texts.[7]

As Lonergan makes clear, this engagement was not just about gaining mastery of the works of a classic author. More significant than this "objective" achievement was the profound personal transformation that this engagement initiated: "On the one hand, that reaching had changed me profoundly. On the other hand, that change was the essential benefit."[8] Lonergan expresses that benefit in terms of "self-appropriation," a sophisticated self-knowledge of one's own cognitional operations. I shall return to this theme when we consider *Insight* in more detail below. For the time being I shall turn my attention to these two earlier projects and their contribution to understanding the "mind of Aquinas."

4. Lonergan, *Insight*, 769.
5. *Grace and Freedom: Operative Grace in the Thought of St. Thomas Aquinas* (London: Darton, Longman & Todd, 1971); *Verbum: Word and Idea in Aquinas* (Notre Dame IND: University of Notre Dame Press, 1967).
6. *Grace and Freedom: Operative Grace in the Thought of St. Thomas Aquinas*, ed. Frederick E. Crowe and Robert M. Doran, Collected Works of Bernard Lonergan (Toronto: University of Toronto Press, 2000); *Verbum: Word and Idea in Aquinas*, ed. Frederick E. Crowe and Robert M. Doran, Collected Works of Bernard Lonergan (Toronto: University of Toronto Press, 1997).
7. I do note however that the Collected Works volume *Grace and Freedom*, contains critical editions of both the book version and thesis version of Lonergan's work.
8. *Insight*, 769.

Grace and Freedom

After undertaking undergraduate studies at Heythrop College in scholastic philosophy and teaching at Montreal, Lonergan was sent in 1933 by his superiors to study theology at the Gregorian University in Rome.[9] After completing his ordination studies, he pursued doctoral work, also at the Gregorian, on the question of the relationship between grace and freedom. In undertaking this topic Lonergan was entering a long-standing debate between Jesuit and Dominican schools of Thomism that had promoted differing interpretations of Thomas on this question.[10] The Jesuit (Molinist) school had stressed human freedom at the expense of divine sovereignty;[11] while the Dominican (Banezian) school so stressed divine sovereignty as to threaten the reality of human freedom.[12] Lonergan, a young Jesuit student, entered into this debate, with an open enough mind as to dismiss the Molinist approach within a few months of starting his study.[13] His researches were also eventually to reject aspects of the Banezian position, but the road was not straightforward. Before exploring the nature of Lonergan's resolution of this historical controversy, however, I would like to draw attention to the two distinct introductions of his project: one in the thesis version, the other in the later book version.[14]

The thesis version begins with bemoaning the inability of theologians to find a suitable method that would resolve the long running debate between the Banezian and Molinist schools. Already at this early stage of his career Lonergan displays what becomes his life-long interest in theological method: "Unless a writer can assign a method that of itself tends to greater objectivity than those hitherto employed, his undertaking may well be regarded as superfluous."[15] To discover such a method he turns to consideration of the way in which speculative thought develops, proposing an "a priori scheme that is capable of synthesizing any possible set of historical data irrespective of their time and place," drawn "solely from a consideration of the nature of

---

9. While studying at Heythrop Lonergan also undertook degrees in mathematics and classics at the University of London. See Frederick E. Crowe, *Lonergan*, Outstanding Christian Thinkers (Collegeville, MN: Liturgical Press, 1992), 6–17.
10. This debate between the rival religious orders had raged for centuries with such ferocity that the pope was forced to intervene to tell each to back down from their mutual recriminations. This debate has parallels with debates in Protestantism between the Calvinists and Arminians.
11. Named after the Jesuit theologian, Luis du Molina (1553–1600).
12. Named after the Dominican theologian, Domingo Banez (1528–1604).
13. See Lonergan, *Grace and Freedom*, xix.
14. The thesis version occurs at ibid., 162–92. The book version occurs at ibid., 3–20.
15. Ibid., 155.

human speculation on a given subject."[16] While the details of this *a priori* scheme need not detain us, they prefigure Lonergan's interest in the turn to the subject, attending to the operations present within any process of "human speculation" in order to answer methodological questions.[17] This approach allows him to view Aquinas's contribution not only within an historical perspective, but within a personal process of Aquinas's own speculative development.

The introduction to the book version takes a different tack. Rather than immediately raise issues of methodology, it begins with a recapitulation of the grace-nature debate. Beginning with Augustine's debates with the Pelagians, and moving through Anselm and Peter Lombard, he identifies a pivotal moment in the contribution of Philip the Chancellor of the University of Paris, whose theoretical breakthrough of the formal distinction of grace and nature as two distinct orders paved the way for the systematic exposition of the question of grace and nature in the work of Thomas Aquinas.

While Augustine left a rich legacy of categories in relation to grace (operative, cooperative, actual, habitual, sufficient etc), his account of the grace-nature issue was marred by an empirical account of human nature. For Augustine, human nature was different before the fall, after the fall, and as redeemed in Christ. This referential fluidity creates a speculative problem. What does it mean, for example, to say that Christ took on our human nature? To which nature is it referring? And how do we conceive of the relationship between grace and freedom, when freedom would seem to mean something different in each variant of human nature? What the distinction of the two orders, grace and nature, made possible was the introduction of a more Aristotelian conception of human nature as a fixed metaphysical principle, constitutive of what it means to be human. It remains stable throughout the various states in which we might find ourselves, though the ability of this nature to express and realize its various potentialities may vary in each state. Lonergan refers to this theoretical breakthrough as the "theorem of the supernatural":

> It no more adds to the data of the problem than the Lorentz transformation puts a new constellation in the heavens. What Philip the Chancellor systematically posited was not the supernatural character of grace, for that was already known and acknowledged, but the validity of a line of

16. Ibid., 156.
17. This scheme itself prefigures elements of what will become Lonergan's notion of a "universal viewpoint" present in *Insight*, 587–91.

reference termed nature. . . . But the whole problem lies in the abstract, in human thinking: the fallacy in early thought had been an unconscious confusion of the metaphysical abstraction "nature" with the concrete data which do not quite correspond.[18]

Lonergan is here identifying the power and necessity of a theoretical perspective if one wants to provide solutions to theological problems. To use an example he often referred to, one can speak of "going faster" in a commonsense manner, but if one wants to do mechanics one needs to talk about "acceleration."[19] With the theoretical distinction of grace and nature in place it became possible "(1) to discuss the nature of grace without discussing liberty, (2) to discuss the nature of liberty without discussing grace, and (3) to work out the relations between grace and liberty."[20]

Both these introductions display a remarkable degree of methodological sophistication for a budding theologian. The first draws our attention to the cognitive aspects of speculative development; it would not be idle speculation to suggest that in some way Lonergan is laying bare his own experience of development in encountering the work of Aquinas. The second lays the ground for what will become a feature of his work in *Insight*—the distinction between descriptive and explanatory understanding. While the first of these will to some extent be transformed into a more comprehensive account of theological method, the second remains a significant yet underappreciated insight within both philosophy and theology.[21]

The actual engagement with the texts of Aquinas is painstaking and detailed, and need not detain us here. The key to Lonergan's resolution to the debate between the Banezian and Molinist positions, however, lies in a clear grasp of the nature of divine transcendence and of the nature of sin and evil as privation. According to Lonergan, the Molinist position failed to grasp the nature of divine transcendence, making God subject to the temporal flow. Hence in reconciling grace and human freedom they needed to limit divine knowledge of "hypothetical future" events.[22] But if God is truly transcendent from creation, God

---

18. *Grace and Freedom*, 17. The reference to the Lorenz transformation is to an important element in Einstein's theory of special relativity. Lonergan's familiarity with science and mathematics is evident.
19. Acceleration is then defined precisely as a second derivative of distance over time.
20. Lonergan, *Method*, 310.
21. Again in terms of personal biography it seems likely that this distinction between descriptive and explanatory accounts arose from Lonergan's first hand familiarity with mathematics and science.
22. Lonergan, *Grace and Freedom*, 111.

is not subject to time. The divine creative act is one and eternal, so that God's knowledge of past, present and future (for us) is complete and infallible. On the other hand God's knowledge, as transcendent and primary cause of being, is not opposed to the genuine secondary causation present within the created order, including the secondary causation of human willing. The fact that God is the primary cause of the will's movement does not negate the genuine secondary causation present when we will to act.[23] How then is God not responsible for human sin (asks the Molinist)? Here we need to clearly grasp the nature of evil as privation. Sin is evil because it lacks the intelligibility proper to being. Since God is the intelligent cause of an intelligible world order, sin is uncaused.

> We can know sin as a fact; we cannot placed it as an intelligible correlation with other things except *per accidens*; that is, one sin can be correlated with another . . . but the metaphysical surd of sin cannot be related explanatorily or causally with the integers that are objective truth; for sin is really irrational, a departure at once from the ordinance of the divine mind and from the dictate of right reason . . . the *mysterium iniquitatis* is mysterious in itself and objectively, because of a defect of intelligibility.[24]

It was the Banezian failure to clearly grasp the unintelligibility of evil that ran the risk of making God the cause not only of salvation but of perdition.[25] According to Lonergan, Aquinas offers three possibilities in relation to the divine will: what God wills to be; what God wills not to be; and what God forbids, but allows to occur. Sin falls into this third possibility. In this way Lonergan resolves the dispute, rejecting both claimants while positing to reclaim Aquinas's genuine position.

What is remarkable about this solution to the long-standing dispute between the two contesting parties is that it falls completely within the realm of a "natural" theology. The issue at stake is not so much about the supernatural order of grace, as the relationship between divine causality and human freedom that belongs to the natural order. Accordingly to speak of divine transcendence from the created order

---

23. More recently this same insight has been given by Kathryn Tanner, using the terminology of a "non-competitive" relationship between divine and human freedom. See Kathryn Tanner, *God and Creation in Christian Theology: Tyranny and Empowerment?* (Minneapolis, MN: Fortress, 2004), 36–48, 62–64.

24. Lonergan, *Grace and Freedom*, 115.

25. Ibid., 111: "Banez offers to solve [the problem of grace and freedom] by means of a two-lane highway: along one lane there is what God effects, and that must be; along the other lane is what God does not effect, and that cannot be." The Banezian position comes close to a double predestination as found in Calvin.

and God's universal causality, is a consequence of knowing God as the efficient cause of being, something which falls properly within natural theology known by natural reason.[26] Similarly the account of human willing as oriented to an intelligible good, though motivated by a theological context of grace and sin, is itself knowable through natural reason. It belongs to the category of discussing "the nature of liberty without discussing grace." This is even more evident in Lonergan's later work, Insight, where he basically reproduces the same arguments in the purely philosophical and natural theological context of that work.[27]

The work itself is a major achievement for a young theologian grappling with a significant theological problem. David Burrell has described Lonergan's resolution of the debate as definitive and his use of the text of Aquinas "comprehensive."[28] In terms of our current project Lonergan's work exemplifies the fruitful conjunction of faith and reason, philosophy and theology. Reason pushes us from description to explanation—in this case drawing on Aquinas's refined Aristotelian metaphysics—to resolve theological issues concerning divine action, grace, and human freedom. While remaining true to its own methods, philosophy has provided invaluable assistance to the theological analysis of the question, strengthening the theological outcome without either faith overriding reason, or reason dominating faith. The dance of faith and reason is herein perfectly balanced and marvelously fertile.

Verbum: Word and Idea in Aquinas

Lonergan's second foray into reaching up to the mind of Aquinas, Verbum: Word and Idea in Aquinas, is another instance of this dance of faith and reason. Ostensibly the presenting issue is a Trinitarian one, to do with the processions of the Word and Spirit, understood analogously in terms of cognitional and volitional operations within human consciousness. Here Lonergan identifies a range of less than successful attempts to interpret the mind of Aquinas on the question, how are we to understand these two processions? However, in responding to this question Lonergan presents a thorough and detailed account of Aquinas's cognitional and epistemological positions, again with the

---

26. As defined by the teaching of Vatican I, De Filius.
27. Lonergan, Insight, 684–87.
28. David Burrell, Faith and Freedom: An Interfaith Perspective (Malden, MA: Wiley, 2008), 93, and n. 3.

view to recovering Aquinas's authentic position from the distortions of his lesser interpreters. Indeed so overwhelming is this predominantly philosophical set of concerns that one can easily lose sight of the theological context in which they are being handled.[29]

The book itself is a collection of articles that had been published in *Theological Studies* in the 1940s. In an introduction to the book, published initially in 1967, Lonergan provided a reflection on the issues the study had to confront. Specifically he identified the tensions between the Aristotelian-Thomistic framework of a metaphysical account of human conscious activities, and a more Augustinian approach based on an interrogation of interiority. The title he gave this introduction was "Subject and Soul." From the perspective of an Aristotelian metaphysics, the *soul* is the form of a living thing to be analyzed in terms of its objects, acts and potencies. From the perspective of Augustinian interiority, the *subject* is a phenomenologically rich field of investigation to be uncovered through self-knowledge gained in inner exploration. The problem, as Lonergan identifies it, is to "find in Aristotle the point of insertion for Augustinian thought."[30] The appeal to interior knowledge is quite explicit in Augustine, particularly in *De Trinitate* Book 10, where he is presenting the justification for his psychological analogy for the Trinity.[31] The question that Lonergan wants to raise is the extent to which both Aristotle and Aquinas will similarly draw on the data of consciousness in their accounts of cognition and volition. This is a startlingly important question in light of the more modern "turn to the subject" which we have seen Gilson vehemently rejects.

Equally startling is that Lonergan's starting point in the main body of the text is not a question about the procession of the Word, but of the procession of the Spirit. Here he notes the conclusion of a study by M. T.-L. Pendio, that theologians who have studied the matter of the Spirit's procession fall into two categories: "those who did not pretend to grasp the matter and those who did [pretend] but failed to be convincing."[32] Nonetheless Lonergan proposes that the solution to this problem is to be found though an investigation of the related and prior question of the procession of the Word. In relation to this procession

---

29. In fact in the first edition of the work published in 1967, the first opening paragraphs found in the Collected Works volume, where Lonergan sets the Trinitarian context of his study, did not appear. This may explain why some readers of his work often neglect its Trinitarian depths.
30. Lonergan, *Verbum*, 4.
31. Already in Book 8 of *De Trinitate*, Augustine runs his reader through a set of five-finger exercises to familiarise themselves with their own cognitional and volitional operations. Also see the extensive footnotes on this work in Lonergan, *Verbum*, 6–9.
32. Ibid., 12.

he expresses his dismay that some theologians hold that the procession of the word in intellect is the same as a procession within the imagination.[33] This question, the procession of the Word, will dominate the discussion in this work.

At the heart of the problem is the meaning of the term *emanatio intelligibilis*, the intelligible emanation, which Aquinas uses to analogously account for the procession of the divine Word.[34] Lonergan analyses this initially in relation to the inner word of definition and understanding. In a telling summary he notes:

> The inner word of the human mind emerges at the end of a process of thoughtful inquiry, that, until it emerges, we do not yet understand but are thinking in order to understand, that it emerges simultaneously with the act of understanding; that it is distinct from understanding, that it is a product and effect of understanding, that it is an expression of the cognitional content of the act of understanding, that more perfect the one act of understanding, the more numerous the inner words it embraces in a single view.[35]

More importantly he notes that arriving at this position does not occur simply from a metaphysical analysis: "to follow Aquinas here one must practice introspective rational psychology."[36] Later in this work he will detail evidence that "from Aristotle Aquinas derived a method of empirical introspection."[37] This is the point of connection between the Aristotelian and Augustinian traditions Lonergan identified in his introduction to the work.

The inner word that emerges from an act of understanding is thus "caused" by the understanding itself. But what is the nature of this causation that Aquinas characterizes as an intelligible emanation? In particular what is the meaning of the term "intelligible" here? After all, all causation is intelligible, the intelligible dependence of the effect on its cause. What distinguishes this form of causation is not that it is simply intelligible, but that it is intelligent, under the intelligent control of the subject:

---

33. Ibid.
34. *STh* I q27.
35. Lonergan, *Verbum*, 22–24. The fact that this relatively short quote is spread over three pages is indicative of the depth of footnoting Lonergan uses to back these assertions in the text of Aquinas.
36. Ibid., 24.
37. Ibid., 87. He details the evidence over the following pages, 87–93.

Natures act intelligibly, not because they are intelligent, for they are not, but because they are concretions of divine ideas and a divine plan. On the other hand, the intelligibility of the processions of the inner word is not passive nor potential; it is active and actual; it is intelligible because it is the activity of intelligence in act; it is intelligible not as the possible object of understanding is intelligible, but as understanding itself and the activity of understanding is intelligible.[38]

The intelligibility of the procession of the word is the intelligibility of intelligence itself, not of a lawfulness imposed from without, but an immanent law in itself. So the word is not just caused, but "because": because I understand I utter an inner word.[39] Understanding the notion of an intelligible emanation is central to understanding how these activities in human consciousness can act as analogues for the procession of the Word and Spirit in the Trinity. Moreover, the notion is applicable not only to the procession of the word from an act of understanding, but also in judgments and acts in the will in relation to such judgments.

While all can acknowledge the scholarly depth of engagement with Aquinas, which is so evident in Lonergan's work here, there has been something of a cleavage in terms of its reception. This is not surprising given, as Lonergan himself has noted, the major historical divisions present within Thomistic scholarship. These divisions arise from certain prior preconceptions which in his later work Lonergan will speak of in terms of one's horizon, and where major changes in one's horizon amount to a "conversion," in particular in dealing with cognitional and related epistemological and metaphysical issues, with intellectual conversion. And so while Douglas Hall will argue that Lonergan overcame "centuries of misinterpretation with boldly insightful yet historically grounded analyses"[40] and Anthony Kenny finds Lonergan's work in *Verbum* one "of the most illuminating books about Aquinas' work in this area"[41], others have been less generous. In an early article in *The Modern Schoolman* Matthew O'Connell launched a scathing attack

---

38. Ibid., 47.
39. An example Lonergan often uses relates to the definition of the circle. One may simply repeat the definition, not because one understands, but simply because one has been taught it; but for the one who understands the definition emerges from the understanding, and is not just repeated from memory. Every teacher of mathematics knows the difference between students that work from memory and those that genuinely understand.
40. Douglas C. Hall, *The Trinity: An Analysis of St. Thomas Aquinas' "Expositio" of the "De Trinitate" of Boethius* (Leiden: Brill, 1992), 2.
41. Anthony Kenny, *Aquinas on Mind* (Routledge, 2013), in the preface. I should also mention the Gilsonian scholar, Gaven Kerr, "Aquinas, Lonergan, and the Isomorphism between Intellect and Reality," *International Philosophical Quarterly* 54, no. 1 (2014): 43–57, who while critical of Lonergan's

on Lonergan's interpretation of Aquinas.[42] More recently John Milbank has been highly critical of Lonergan's work, but there are good grounds for holding that he understands neither Lonergan's position on Aquinas, nor Aquinas himself.[43]

The Transposition to the Modern Context – Lonergan's *Insight*

If these two studies represent Lonergan's immersion in the thought world of Aquinas, his major study, *Insight: A Study of Human Understanding*, is the fruit of that immersion brought into engagement with the modern world. Two major aspects of that engagement are with modern science (at the time of Lonergan's writing, science up to the mid-1950s) and modern philosophy (notably with Kant and Hegel). However, while the work is the fruit of his immersion in Aquinas, the latter is hardly present in the text except occasionally and parenthetically. Aquinas is not an authority to be quoted to establish a case, though he has an honored place in the history of philosophy as Lonergan understands it. Rather we have Lonergan speaking definitively in his own voice as a philosopher, on a range of topics: science; common sense; society; cognitional, epistemological and metaphysical issues; ethics; and finally natural theology. Lonergan is not attempting to say what Aquinas might have said if he were alive today, but to say what Lonergan holds in transposing Aquinas into the present context.[44]

In terms of the nature of the present project on the possibility of a Christian philosophy, Lonergan's work in *Insight* is important because as was noted earlier in chapter 1, if we are to give a coherent account of the relationship between faith and reason, one thing we need to do

---

metaphysical claims, finds Lonergan's account of Aquinas on cognitional theory "consistent and coherent" (57).

42. Matthew J. O'Connell, "St Thomas and the Verbum: An Interpretation," *Modern Schoolman* 24 (1946-47): 224–34. O'Connell's opening lines are: "In a recent article in *Theological Studies*, there appeared an article concerning St Thomas's doctrine on the verbum. It is of interest to Thomistic philosophers as an example of how easily a concatenation of text from St Thomas can easily be made to support a theory he could never have accepted" (224). For an effective rebuttal of O'Connell's position see J. Quentin Lauer, "Comment on 'An Interpretation'," *Modern Schoolman* 25 (1947–48): 251–59. O'Connell was responding to the first of the verbum articles that appeared in *Theological Studies*. Lonergan was later to footnote O'Connell's article in his later articles as representing "the other side of the ledger." See Lonergan, *Verbum*, 107n2.

43. See the major rebuttal by Paul J. DeHart, *Aquinas and Radical Orthodoxy: A Critical Inquiry* (New York: Routledge, 2012). Less extensively, see Neil Ormerod, "'It is Easy to See': The Footnotes of John Milbank," *Philosophy and Theology* 11, no. 2 (1999): 257–64.

44. On Lonergan's notion of transposition see Christiaan Jacobs-Vandegeer, "The Hermeneutics of Interiority: Transpositions in the Third Stage of Meaning," in *Meaning and History in Systematic Theology: Essays in Honor of Robert Doran, SJ*, ed. John Dadosky (Milwaukee: Marquette University Press, 2009).

is sort out what exactly we mean by reason itself. Without a genuinely explanatory account of reason, any attempt to either oppose faith and reason, or subsume one within the other, will rest on little more than assertion and counter-assertion. Just as in *Grace and Freedom*, where Lonergan identified the three-fold task of (1) discussing the nature of grace without discussing liberty, (2) discussing the nature of liberty without discussing grace, and (3) working out the relations between grace and liberty, so too unless we have a thorough account of the nature of reason, we will be hard pressed to give a solid analysis of the relationship between faith and reason.

For Lonergan the key to all philosophy is nothing less than an understanding of understanding. We have already witnessed how his account of Aquinas's notion of an intelligible emanation was the key to understanding the underlying cognitional theory behind the psychological analogy for the Trinity. Here that same issue becomes the key to all knowledge: "*Thoroughly understand what it is to understand, and not only will you understand the broad lines of all there is to be understood but also you will possess a fixed base, an invariant pattern, opening upon all further developments of understanding.*" This sums up the "positive content" of his book.[45] Again, however, our purpose will not be to explore all the riches of this major work, but to focus on those elements of particular relevance to our exploration of the possibility of a Christian philosophy.

Modern Science

Many a reader has been put off reading *Insight* because of the demands made in the first five chapters.[46] Here Lonergan draws on mathematical and scientific examples that those with no facility in the area may find alienating. He begins with an account of insight drawing on the example of Archimedes jumping out of his bath shouting eureka and running naked down the streets of Syracuse. He moves quickly to the definition of the circle, and then to arithmetic, algebra, nominal and implicit definitions (a favorite tool of the mathematician David Hilbert), inverse insights (which grasp that there is no direct insight to be gained and so one must seek a higher viewpoint), and the notion of the empirical residue (the residual data from which science abstracts).[47] Throughout this journey Lonergan is asking us to attend

---

45. Lonergan, *Insight*, 22. Emphasis in the original.
46. Anecdotally this appears to be one reason for Lonergan's reputation for being "difficult" to read.
47. All this is introduced in chapter 1, Lonergan, *Insight*, 27–56.

to our own performance as subjects experiencing insights, in all their variety. As the title of the first section of the book explains, it is concerned with "Insight as *Activity*."[48]

This focus on insight as activity then turns our attention for the next four chapters to questions of science: scientific understanding and its method. Using his distinction between direct and inverse insights Lonergan distinguishes between classical scientific accounts, wherein there are direct correlations between variables,[49] and statistical scientific accounts, wherein the correlations are of a statistical nature.[50] In both cases, classical and statistical laws, there is an intelligibility found in the data, though that intelligibility differs in each case. He then argues that these two types of scientific laws are complementary, that both are needed and both combine to produce what he calls schemes of recurrence, leading to his notion of emergent probability, a generalized form of evolutionary thinking.[51] Finally, in Chapter 5, drawing on the notion of insight and the necessary invariance of physical laws, he provides a philosophical analysis of special and general relativity.[52]

All this is an intellectual *tour de force* and on its own would be enough to establish Lonergan as an original and profound philosopher of science. Lonergan speaks of science and mathematics as someone with a genuine feel for his topic. However, *Insight* is not a work in the philosophy of science but in cognitional theory. Lonergan takes his reader through this material because it allows him to stretch out the various components of cognitional activity.[53] Science requires that we attend to the data; in struggling to understand this data we experience insights that are formulated as hypotheses, often in mathematical form; these hypotheses must then be subject to verification and judgment as to their validity. These three elements, experience (attending to the data), understanding, and judgment become a refrain throughout the work. They were present in Lonergan's account of Aquinas's

---

48. With this starting point Lonergan is not trying to justify knowing. He takes knowing as given and asks about its processes. Thus his starting point is not scepticism about knowing as in Descartes.
49. Lonergan, *Insight*, 60–76. One might think of the scientific paradigms of Newton and Einstein, often associated with a deterministic understanding of scientific laws.
50. Ibid., 76–92. One might think here of areas such as quantum mechanics or evolution where there appears to be an irreducibly statistical component to the laws they enunciate.
51. Ibid., 126–62. For an account of these notions and their implications in contemporary science and religious debates see Neil Ormerod and Cynthia S. W. Crysdale, *Creator God, Evolving World* (Minneapolis, MN: Fortress Press, 2013).
52. Lonergan, *Insight*, 163–95.
53. Bernard J. F. Lonergan et al., *Caring about Meaning: Patterns in the Life of Bernard Lonergan* (Montreal: Thomas More Institute, 1982), 221.

cognitional theory, but here they are presented through an analysis of modern science and its method.

The other hard gained goal of this material is the distinction between descriptive and explanatory insight. Descriptive insights relate things to us, while explanatory insights relate things to other things. The explanatory power of science lies in its movement from descriptive to explanatory insights, to develop hypothcses that relate things to other things. Lonergan already refers to this movement in his Introductory material in *Grace and Freedom* in his discussion of the theorem of the supernatural. Here we come closer to the source of this distinction in his familiarity with science and mathematics. Both these disciplines are able to advance by moving from descriptive accounts to provide a tight control of meaning of their basic terms and relations which are mutually defined.[54] This approach is the notion of implicit definition, something Lonergan learnt from the mathematician David Hilbert.[55]

Cognitional Theory

These three elements (experience, understanding, and judgment) become the basic components of Lonergan's account of cognition. Each of these activities is a conscious activity, that is, they relate to operations we perform while conscious, not asleep or in a coma.[56] We become familiar with our cognitional operations through attending to them as conscious operations. Still this is not a Cartesian withdrawal from the world to contemplate ourselves through some inward look. Rather it is a heightening of consciousness to attend to its operations while they are occurring. We experience ourselves having an insight: we experience the struggle to understand, the sudden and at times unexpected arrival of the insight, the falling into place of the pieces of the puzzle, the release of tension that accompanies its arrival. I can so attend

54. This is very evident in the so-called Standard Model of particle physics where particles and fields are defined in terms of their mutual relations to one another. See Robert Oerter, *The Theory of Almost Everything: The Standard Model, the Unsung Triumph of Modern Physics* (New York: Penguin Group US, 2006).

55. William A. Mathews, *Lonergan's Quest: A Study of Desire in the Authoring of Insight* (Toronto: University of Toronto Press, 2005), notes "Lonergan's style is heavily mathematical, the method of implicit definition developed by Hilbert, the mathematician, being constantly in the background" (12).

56. Lonergan distinguishes between "consciousness as presence" and "consciousness as perception." Lonergan, *Insight*, 344–46. When these are confused it leads to various incoherencies in one's account of consciousness. When Lonergan uses the term consciousness he is always referring to consciousness as presence.

to these experiences because insight is a *conscious* operation and it is *my* insight.[57] Lonergan will refer to these three types of activities as corresponding to levels of consciousness—experiential, intelligent and rational consciousness. Each "higher" level subsumes or sublates the "lower" level, not leaving behind the prior levels but taking them into a larger richer context.[58]

Lonergan spends two chapters spelling out in more detail the nature of judgment.[59] If insight arises in relation to the question "what is it?" judgment arises as we move through the insight and its conceptual formulation to ask "is it so?" If we attend to this process we can notice that the referents in these two questions are different. When we ask "what is it?" the referent "it" relates to a particular set of data which we have singled out for attention—a sound, a noise, some visual phenomenon we encounter. However, when we ask "is it so?" the "it" now refers to the intelligibility that arises from the insight in relation to the data. Is this intelligibility truly the intelligibility of the data? Judgments pass judgment on insights in relation to data. Insights are, as Lonergan often notes, "a dime a dozen."[60] The same desire to know that drives our initial question about the nature of the experience now pushes us to seek to verify our insights as true or false. The question is, how do we make such judgments? What are the cognitional steps we engage to reach the point where we say yes or no? It is important to note that this is not an epistemological question about the validity of judgments, but first and foremost a question of cognitional performance. What am I doing in making a judgment?

Of course there are all sorts of judgments that we make: common-sense judgments, scientific judgments, mathematical judgments and so on. In order to uncover the basic pattern of all these judgments, Lonergan draws our attention to the basic form of the syllogism:

> If A, then B
> But A
> Therefore B.

57. This notion of the self-presence of the subject in their own cognitional activity is also present in Augustine, *De Trinitate*, Book 10.
58. Lonergan introduces the notion of sublation to describe this relationship between levels of consciousness in his later work, Lonergan, *Method*, 241.
59. David Tracy notes that many commentators think that Lonergan's work on judgment is among the more original of his contributions to cognitional theory. See David Tracy, *The Achievement of Bernard Lonergan* (Herder and Herder, 1970), 128.
60. Frederick E. Crowe, *Developing the Lonergan Legacy: Historical, Theoretical and Existential Themes*, ed. Michael Vertin (Toronto: University of Toronto Press, 2004), 281.

The point is not to try to make cognition a logical deductive process as is often meant when people refer to "reason" or "rationality." Such would be a severe misunderstanding of Lonergan's point. Rather as he states:

> Now the conclusion is a conditioned, for an argument is needed to support it. The major premise links this conditioned to its conditions, for it affirms 'If A, then B.' The minor premise presents the fulfilment of the conditions, for it affirms the antecedent A. The function, then, of the form of deductive inference is to exhibit a conclusion as virtually unconditioned. Reflective insight grasps the pattern, and by rational compulsion there follows the judgment.[61]

The conclusion, B, is a condition whose conditions have been fulfilled; in Lonergan's terms, it is a "virtually unconditioned." The terminus of the cognitional process lies in a different type of insight, not direct or inverse, but reflective, which grasps that there is a connection between the conclusion and the conditions to be fulfilled, and in fact they are fulfilled. Still if the conclusion is a judgment, we cannot think of the premise and minor premise as also representing judgments or we end up with an infinite regression of prior judgments. Rather,

> Before the link between conditioned and conditions appears in the act of judgment, it existed in a more rudimentary state within cognitional process itself. Before the fulfilment of conditions appears in another act of judgment, it too was present in a more rudimentary state within cognitional process. The remarkable fact about reflective insight is that it can make use of those more rudimentary elements in cognitional process to reach the virtually unconditioned.[62]

The operative criterion for the termination of the cognitional process leading to judgment is located in the distinction between vulnerable and invulnerable insights. Insights are invulnerable when there are no further relevant questions to be asked. Once this stage is reached a judgment is a matter of "rational compulsion."[63] Still as Lonergan notes, the judgment is a personal act and commitment. As he notes, "everyone complains of his memory, but no one of his judgment."[64] Rational compulsion does not make it automatic. Just as some may

---

61. Lonergan, *Insight*, 306.
62. Ibid.
63. Or in the earlier terminology of *Verbum*, this is an intelligible emanation.
64. Lonergan, *Insight*, 297.

judge hastily, jumping the gun before their insight is invulnerable; while others may delay judgment because they fear error.

One may trace Lonergan's account of judgment to antecedents in John Henry Newman, in particular his *Grammar of Assent*.[65] Lonergan notes that he read sections of Newman's essay several times, notably those sections where Newman speaks of the "illative sense."[66] As with Lonergan, Newman is searching for the cognitive criterion by which we come to a judgment. Newman too is very aware of the personal nature of judgment, and the finely balanced process by which a judgment is formed. Lonergan adds precision to Newman's account through his distinction between vulnerable and invulnerable insight.

With the addition of judgment we arrive at the basic outline of Lonergan's cognitional theory. We move through experience, through inquiry to insight and formulation, to reflective insight and judgment. At this stage cognitional process has come to its term. Once we reach a judgment we can say we know. This does not tell us what we know or why this process is knowing, but an account of knowing as an *activity*. Lonergan makes two strong claims in relation to his account of the structure of cognitional activity. The first is that it is self-verifiable. In Chapter 11 of *Insight*, entitled "Self-affirmation of the knower," he asks his readers to affirm themselves as knowers through this three-fold structure. This involves: experiencing oneself as experiencing, understanding and judging; understanding oneself as experiencing, understanding and judging; and judging oneself as experiencing, understanding and judging. Each of us, he claims, is able to affirm ourselves as a knower engaged in experiencing, understanding, and judging. For Lonergan this three-fold structure defines what it means to know. This claim is the climax of the first half of the book, and initiates a transition from insight as *activity* to insight as *knowledge*.

The second claim is that this structure is irrevisable. He asks his reader to suppose how one might propose a revision to the structure. First, one would point out some data which the structure overlooks. Then one would propose a different understanding on the basis of the new data. Finally, one would propose that there is sufficient evidence to pass a judgment that this proposed revision is superior to the old proposal. However, in doing so one would be implicitly adopting Lonergan's structure of experience, understanding and judgment. Any

65. John Henry Newman, *An Essay in Aid of a Grammar of Assent* (London: Burns, Oates and Co, 1874), Chapter 9.
66. Lonergan et al., *Caring about Meaning*, 45–46, 107.

proposed revision would thus implicitly affirm what explicitly it was denying. This would be a performative contradiction, a contradiction between one's performance and one's claim made in the act of performance. Philosophically this is referred to as a retortion argument.

This explication of the structure of cognitional activity fulfils what Lonergan identifies as the main goal of his book, to find "*a fixed base, an invariant pattern, opening upon all further developments of understanding.*"[67] Everything else in Lonergan's work revolves around this fixed base. From this base Lonergan will move into metaphysics, epistemology and questions of objectivity.

Knowing, the Known, and Being

To know the structure of knowing is to also know the structure of the known; indeed there is an isomorphism between the knowing and the known.[68] This assertion is the first step in a movement from questions of cognition to questions of epistemology and metaphysics. While a traditional Thomistic approach, as we found in Gilson, will place enormous emphasis on the priority of metaphysics, Lonergan will seek to ground his metaphysics in his cognitional theory. His argument is that his more precise account of cognitional activity will then allow for a more precise control of metaphysical meaning than Thomism was able to provide.[69] From cognitional theory Lonergan will develop a *critical* metaphysics.

If knowing consists of experience, understanding, and judgment, then the known has an empirical component grasped in experience, and intelligible component grasped in insight, and a rational component grasped in judgment. To someone trained in Aristotelian-Thomistic metaphysics, this three-fold constitution of the known begins to look like the metaphysical account of being in terms of potency, form, and act. Indeed Lonergan will make this connection when he makes the further claim that the isomorphism of knowing and the known is in fact an isomorphism between knowing and proportionate being, that is, being that is proportionate to our knowing.[70]

---

67. Lonergan, *Insight*, 22.
68. Ibid.
69. As he notes in the Preface to *Insight*, "the philosophy and metaphysics that result from insight into insight will be verifiable." Further, "every statement in philosophy and metaphysics can be shown to imply statements regarding cognitional fact." Ibid., 5.
70. Ibid., 416.

Of course we can ask whether proportionate being is the whole of being, which is to ask about the possible existence of transcendent being, being for which there is no empirical component to be had. But prior to that we must grant that being itself is the goal of all our cognitional activity, whatever can be intelligently grasped and reasonably affirmed. Or as Lonergan puts the matter, being is the objective of the pure desire to know.[71] As he notes, this "definition" is not a concept of being, because to form a concept one must first understand, and to understand being would be to understand everything that is, and this we cannot do. Rather it is a *notion*, an expression of our dynamic, conscious, intelligent and reasonable orientation to being. It tells us not what being is, so much as how we arrive at being, through intelligent grasp and reasonable affirmation. Still, it is an unrestricted notion because we can ask questions about anything and everything, and in asking questions we expect, indeed demand, intelligent and reasonable answers.[72] It is a spontaneous notion because it arises with the spontaneity of our questioning. In that sense it is prior to whatever philosophical formulations that might arise in relation to being.[73] It is an all-pervasive notion because it drives all our cognitional activities: "it underpins all cognitional contents; it penetrates them all; it constitutes them as cognitional."[74] Finally it is a puzzling notion, because though it intends the concrete universe of being, of itself the notion is completely indeterminate. Determinacy can only be achieved through specific insights and judgments, which the notion intends, but does not of itself achieve.[75]

At this stage we might be tempted to concede that Gilson's fears about a transcendental Thomism have been fully realized in Lonergan. Knowing is not defined in terms of being; rather being is defined in terms of knowing. Is this not the very transcendental solipsism that Gilson warned us about? Has idealism excluded any possibility of a genuine realism here? The anxiety behind such questions cannot be pre-emptively dismissed but nonetheless this is a point we do not and cannot concede. In order to address this anxiety we need to push further into the question of reality and objectivity and to do so requires what Lonergan will in his later writings call "intellectual conversion,"

71. Ibid., 372.
72. Ibid., 375–76.
73. Ibid., 377–80.
74. Ibid., 380.
75. Ibid., 383–88.

but which in *Insight* he deals with through what he calls three positions and their corresponding counter-positions.

Intellectual Conversion and Reality

In his later writings Lonergan speaks of the need for an intellectual conversion in terms of a rejection of the "exceedingly stubborn and misleading myth" that reality is already out there now, to be known through taking a good look, and replacing it with reality as the universe of being, known through intelligent grasp and reasonable affirmation.[76] However, in *Insight,* he does not refer directly to such a conversion. Rather he develops three "positional" claims, which are largely constitutive of what he means by his later term, intellectual conversion. We shall consider each of these positions in turn.[77]

"The real is the concrete universe of being and not a subdivision of the 'already out there now'."[78] In the introduction to *Insight* Lonergan speaks of a duality in our knowing, one based on animal extroversion, the other based on a fully human knowing through intelligence and reason.[79] To the "knowing" of animal extroversion, the world is already out there now, just waiting for us to open our eyes, to sharpen our hearing, to ready our taste buds. It is a world dominated by our animal wants and needs, but it is not a fully human world, a world of institutions, relationships, culture, history and so on. This human world is a real world but it is not known through taking a look, but through intelligence and reason.[80] The equation of reality with the concrete universe of being, itself defined in terms of the intentionality of our knowing, lies at the heart of intellectual conversion. It involves a radical shift in one's criteria for reality. As with the self-affirmation of the knower, it is a difficult position to argue against, because any argument is premised upon questions and answers, on intelligence and reason. Once we begin to argue, inasmuch as we do so intelligently and reasonably, we are immediately moving within the universe of being.[81] While we may assert a separation of reality from being (as the objective of the

---

76. *Method*, 238.
77. In fact Lonergan did use the term "intellectual conversion" in lectures preparatory to *Insight*, but it did not find its way into the published version. See Crowe, *Lonergan*, 68.
78. Lonergan, *Insight*, 413.
79. Ibid., 13.
80. In his later writings Lonergan will refer to this as a world mediated by meaning. See *Method*, 28–29.
81. As Lonergan notes the best way to deal with skeptics is to get them talking. "It is this conditional necessity of contingent fact that involves the talking sceptic in contradiction." *Insight*, 353.

desire to know), we cannot argue the case without some level of inco-
herence.

*"The subject becomes known when it affirms itself intelligently and rea-
sonably and so is not known yet in any prior 'existential' state."*[82] Here Lonergan distinguishes himself from the approach of Descartes. Far from
claiming that self-knowledge is some privileged source of knowledge
immediately available through an act of introspection, for Lonergan
self-knowledge is attained in exactly the same way as all other knowledge, through intelligence and reason. Just as our knowledge of the
world begins with the data of sense, our self-knowledge begins with the
data of consciousness. For Lonergan consciousness is not self-knowledge, but mere self-presence, which can come to be known through
intelligence and reason. To push the matter further, to even distinguish between the data of sense and the data of consciousness requires
intelligence and reason to properly make the distinction. This position
abolishes the priority of the subject-object split found in idealism and
to some extent presumed by Gilson. For Lonergan the distinction is
constructed, indeed hard won, not given immediately in the data itself.
And as we noted above, access to the data of consciousness is not
achieved through a withdrawal from the world of the senses, but is discovered through a heightening of awareness in the act of engagement
with the world of the senses.

*"Objectivity is conceived as a consequence of intelligent inquiry and critical
reflection, and not as a property of vital anticipation, extroversion, and satisfaction."*[83] Given Lonergan has abolished the priority of the subject-
object split he must also reject the subjectivity-objectivity dichotomy.
If we reject the first and second position, objectivity means knowing
the already out there now real through taking a good look and seeing
what there is to be seen, and of course, not seeing what isn't there to
be seen. Objectivity is then a function of extroversion and one appeals
to objectivity over and against subjectivity. However, if one adopts
the first and second positions, it would be inconsistent to conceive
of objectivity in the terms one has rejected in those positions. Objectivity can only be conceived in terms of allowing the desire to know
its full intention, through intelligent inquiry and critical reflection. As
these are the activities of the human subject they are "subjective" but
not merely subjective in the sense of arbitrary or self-serving. What is
opposed to objectivity is not the fact that the operations of intelligence

82. Ibid., 413.
83. Ibid.

and reason are those of a conscious subject, but the elements within the subject that interfere with the proper operation of intelligence and reason. These elements are the biases which turn away from particular data, truncate the scope of our questioning, and terminate the knowing process before it has come to its proper term.[84] Or as Lonergan so succinctly puts the matter in his later writings, "genuine objectivity is the fruit of authentic subjectivity."[85]

A Lonerganian response to the Gilsonian concern would be to suggest that this concern arises inasmuch as one has not clarified the distinction between animal and fully human knowing, so that the real remains the already out there now real of extroverted consciousness; that one has incorrectly accepted that the subject-object split as primordial rather than constructed by intelligence and reason; and so one is still operating with a false notion of objectivity conceived in terms of extroversion.[86] I shall argue this more fully in the next chapter.

General and Special Transcendent Knowledge

We have already introduced the distinction between being in general as the objective of the pure desire to know, and proportionate being, that is, being proportionate to our knowing. Human knowledge always begins with the empirical, the data of the senses or the data of consciousness. Interrogation of the data leads to insight, hypothesis/concept, asking the further question "is it so?" to the formation of judgment—yes/no/maybe. The question that naturally arises for an inquiring mind is whether there is any being other than proportionate being? Is there being that transcends the limits of human knowing and if so are we able to know of the existence of such being which by definition transcends the normal structure of that knowing? To raise such a question is to raise the question of God. In two chapters at the conclusion of *Insight*, Lonergan addresses the question of God (chapter 19: General Transcendent Knowledge) and the question of God in relation to the problem of evil (chapter 20: Special Transcendent Knowledge).

To pose the question of God as we have above is to face a conundrum. How can we know the existence of transcendent being when it tran-

---

84. Lonergan provides a thorough account of these biases as dramatic, individual, group and general, each of which distorts or truncates our orientation to being in specific ways. See ibid., 214–31, 244–67. While important in themselves, they are not necessary for our present work.
85. *Method*, 292.
86. For a solid exposition of the differences see Paul St. Amour, "Lonergan and Gilson on the Problem of Critical Realism," *Thomist* 69 (2005): 557–92.

scends the normal operation of that knowing? In the current cultural context, the answer is usually a flat rejection of such a possibility. The most common claim is that it is not possible to prove the existence of God, something both Christian theologians and atheists seem to agree upon. However, Lonergan remains faithful to the standard Catholic position that it is possible to know the existence of God and so proceeds to make his argument.[87] Given the restriction of our knowing to proportionate being, if we are to move to transcendent being it must be through some form of inference based on features of proportionate being that require or even demand further explanation. Such an inference will not be a direct insight into the nature of transcendent being, but rather a judgment of existence based on features of proportionate being. Or as Aquinas would say, we can know that God is, but not what God is.[88]

In order to draw the needed inference Lonergan introduces the notion of causality. True to his method of correlating metaphysical terms with psychological acts, Lonergan defines causality as "the objective and real counterpart of the questions and further questions raised by the detached, disinterested, and unrestricted desire to know."[89] Different types of questioning then lead to different types of causality. Internal causes are the metaphysical elements of potency, form and act, while external causes are efficient, final and exemplary causality. While the internal causes relate to proportionate being, the issue that needs resolution is whether the external forms of causality are general principles of being itself. Because being is the objective of the desire to know, being is completely intelligible. For what is unintelligible cannot be, and certainly cannot be the objective of a desire to know. Causality then is not to be conceived in terms of imagined pushes and pulls, or emanations from cause to effect, but as an intelligible relationship of dependence. If we can affirm such an intelligible relationship, then we have a form of causality. If however we restrict the field of causality to the empirical realm of proportionate being, then all our questioning hits up against a brick wall of brute fact—the brute facts of existence and occurrence. If proportionate being is the full scope of being, then being is no longer intelligible in itself, for the brute fact of existence and occurrence allows for no further answers

---

87. The standard Catholic position was enunciated at Vatican I, and essentially repeated verbatim by Vatican II.
88. Lonergan, *Insight*, 657.
89. Ibid., 674.

to emerge. Ultimately the intelligibility of the realm of proportionate being must lie beyond itself, in a transcendent being who is the external cause of existence of proportionate being.

The summary argument that Lonergan then gives for the existence of God is as follows: "If the real is completely intelligible, God exists. But the real is completely intelligible. Therefore, God exists."[90] This brings together various elements of Lonergan's overall developing position in *Insight*. The real is completely intelligible because through intellectual conversion we equate the real with being. Being is completely intelligible because we affirm and commit to ourselves as knowers through intelligent grasp and reasonable affirmation.[91] However, the real can only be completely intelligible if there is an extrinsic cause to make it exist, otherwise its incomplete intelligibility means it sinks into non-being. Our commitment to ourselves as fully oriented to being through intelligent grasp and reasonable affirmation commits us to an affirmation of the existence of God.

While there are nuances to the discussion that are beyond the scope of this present exposition, I will make two comments as to the relationship between Lonergan's approach and that of St Thomas.[92] First, Lonergan notes the similarities between the approach he has adopted above and the well-known "five ways" of Aquinas's *Summa Theologiae*: "the five ways in which Aquinas proves the existence of God are so many particular cases of the general statement that the proportionate universe is incompletely intelligible and that complete intelligibility is demanded." Further "besides Aquinas's five ways, there are as many other proofs of the existence of God as there are aspects of incomplete intelligibility in the universe of proportionate being."[93] Lonergan thus envisages his approach to proving the existence of God as entirely congruent with and in fact the foundation of Aquinas's approaches to the question. The second comment is to note that in enumerating the various consequences of his approach to the question of God, Lonergan rehearses in a few brief paragraphs the basic conclusions of his study

---

90. Ibid., 695.
91. As Lonergan notes, the chapter on the self-affirmation of the knower is in fact central to his argument at this stage. Ibid., 698: "It is a fair question, but to answer it a distinction has to be drawn between (1) affirming a link between other existence and God's and (2) affirming the other existence that is linked to God's existence. The second element lies in the affirmation of some reality: it took place in the chapter on self-affirmation, and it was expanded to the universe of proportionate being in subsequent chapters."
92. For a fuller exposition and analysis see Bernard Tyrrell, *Bernard Lonergan's Philosophy of God* (Notre Dame, IN: University of Notre Dame Press, 1974).
93. Lonergan, *Insight*, 701.

on grace and freedom in Aquinas.[94] Again we can grasp the continuity of Lonergan's position with that of Aquinas.

In the following chapter, on "special transcendent knowledge," Lonergan departs from the more familiar questions in relation to proving the existence of God, to ask what God is doing in relation to the problem of sin and evil.

> Because God is omniscient, he knows man's plight. Because he is omnipotent, he can remedy it. Because he is good, he wills to do so. The fact of evil is not the whole story. It also is a problem. Because God exists, there is a further intelligibility to be grasped.[95]

Here as a philosopher Lonergan cannot move beyond his brief to point to the Incarnation, redemption and the church as providing God's response to our plight. This would involve an appeal to revelation and hence be theological in the strict sense. However, as a philosopher he begins to speculate as to what a possible solution might look like, in order to establish an anticipation of the "heuristic structure" of a solution to the problem of evil. He specifies three possible solutions: a natural solution, a relatively supernatural solution, and an absolutely supernatural solution to the problem of evil. While there are differences between these, and as a philosopher one cannot pass judgment as to which is in fact operative in the actual universe of being, still each will involve three "conjugate forms" within human consciousness: faith in the intellect to believe in the solution offered by God and the various truths that emerge from it; hope in our conscious sensitivity to face the difficulties that emerge in living out the solution; and charity in the will which meets the fact of evil with self-sacrificing generosity, healing, and compassion. The fact that this aligns with the traditional theological virtues would escape the attention of no one. In his discussion of these conjugate forms Lonergan provides a long excursus on the nature of belief.[96] I shall engage with this more fully below, because it provides an excellent response to many of the questions that emerge around faith and reason lying at the heart of debates on the possibility of a Christian philosophy.

By any measure *Insight* is a philosophical masterpiece and the above material barely scratches its surface. Here Lonergan is not just seeking to "reach up to the mind of Aquinas" but to speak in his own voice,

94. Ibid., 684–87.
95. Ibid., 716.
96. Ibid., 725–40.

engaging what he had learnt in that reaching up to bring it to bear on our modern context. Aquinas knew nothing of the advances of modern science, whereas Lonergan regarded the modern scientific revolution as one of the most important cultural advances of our age.[97] Lonergan's comfort with both the content and method of science distinguishes him from the majority of his contemporary theologians and Thomistic philosophers for whom science remained an undiscovered country. Lonergan was also willing to engage with major philosophical trends, particularly the Kantian transcendental idealism and the Hegelian challenge of absolute idealism, not just view them as adversaries to be overcome.[98] Lonergan was clearly not unaware of the dangers Gilson identified in terms of a self-enclosed subjectivity knowing only its own thoughts and not reality. But as I noted in Chapter 1, Eric Mascall, himself influenced by Gilson, thought that Lonergan survived the charge of Kantian idealism.[99] Finally in this Lonergan's most philosophical work, in its concluding Chapter 20 and the epilogue that follows, we find Lonergan the theologian emerging, bringing theological questions into the discussion, mapping out a heuristic anticipation of theological issues that can only be fully addressed through revelation.[100] These concluding sections in a way provide the overall context and climax of the whole project. As Lonergan himself describes it, that project is not one of faith seeking understanding [*fides quaerens intellectum*], but of understanding seeking faith [*intellectus quaerens fidem*].[101] Only in the light of faith can the dynamism of intellect toward being reach its final goal.

Integrating the Existential – an Augustinian Turn?

Though as I have indicated, *Insight* is a major philosophical achievement, it would be wrong to think that Lonergan's thought ceased to

97. In later writings Lonergan voices the opinion that the scientific revolution "outshines everything since the rise of Christianity and reduces the Renaissance and the Reformation to mere episodes, mere internal displacements, within the system of medieval Christendom." See "Theology in its new context," in *A Second Collection*, ed. William Ryan and Bernard Tyrrell (Philadelphia: Westminster, 1974), 55–67, at 56.
98. Mark Morelli has made a strong case for Lonergan's engagement with the Hegelian challenge. See Mark Morelli, "Lonergan's Debt to Hegel and the Appropriation of Critical Realism," in *Meaning and History in Systematic Theology: Essays in Honor of Robert Doran, SJ*, ed. John Dadosky (Marquette: Marquette University Press, 2009).
99. Eric Mascall, *The Openness of Being: Natural Theology Today* (London: Darton, Longman and Todd, 1971), 90.
100. Lonergan himself will describe *Insight* as a prolegomenon to his later work on theological method.
101. See Lonergan, *Insight*, 753: "a problem of evil . . . demands the transformation of self-reliant intelligence into an *intellectus quaerens fidem*."

develop after this work. While *Insight* represents the modern transposition of the work of Aquinas, we can also suggest that as Lonergan's thought developed, it is Augustine who becomes a stronger voice. We have already noted in the discussion of *Verbum* that Lonergan seeks to integrate the method of interiority found in Augustine with the more metaphysical account of cognition to be found in Aristotle and Aquinas.[102] However, the world of interiority is not just one of thought, but also of feeling. Whereas affectivity gets less attention in *Insight*, it begins to emerge as a significant theme as Lonergan extends his range beyond the cognitional to the more existential scope of human living. If for Augustine it is our restless heart that rests not, until it rests in God, for the earlier Lonergan and for Aquinas, it is more the restlessness of our minds than never settles. Now in the post-*Insight* era Lonergan discovers (and thematizes) the restlessness of the heart. In his latter writings Lonergan will speak of feelings as providing the "mass, momentum, drive [and] power" of intentional consciousness.[103] Whereas *Insight* is dominated by the three-fold structure of experience, understanding and judgment, in later writings he will speak of *four* "transcendental precepts": "Be attentive, be intelligent, be reasonable, be responsible."[104] More and more the question of existential, rather than cognitional, authenticity comes to the fore. And rather than the question of God's existence being at the climax of the investigations, concerns with religious experience and religious conversion take a center stage.

These shifts are enormously enriching, filling out the more intellectualist stance of Lonergan's earlier work. Nonetheless none of these developments is a repudiation of his earlier gains; it is an expansion of Lonergan's horizon, an expansion which more fully prepares us for the movement into strictly theological concerns. However, for the sake of keeping some degree of control of the present project, on the possibility of a Christian philosophy, I shall keep the focus on his writings up to and including *Insight*, and whatever later writings may contribute to a better understanding of those works.

102. *Verbum*, 4.
103. *Method*, 30.
104. Ibid., 231.

Lonergan as a "Christian Philosopher"

Now all would accept that Lonergan was a Christian and a philosopher. The question we now turn our attention to is whether we can think of him as a "Christian philosopher" more or less in the terms spelt out by Gilson in the previous chapter. Lonergan himself never used the term to describe his work, though he does adopt a perhaps related term "Christian realism," which we shall consider below. And as we shall spell out more fully in the subsequent chapter there are philosophical differences between Gilson and Lonergan in terms of philosophy's starting point (metaphysics or cognitional theory) as well as differences in their accounts of these two topics. Both however have claims to carrying on the tradition of Aquinas. These differences need further exploration. But in the meantime I would like to explore Lonergan's credentials to be a Christian philosopher.

Natural Desire to see God[105]

One of the major debates around the *nouvelle théologie* is the status of a purported "natural desire to see God." Few questions have generated as much debate,[106] a debate that extends even into contemporary authors such as Lawrence Feingold[107] and John Milbank. As a question it touches on the range and scope of our orientation to the world of existence. Are we oriented to the source of all existence and if so is this orientation "natural" in the sense of a constitutive element in human nature, or is it supernatural, something implanted in us by God without which we would still be human, however diminished we might be? And so we have two questions: Does the scope of our orientation to the world extend to the source of the world, to God? Is this orientation natural or supernatural? The answer to the first is best captured by Augustine's observation that our restless hearts can only truly rest in God. The answer to the second is where things get interesting.

Without exploring the depths of this debate I shall set forth Lonergan's approach to the question. We have already seen how in *Insight*

---

105. For an excellent account of Lonergan's position on this issue see Brian Himes, "Lonergan's Position on the Natural Desire to See God and Aquinas' Metaphysical Theology of Creation and Participation," *Heythrop Journal* 54, no. 5 (2013): 767–83.

106. See for example the account of the debate surrounding the *nouvelle théologie* in Stephen Duffy, *The Graced Horizon: Nature and Grace in Modern Catholic Thought* (Collegeville, MN: Liturgical Press, 1992).

107. Lawrence Feingold, *The Natural Desire to See God According to St. Thomas Aquinas and His Interpreters* (Naples, FL: Sapientia Press of Ave Maria University, 2010).

Lonergan speaks of the detached disinterested desire to know, which has as its objective, being, everything that exists. This desire is a *potentia omnia*—a potency to all things, though of limited attainment. While the intentional reach of our questioning is all being, the actual attainment is of proportionate being. As Lonergan poses the question of God, does there exist transcendent being, being that transcends the reach of our actual attainment, and if so can we know of its existence? However, rather than start with *Insight* I will consider one of Lonergan's early Latin works, *De ente supernaturalis* (1946),[108] and the related article "On the Natural Desire to see God"[109] in which Lonergan considers the question of whether we possess "natural desire to see God." This question directly touches on problems raised by the *nouvelle théologie* debates on the grace-nature distinction.

Lonergan defines desire as "an appetite for, or an act of striving after an object that is absent or not possessed."[110] Within the range of desires he distinguishes between "natural appetite, on the one hand, and appetitive acts, whether sensitive or intellectual, on the other." These latter appetitive acts are "elicited," that is, it "is an act of desiring some object; it is caused and specified by that object as apprehended . . . and so is found only in sensitive and intellectual beings."[111] In this sense the word natural, when speaking of a "natural desire," has a double meaning, that is, natural as distinct from elicited, and natural as distinct from supernatural. And so, to speak of a natural desire to see God is to say the desire is neither elicited nor supernatural.

In what then does the natural desire consist? Lonergan argues that natural desires are revealed by their acts and the acts which he identifies as revealing this natural desire are acts of questioning.

> The radical inclination or tendency of the intellect is manifested principally by the occurrence of the question *quid sit* ('What is it?' or 'Why is it so?') and *an sit* ('Is it so?'), to which all other questions can ultimately be reduced. Such questioning is a natural activity. . . . If questioning is natural, then so is the antecedent desire from which it wells up.[112]

---

108. The Latin work is not yet available in Lonergan's Collected Works, but a detailed analysis of this work can be found in J. Michael Stebbins, *The Divine Initiative: Grace, World-order, and Human Freedom in the Early Writings of Bernard Lonergan* (Toronto: University of Toronto Press, 1995). I draw from Stebbins's analysis.
109. Bernard J. F. Lonergan, "The Natural Desire to see God," in *Collection*, ed. Frederick E. Crowe and Robert M. Doran, Collected Works of Bernard Lonergan (Toronto: Toronto University Press, 1988), 81–91.
110. Stebbins, *The Divine Initiative*, 150.
111. Ibid., 151.
112. Ibid., 154.

And so for Lonergan, "the question, *quid sit Deus*, expresses a desire that naturally arises as soon as one knows the existence of God."[113] In summary then, "the intellect's desire to know is at root a desire to know God."[114]

The desire to know that Lonergan thus identifies as a desire for God becomes the central theme of *Insight*. It is manifest in questions for understanding and questions of judgment. This questioning drives all our science, mathematics, scholarship, philosophy and theology. Its proper object is being itself, with the desire to know constituting a "notion of being" within consciousness. Lonergan often refers to the desire to know as "detached and disinterested" to distinguish it from the various other desires/attachments which create a polyphony within consciousness. Human desires are "polymorphous" and it is a constant struggle to allow full reign to the desire to know. The desire to know is unrestricted, as revealed in our constant questioning and the never ending flow of books which fill our libraries. Attempts to limit the scope of questions are immediately overcome by further questioning of those limits. The desire to know is itself a "pure" question, a question without preconditions, without boundaries. Left to its own internal dynamism it will raise the question of God, and fidelity to that dynamism will lead one to inevitably affirm the existence of God. To properly grasp the significance of this desire to know is the core of all philosophy.[115]

The Possibility of Natural Knowledge of God

As we can see from above, not unrelated to the question of the natural desire to see God, is that of the possibility of natural knowledge of God. We have already witnessed Lonergan's commitment to a natural theology in the concluding chapters of *Insight*. His proof of the existence of God comes as the culmination and climax of a moving viewpoint, which begins with cognitional theory and moves to epistemological and metaphysical accounts, in such a way that God's existence is the ultimate underpinning of the intelligibility of reality. Without God, reality remains unintelligible and what is unintelligible falls away into non-existence. In more traditional terms God is the necessary ground of being for the universe of contingent being. Lonergan would view his

---

113. Lonergan, "The Natural Desire to see God," 83.
114. Stebbins, *The Divine Initiative*, 155.
115. The references here to *Insight* are too numerous to list, but can easily be traced through the index to that work.

argument as fulfilling the teaching of Vatican I on the possibility of natural knowledge of God.

Still it is a "proof" that depends on pre-conditions and commitments, the culmination of a moving viewpoint, which includes the self-affirmation of the knower in chapter 11 of *Insight*. This viewpoint also requires the adoption of the three positions and a rejection of the counter-positions. In his later writings Lonergan will refer to these requirements as amounting to a need for "intellectual conversion." In other writings he notes that, "One cannot prove the existence of God to a Kantian without first breaking his allegiance to Kant. One cannot prove the existence of God to a positivist without first converting him from positivism."[116] So in that sense the argument begins within a horizon with certain presuppositions which may not be present in every subject. If one does not accept these presuppositions the argument has no traction. As Tyrrell notes:

> The extrapolation from restricted acts of understanding to the unrestricted act of understanding is a subtle and refined intellectual accomplishment doomed to failure from the outset unless attempted by one who is operating from the basis of fully developed intellectual conversion.[117]

This recognition marks a development on the standard Thomist position which tends to take somewhat for granted the correct disposition within the subject asking the question of God's existence. Here the basic presuppositions of any proof for the existence of God are not the basic principles of being (such as the principles of non-contradiction and identity) but the correct alignment of our native orientation to being with our stance on knowing, objectivity and reality. In his later writings Lonergan shifts even further to claim that it is not the answer, but the question about God that is most significant, because it is our questions about God that provide a basic heuristic as to the meaning of the word God itself.[118] What emerges here is that in the debate between faith and reason, there is an important distinction between the native operations of intellect (performance) and our accounts of the opera-

---

116. Bernard J. F. Lonergan, "The General Character of the Natural Theology of *Insight*," in *Philosophical and Theological Papers 1965–1980*, ed. Robert M. Doran and Frederick E. Crowe, Collected Works of Bernard Lonergan (Toronto: University of Toronto Press, 2004), 6.

117. Tyrrell, *Bernard Lonergan's Philosophy of God*, 136. Note the similarities with Taylor's comments that a conclusion of an argument for the existence of God comes at the end of an "extreme and most fragile end of a chain of inferences." Charles Taylor, *A Secular Age* (Cambridge, MA: Belknap Press, 2007), 558.

118. Lonergan, *Method*, 101–3.

tions of intellect (reflection on performance). When we talk about reason we often have in mind some account of what reason is, which may or may not accurately grasp the actual performance of intellect. This is very evident in debates with the "new atheists" who often put forward an empiricist or positivist account of reason, as if that is what reason actually is. Further, a distorted account of reason feeds back into our own performance, distorting our reasoning in the process. Without attending to these "subjective" aspects of proving the existence of God, we can find our intellectual wheels spinning but nothing moves forward.

Cognitional Theory or Metaphysics

In reviewing his achievement in *Insight*, it is clear that Lonergan is well aware that he is breaking with the received tradition in taking cognitional theory as his starting point. Indeed he notes that "the most shocking aspect of the book, *Insight*, is the primacy it accords to knowledge" while "in the writings of St Thomas, cognitional theory is expressed in metaphysical terms and established by metaphysical principles." As he states in it, "I have turned everything upside down."[119] On the other hand, as he does in his more fulsome study, *Verbum*, he identifies times in the work of Aquinas where an appeal is made to our experience of cognitional processes. In particular he quotes *STh* I q88, a2, ad3, which he translates as "the human soul understands itself by its understanding, which is its proper act, perfectly demonstrating its power and its nature."[120] He goes further to justify this appeal to experience by using the standard Aristotelian and Thomist distinction between the *quoad se* (what is first in itself) and *quoad nos* (what is first for us). While being is first in itself, knowing is first for us. If we take the *quoad se* as a starting point, then metaphysics has priority over cognitional theory; however if we take the *quoad nos* as a starting point, then cognitional theory takes precedence. Both are equally valid starting points, however, and both lead to isomorphic conclusions. As he notes, "on this showing, then, the ontological and the cognitional are not incompatible alternatives but interdependent procedures."[121] He further appeals to the needs of the present day to go beyond the desire to "select a minimum number of certitudes on which all agree,

119. "*Insight*: Preface to a Discussion," in *Collection*, ed. Frederick E. Crowe and Robert M. Doran, Collected Works of Bernard Lonergan (Toronto: University of Toronto Press, 1993), 142.
120. Ibid., 143.
121. Ibid., 144.

to strive for a thorough knowledge of medieval thought, to deduce new conclusions from old premises" all drawn from the writings of Aristotle and Aquinas. Rather there is a need to implement "Aristotelian and Thomist method." This demands "a developed understanding of understanding itself, and to use that developed understanding of human understanding to bring order and light and unity to a totality of disciplines and modes of knowledge."[122]

Lonergan's relationship then to the position of Aquinas is not one of repetition, but of transposition. In the light of so many modern developments—the emergence of modern science,[123] of historical consciousness,[124] of the turn to the subject[125]—simple repetition is not enough. While there are undoubtedly dangers in such an approach, amply spelt out by Gilson in the previous chapter, there are also many gains to be had, particularly for a Christian philosophy that will need to deal with questions of religious experience. The Christian tradition is replete with explorations of the interior life, be it Augustine, Ignatius of Loyola or the Rhineland mystics. Lonergan was himself a son of Ignatius, and there are those who argue that his own method finds its grounding in the Ignatian spiritual exercises.[126] Such a turn to the concrete experience of the subject runs the risk not so much of idealism, but of blurring the distinction between grace and nature. I shall return to this issue in the final chapter.

The Reasonableness of Believing

As I noted in chapter 1, if you want to develop a more precise account of the relationship between faith and reason, one must first provide a fairly precise account of reason, in order to be able to differentiate it from faith. Lonergan provides just such a precise account of reason through his structure of experience, understanding and judgment. However, he pushes the matter further by providing a far more

---

122. Ibid., 145.
123. Here Lonergan concurs with the judgment of the historian of science, Herbert Butterfield, that the emergence of modern science "outshines everything since the rise of Christianity and reduces the Renaissance and the Reformation to mere episodes, mere internal displacements, within the system of medieval Christendom." "Theology in its New Context," 56. Lonergan is referring to Herbert Butterfield, *The Origins of Modern Science, 1300–1800*, 2nd ed. (New York: Free Press, 1966).
124. See Bernard J. F. Lonergan, "The Transition from a Classicist World-View to Historical Mindedness," in *A Second Collection*, ed. William F. Ryan and Bernard Tyrrell (Philadelphia: Westminster, 1974).
125. "The Subject."
126. Robert Doran, "Ignatian Themes in the Thought of Bernard Lonergan," *Toronto Journal of Theology* 22, no. 1 (2006): 39–54.

nuanced and precise account of faith as well, in a way that takes the debate in a surprising direction. To those who would oppose faith and reason, especially those who promote reason against faith, Lonergan demonstrates the reasonableness of believing. Without some form of belief all that we can claim to know is that which we ourselves can generate from our own experience, understanding and judgment. In fact if that is all we can legitimately claim to know, in the strict sense, if belief were to be excluded, we would all be most ignorant. Indeed most of what we claim to "know" is not immanently generated at all, but is material we take "on trust" as part of the common store of knowledge offered to us through our education, reading, and heritage. These are the general plausibility structures and background beliefs constitutive of a society or particular community. For Lonergan, the "general context of belief is the collaboration of mankind in the advancement and the dissemination of knowledge."[127] Without such belief we would be condemned to primitivism.[128]

As with his account of cognition, Lonergan also provides a precise account of the stages that lead to a belief:

> Five stages are to be distinguished, namely, (1) preliminary judgments on the value of belief in general, on the reliability of the source for this belief, and on the accuracy of the communication from the source, (2) a reflective act of understanding that, in virtue of the preliminary judgments, grasps as virtually unconditioned the value of deciding to believe some particular proposition, (3) the consequent judgment of value, (4) the consequent decision of the will, and (5) the assent that is the act of believing.[129]

If we focus on the first of these stages, two important elements emerge. The first is a general judgment of the value of belief in general. Belief permeates all our attempts to know. The scientist who thought it necessary to recapitulate all previous scientific discoveries for herself before she could made a genuine advance of her own would be a scientist who never made an advance![130] Those physicists working at the Large Hadron Collider believe all the theoretical and practical intel-

---

127. Lonergan, *Insight*, 725.
128. It is the startling discovery that much of what we think we "know" is in fact a matter of belief that leaves the door open for the very modern phenomenon of widespread suspicion of generally trustworthy authorities. This is very evident in the climate change debate where large portions of the population feel justified in questioning and rejecting the scientific consensus on climate change.
129. Lonergan, *Insight*, 729–30.

ligence of the engineers who built their massive device. In our more mundane daily lives we believe in the theoretical and practical intelligence of those who build our cars, our electrical and electronic devices, and so on. If we had to verify for ourselves all the insights that went into producing them all before we trusted their operation, life would be a tedious and dull affair. As Lonergan notes, belief allows for "the collaboration of mankind in the advancement and the dissemination of knowledge."[131] The second element is that belief involves *someone* believed. Any act of belief involves a judgment as to the trustworthiness of the one we believe. Is this a reliable person? Have they communicated the facts accurately? Belief then is always about an interpersonal relationship to some degree. We may trust the other person's professionalism or simply their virtue.

Clearly believing is not infallible. We can and do have false beliefs. "Mistaken beliefs exist, and the function of an analysis of belief is overlooked if it fails to explain how mistaken beliefs arise and how they are to be eliminated."[132] Rather than reject the contribution of belief to our knowing, Lonergan counsels a methodology for eliminating false belief:

> It takes as its starting point and clue the discovery of some precise issue on which undoubtedly one was mistaken. It advances by inquiring into the sources that may have contributed to that error and, perhaps, contributed to other errors as well. It asks about the motives and the supporting judgments that, as they once confirmed one in that error, may still be holding one in others. It investigates the consequences of the view one now rejects, and it seeks to determine whether or not they too are to be rejected. The process is cumulative. The discovery of one error is exploited to lead to the discovery of others; and the discovery of the others provides a still larger base to proceed to the discovery of still more.[133]

Lonergan is taking forward a suggestion of Newman, that it is better to believe everything, and set about correcting false belief, than to adopt the universal doubt of Descartes which runs the risk of emptying the mind of essential knowledge along with error.[134]

Lonergan's argument for the rationality of belief cuts across the dichotomy of faith and reason so prevalent in many current debates,

130. As one example Lonergan gives states, "Perhaps no one has immanently generated knowledge that general relativity is more accurate than Newtonian theory on the perihelion of Mercury. But it does not follow that for everyone it is purely a matter of belief." Ibid., 728.
131. Ibid., 725.
132. Ibid., 735.
133. Ibid., 736.
134. "Universal doubt leads the philosopher to reject what he is not equipped to restore." Ibid., 436.

particularly in the science-religion context. It is a reminder that even the "knowledge" of the scientist is suffused with belief.[135] In contexts of both science and religion people can make a reasonable decision to believe others, based on our assessment of their reliability and the value of believing in general as a way of transmitting knowledge from one person to another. What is important is that someone actually knows in the chain of believing.

Christian Realism

While Lonergan does not directly use the term "Christian philosophy" of his own position, he uses a similar and perhaps more precise term, that of "Christian realism" to identify a position he finds congruent with his own thinking. What we can grasp in this designation is the close connection operating between doctrinal commitments and philosophical outcomes, all the time maintaining the clear distinction between faith and reason, between theology and philosophy. Lonergan argues that Christian doctrine contains an implicit realism which becomes increasingly explicit in the history of Christian theological attempts to understand these doctrines. Just as Gilson draws philosophical implications from the story of Exodus 3:14, Lonergan will draw on various theological positions to make explicit implications that can philosophically stand in their own right.

Impact of Christology

The first example arises from autobiographical comments Lonergan made in relation to his own intellectual development. These comments have been brought together in William Mathews's book, *Lonergan's Quest*, and in Richard Liddy's book, *Transforming Light*.[136] As noted by these authors Lonergan attributes his own grasp of the distinction between essence and existence to working through a serious dogmatic question in theology:

135. This is very evident in the climate change debate. It is not unreasonable to believe the position of climate scientists on the basis of their special expertise. Even other scientists will trust their judgments and the process of scientific peer review that supports their research. But few actually have the immanently generated knowledge about climate change. In later works Lonergan refers to this insight as to do with the "sociology of knowledge" as propounded by Peter L. Berger and Thomas Luckmann, *The Social Construction of Reality: a Treatise in the Sociology of Knowledge* (New York: Anchor Books, 1990).
136. Mathews, *Lonergan's Quest*, 82–84; Richard M. Liddy, *Transforming Light: Intellectual Conversion in the early Lonergan* (Collegeville, Minn.: Liturgical Press, 1993), 114–16.

Can one have one person who has two natures? The argument given me by a good Thomist, Father Bernard Leeming, was that if you have a real distinction between *esse* (existence) and essence, the *esse* can be the ground of the person and of the essence too. If the *esse* is relevant to two essences, then you can have one person in two natures. On that basis I solved the problem of Christ's consciousness: one subject and two subjectivities.[137]

Now the question of the person and natures of Christ is something that could not be known unless it were revealed to us; on this both Gilson and Lonergan would concur. While Gilson finds the distinction between essence and existence in the revelation of the divine name, for Lonergan the basic dogmatic formulation of Chalcedon is rendered unintelligible without such a distinction. For both thinkers what drives the emergence of the distinction is not just abstract philosophical reasoning, but personal engagement with revelation within a context of an historical practice of such engagement. Still, both would hold that as something knowable in itself, the distinction is a purely philosophical position that is at least potentially accessible through reason alone. I shall return to this example below in discussing Lonergan's notion of Christian realism.

The Relationship Between Trinitarian Theology and Epistemology

The second example is in relation to the role of Trinitarian theology in Lonergan's philosophical development. In the epilogue to *Insight* Lonergan notes that his position in that work draws on his historical study of the work of Aquinas: "So it is that my detailed investigations of the thought of Aquinas on *gratia operans* and on *verbum* have been followed by the present essay in aid of a personal appropriation of one's own rational self-consciousness."[138] Yet both these works depend heavily on Christian dogmatic teachings: the first on grace and free will; the second on the Trinity. To focus on the second of these, Lonergan's work, *Verbum: Word and Idea in Aquinas*, is often related to by philosophers for its rejection of Scotist conceptualism, its affirmation of Aquinas's intellectualism, and for its proposed resolution of questions in Thomist epistemology. Now it is undoubtedly true that these elements are to be found in that work. However, the immediate question that Lonergan is seeking to address, as we have noted above, is that of the Trinitarian processions. He begins the work with some general comments about

137. Mathews, *Lonergan's Quest*, 82.
138. Lonergan, *Insight*, 769.

the then state of play in relation to the question of the Trinitarian processions. He notes the conflict between those who hold that the procession of the Word may be found in the "sensitive potency" in contrast to those who hold it may only be found in the intellect. He identifies the difference between these two positions as arising from a "neglect of what is peculiar to rational creatures." He concludes, "I believe these questions to be significant. It is to discuss them that I have undertaken the present inquiry into the concept of *verbum* in the writings of St Thomas."[139]

In undertaking this study Lonergan is engaging in a practice of reflection going back at least as far as Augustine's *De Trinitate*. This practice is driven by a theological desire to find some way of approaching the doctrine of the Trinity in an intellectually coherent manner, not in order to prove it as a doctrine, but to make sense of what is believed (*fides quaerens intellectum*). This practice seeks analogies for the two divine processions in various operations within human consciousness. Yet in order for the analogy to work as an analogy various philosophical assumptions must be in place. For example, unless knowing attains reality, the analogy for the divine Word proceeding from the Father as a concept proceeds from an act of understanding, cannot help us understand how the Word is consubstantial with the Father. Similarly unless judgments of value are grounded in reason, the analogy cannot help us understand how the Spirit proceeds from the Father and the Son.[140]

What we find here is an intimate connection between revelation and philosophical development in Lonergan's work. Dogmatic belief in the Trinity is driving greater and greater precision in relation to questions of cognitional structure and epistemology through the speculative hypothesis of the psychological analogy. This precision could be derived from reason alone, but more obscurely and with greater difficulty. In fact in *Insight* we can witness the effort needed to attain some of these positions on the basis of philosophical reason alone. However, from the point of view of the present discussion, what is important is the way in which this element of Lonergan's work exemplifies Gilson's notion of a Christian philosophy.

---

139. *Verbum*, 13.
140. For a fuller account of the philosophical assumptions embedded in the psychological analogy see Neil Ormerod, "The Psychological Analogy for the Trinity – At Odds with Modernity," *Pacifica* 14 (2001): 281–94.

Origins of Christian Realism

In an essay entitled, "The Origins of Christian Realism," Lonergan develops further this interaction between dogmatic teaching and philosophical thought.[141] This essay was written in response to certain proposals by Ansfried Hulsbosch, Edward Schillebeeckx and Piet Schoonenberg for a revision of Christological doctrine. Lonergan meets these proposals with a discussion of Christianity's engagement with the problems of realism since the time of the early Trinitarian and Christological debates. He outlines how Christianity is inextricably involved in the problems of realism. In fact, Christian meanings demand a critical, or at least, dogmatic realism to make sense of its basic doctrines. And so, after reviewing the distinction between the world of immediacy and the world mediated by meaning, he considers the early Trinitarian debates, to grasp how different philosophical positions handle the question of the relationship between the Father and the Son. The way in which to understand "what was moving forward" is, he argues, to observe that Tertullian was a naïve realist, that Origen was a neo-Platonic idealist, while Athanasius, and the definition of Nicaea, demand at least a dogmatic realism, to be able to properly affirm the *homoousios*. This realism is based on accepting the assertion that reality corresponds to true meaning, mediated by propositions, as summarized in the Athanasian rule for the *homoousios*: "all that is said of the Father also is to be said of the Son, except that the Son is Son and not the Father."[142] Such a formulation operates within a world mediated by meaning but is problematic as long as one remains within the world of immediacy.

Turning to Christological doctrine Lonergan then seeks to explain the distinction between person and nature in the Chalcedonian definition by considering three meanings of the term "one." There is one, in the numerical sense, corresponding to experiential activity. There is one, grasped in terms of the unity of a thing, corresponding to intellectual activity. And then there is one, as in one and the same, as distinct from another, corresponding to judging. Here Lonergan is clearly

141. Lonergan, "The Origins of Christian Realism."
142. Ibid., 250. The reference to Athanasius is to his *Against the Arians*, Discourse III.4. Lonergan develops the same point more fully in *The Way to Nicea: the Dialectical Development of Trinitarian Theology*, trans. Conn O'Donovan (London: Darton, Longman & Todd, 1976). This material is now available in its fuller context of Lonergan's work on the Trinity, *The Triune God: Doctrines*, ed. Robert M. Doran and H. Daniel Monsour, trans. Michael Shields, Collected Works of Bernard Lonergan (Toronto: University of Toronto Press, 2009).

invoking the three levels of cognitional structure in a way that transposes into cognitional terms the classical distinction between essence and existence. Person is then defined in terms of the one and the same identity affirmed in judgment. This account gives more precision to his autobiographical comments noted earlier that the distinction between person and nature in the Chalcedonian definition requires a real distinction between existence (grounded in judgment) and essence (grounded in understanding).

Lonergan makes this connection, between religious experience and belief on the one hand, and philosophical development on the other, explicit in his notions of religious and intellectual conversion. In *Method in Theology* Lonergan speaks of religious conversion in terms of an other-worldly falling in love, the gift of God's love poured into our hearts by the Holy Spirit (Rom 5:5). This experience of God's love grounds faith as a knowledge borne of that love. This faith is expressed as religious beliefs which are the cultural and historical expression of that faith. As we can see in the above examples, for Lonergan the teachings of Nicea and Constantinople elicit an intellectual conversion as the depths of that revelation are uncovered through the ongoing reflection of the Christian community. As Lonergan states it:

> First there is God's gift of his love. Next, the eye of this love reveals values in their splendor, while the strength of this love brings about their realization, and that is moral conversion. Finally, *among the values discerned by the eye of love is the value of believing the truths taught by the religious tradition, and in such tradition and belief are the seeds of intellectual conversion.* For the word, spoken and heard, proceeds from and penetrates to all four levels of intentional consciousness. Its content is not just a content of experience but a content of experience and understanding and judging and deciding. The analogy of sight yields the cognitional myth. But fidelity to the word engages the whole man. [emphasis added][143]

In summary then we have noted a number of ways in which Lonergan conceives the interaction of philosophical reasoning with revealed truths. In terms that MacIntyre might use we can say that revelation initiates, prolongs and sustains a tradition of rationality we can locate in the philosophical realism of the Thomistic tradition, and its modern transposition in the work of Lonergan. This achieves, I would argue, what Gilson sought to articulate in his notion of a Christian philosophy, even though Lonergan himself does not use the term.

143. *Method*, 243.

Lonergan on Gilson

In the previous chapter I outlined Gilson's critique of the turn to the subject, as exemplified by the transcendental Thomists of the Leuven school. Many have seen this critique as extending to the position of Lonergan as spelt out above. Lonergan is a strong proponent of the turn to the subject, taking as his starting point cognitional theory to ground his metaphysics. In fairness we should also present Lonergan's account of Gilson, in order to place it within a Lonerganian perspective. Now Lonergan has not provided us with extensive commentary on Gilson's work, but he did write two essays, a book review of *Being and Some Philosophers*,[144] and an essay entitled "Metaphysics as Horizon," a critical response to work of Emerich Coreth.[145]

Lonergan is clearly appreciative of Gilson's work in *Being and Some Philosophers*. He describes it as "extraordinarily erudite" and as containing an "amazing wealth of insights."[146] After presenting a summary of the argument of the book and noting a few areas of disagreement, Lonergan expresses his agreement with the "central contentions" of the work: "Being is existing, and thinking is not knowing." In so arguing he has placed "the old disputed question of essence and existence" into a new context by Gilson's appeal to the historical experiment of past philosophies: "For an appeal to history as experiment is not more argument or more theory. It is an appeal to fact and possesses the peculiar decisiveness of that appeal."[147] Indeed it may be that Gilson's historical method here provided Lonergan with something of a model for his own brief discussion of "Theories of the Notion of Being" and his fuller discussion of "The Dialectic of Method in Metaphysics" in *Insight*,[148] though both go back in some way to Aristotle's use of historical dialectic in philosophy.

As Lonergan notes the decisive step in Gilson's argument is the role of judgment. As he quotes Gilson, "'All real knowledge includes a judgment of existence' (p. 204)." Judgment moves us beyond substantial form, individuating matter, and accidents to "a further ontological

---

144. "Review of Étienne Gilson, *Being and Some Philosophers*," in *Shorter Papers*, ed. Robert Croken, Robert M. Doran, and H. Daniel Monsour, Collected Works of Bernard Lonergan (Toronto: University of Toronto, 2007), 185–88. The original review appeared in 1950 in *Theological Studies*.
145. "Metaphysics as Horizon," in *Collection*, ed. Frederick E. Crowe and Robert M. Doran, Collected Works of Bernard Lonergan (Toronto: University of Toronto, 1988), 188–204. The original article was published in 1963 in *Gregorianum*.
146. "Review of Étienne Gilson, *Being and Some Philosophers*," 185.
147. Ibid., 188.
148. *Insight*, 388–98, 426–55.

component named 'existence'." Nonetheless Lonergan expresses some concern about Gilson's precise understanding of the act of judgment: "Finally, the insistence upon a 'return to sense' and the affirmation of an intuitive experience of acts of existing (pp. 206–7) are strangely reminiscent of something like Kierkegaard's aesthetic sphere of existential subjectivity."[149] Still he does not view this quibble as invalidating Gilson's overall argument.

In his later essay, "Metaphysics as Horizon" we find a more extended and critical engagement with Gilson's earlier work, *Thomistic Realism and the Critique of Knowledge*. The context of this engagement is an extended review of the work of Coreth in developing a transcendental metaphysics. Coreth's project is within what he identifies as "transcendental Thomism" as exemplified by the Leuven Thomists that Gilson has so thoroughly critiqued in his work *Thomistic Realism*. Lonergan engages in a three-way dialectic between Coreth, Kant, and Gilson, to highlight the similarities and differences between the three approaches. Lonergan is clearly far more sympathetic to the approach of Coreth, which in many ways parallels his own. In relation to Gilson, however, he makes a number of critical comments.

Firstly he compares Gilson's appeal to perception to Kant's notion of *Anschauung* or "intuition." Both provide these philosophers with a door to the real world, in an attempt to provide some basis for objectivity. For Kant this basis must fail because our *Anschauung* is only sensitive (phenomenal) and so does not reach the thing-in-itself (*noumena*). Human knowing is then confined to the phenomena. Gilson avoids this idealist trap by his assertion that there exists "an intellectual vision of the concept of being in any sensible datum . . . predicated in perceptual judgments of existence."[150] For Gilson there can be no mediation of the real, for any such meditation leads inevitably to idealism and the problem of the bridge—how to get the outside inside. "It follows that [for Gilson] realism is possible if and only if we *perceive* reality."[151] As we noted in the previous chapter, Gilson himself refers to this position as a dogmatic realism, indeed "the brute reaffirmation of dogmatic real-

149. "Review of Étienne Gilson, *Being and Some Philosophers*," 187. The page references within the quote are to Étienne Gilson, *Being and Some Philosophers*, 2nd ed. (Toronto: Pontifical Institute of Mediaeval Studies, 1952).
150. Lonergan, "Metaphysics as Horizon," 195.
151. Ibid., 196.

ism, the validity of which had been denied by Kant's critique."[152] In this way Gilson can save the objectivity of human knowing.

However, what can be dogmatically asserted can equally dogmatically be denied, so how are we to decide between the Kantian and Gilsonian position? Coreth provides an alternative approach, one congruent with Lonergan's own position in *Insight*. Lonergan takes as his starting point two different ways of reading the Thomist principle, *Nihil in intellectu nisi prius fuerit in sensu* (nothing in the intellect unless first in sense). He notes however there is a difference between a box being empty and a stomach being empty. "When there is nothing in a box, a box does not feel empty; when there is nothing in a stomach, the stomach does feel empty. Human intelligence is more like a stomach than a box."[153] While empty, the mind still can ask questions, and "the analysis of questioning forces one to conceive of human intelligence, not on the analogy of sense, but properly in terms of intelligence itself."[154] While for Gilson being is perceived through the senses, for Coreth and Lonergan being is intended in questions that arise from the sense data. This "intention of being" in questioning is an *a priori* within the subject that eliminates the problem of the bridge: "there can be no problem of the 'extramental,' of getting outside the mind, for as soon as a question is asked, being is intended, being includes everything, and so everything is already within the mind's intention."[155] In terms Lonergan uses in *Insight*, Gilson's position is based on an extroverted conception of reality as already-out-there-now, a counter-position inviting reversal through attention to the dynamic intention of being found in human questioning.

This is not to say that Lonergan endorses the whole of Coreth's program, and the point of disagreement is instructive for the present work. Coreth is seeking to define metaphysics as a basic position that "accepts no presuppositions that it itself does not justify."[156] As we have seen however in *Insight*, for Lonergan metaphysics is a derived science, one whose ultimate basis lies in cognitional theory.

---

152. Étienne Gilson, *Thomist Realism and the Critique of Knowledge* (San Francisco: Ignatius Press, 2012), 154.
153. Lonergan, "Metaphysics as Horizon," 200.
154. Ibid., 201.
155. Ibid., 202.
156. Ibid., 189.

Conclusion

As with Gilson, Lonergan has had his share of critics, not least among them those who have taken the Gilsonian critique to heart. Given the diversity of Lonergan's writings, in theology, philosophy, economics, art, education to name a few, critics can find ample points of disagreement and criticism. The one constant in all Lonergan's work is the turn to the subject, the exploration of interiority or human consciousness. This is the basis on which his life's work stands or falls. Nonetheless, in contrast with the faltering reception of Gilson's legacy, the reception of Lonergan's work remains relatively robust, both philosophically and theologically. While much of the early reception focused on his philosophical contributions, increasingly Lonergan's theological work is being taken up.[157] Lonergan's *Insight* and its related works have a certain timeless quality to them that transcends much of their historical and cultural context. They are likely to continue to provoke both admiration and dissent for some time to come. While I have already indicated some mutual dialogue between our two thinkers, it is now time for a more thorough engagement between them with a particular focus on whether Lonergan falls under the Gilsonian critique of idealism and their potential common ground in relation to the possibility of a Christian philosophy.

---

157. To my mind this theological reception has been greatly facilitated by the writings of Robert Doran.

4

––––––

Lonergan and Gilson in Dialogue

In the previous two chapters I have attempted to give some overview
of the positions of both Gilson and Lonergan on the issue of the possibility of a Christian philosophy and more generally on the relationship between faith and reason. I shall now bring them into a more
active dialogue, bringing out the similarities and differences in their
approach. Both these authors have something to bring to the table of
contemporary debates, which we shall explore in the next chapter.
However in this chapter I will argue for the rational superiority (in
MacIntyre's sense) of Lonergan's philosophical position over that of
Gilson. For MacIntyre, a position is rationally superior when it can
resolve unsolved problems in another's account, while preserving the
major achievements of the earlier tradition:

> Just as a later stage within [a] tradition is held to be superior to an earlier
> stage only if and insofar as it is able to transcend the limitations and fail-
> ures of that earlier stage, limitations and failures by the standards of ratio-
> nality of that earlier stage itself, so the rational superiority of [a] tradition
> to rival traditions is held to reside in its capacity not only for identify-
> ing and characterizing the limitations and failures of that rival tradition
> as judged by that rival tradition's own standards, limitations and failures
> which that rival tradition itself lacks the resources to explain or under-
> stand, but also for the explaining and understanding of those limitations
> and failures in some tolerably precise way.[1]

In this case the problem lies in Gilson's account of judgment and its relationship to existence. This will be illustrated through reference to a particular contemporary scientific issue. However, before we arrive at that place we need to identify both the common ground and points of disagreement between our two thinkers.

The Puzzling Notion of Being

At the heart of both philosophers' concerns lies the puzzling notion of being. In an age accused of the "forgetfulness of being"[2] (largely a legacy of the type of Suarezian metaphysics Gilson criticized in *Being and Some Philosophers*) both Gilson and Lonergan draw our attention to the difficulty we all have with trying to conceptualize being. As Gilson states in the introduction to *Being and Some Philosophers*, "the truth about [being] cannot be proved, it can only be seen—or overlooked."[3] His frustration is fully on display in attempting to present Suarez's account of metaphysics with its fatal oversight in relation to being. "There would be no point in protracting a discussion which is obviously marking time. It now resembles one of those conversations in which one man says to another: 'Don't you see it?' 'No.' 'Well, have a better look. Do you see it now?' Then what? All that is left to do is for the man who thinks he sees to account for the fact that the other does not."[4] Gilson's reading of the history of philosophy is one of so many failed experiments that arise because of this oversight of being. Some of the difficulty can be found in Gilson's own terminology. He at times refers to a "concept of being." On the other hand he notes: "What he [Suarez] would like to know is *quid existentia sit*: what is existence, as if existence could be a *what*."[5] We do not know the "what" of existence, only the fact of it. As Gilson notes, concepts arise from "an intellectual act of conceiving" which grasps the quiddity or what-ness of something.[6] Existence is known not through such an intellectual act,

---

1. Alasdair MacIntyre, *Three Rival Versions of Moral Enquiry: Encyclopaedia, Genealogy, and Tradition* (Notre Dame, Ind.: University of Notre Dame Press, 1990), 180–81.
2. This of course is the famous philosophical phrase of Martin Heidegger, who accused western metaphysics of such a forgetfulness. See Martin Heidegger, *Being and Time*, trans. Joan Stambaugh (New York: State University of New York, 1996). It would go beyond the scope of the present work to engage Heidegger on this issue. There has been a spirited debate between Thomists and Heideggerians as to whether Aquinas falls under such a forgetfulness, or whether it is Heidegger himself who has been forgetful of Aquinas's definitive breakthrough in metaphysics.
3. Étienne Gilson, *Being and Some Philosophers*, 2d ed. (Toronto: Pontifical Institute of Mediaeval Studies, 1952), x.
4. Ibid., 104.
5. Ibid., 105.
6. Ibid., 190.

but through a different act, that of judgment. In that sense we have no "concept" of being *per se*, no direct insight into its nature.

For this reason, in *Insight,* Lonergan only uses the term "concept of being" in relation to the position of other thinkers. His preferred term is a "notion of being" by which he means our dynamic, conscious, intelligent and reasonable orientation to being. This notion is revealed in our questioning and forms an *a priori* in the subject, a conscious reaching out to being not yet known. As with Gilson, Lonergan holds that "the notion of being is not the notion of some essence."[7] Strictly then we have no concept of being. Since everything that is has being, to form a concept of being one would have to understand everything about everything, something only available to God. So Lonergan refers to it as a "puzzling notion."[8] He notes that, "By mistaken analogy it is inferred that the notion of being resembles concepts in their other aspects. But in fact the notion of being is unique; for it is the core of all acts of meaning; and it underpins, penetrates, and goes beyond all other cognitional contents."[9] Being is the objective of intelligent grasp and reasonable affirmation, and so one can arrive at determinate content only through the use of intelligence and reason. In fact, being is only known in the "totality of correct judgments" indicating that for both Lonergan and Gilson, judgment is the decisive cognitional activity in relation to being. Moreover, Lonergan would claim that his notion of being prescinds from any particular metaphysical commitment. As a notion it is not yet determinate; it becomes determinate through judgments. It is possible that we could determine that all being is material, or ideal. Such determinations can only come later, once the full implications of the notion are unpacked in relation to the universe that actually exists, through forming concrete judgments. This puzzling quality of being is further highlighted by Lonergan's later language of "intellectual conversion."[10] Conversion is an extremely personal event, and what is evident to the converted person remains obscure or simply wrong to the unconverted. One is not argued into conversion; it is not the result of a logical argument, because any such argument occurs within a particular horizon, and conversion is a radical shift in one's horizon. This perspective echoes Gilson's frustration

---

7. Bernard J. F. Lonergan, *Insight: A Study of Human Understanding,* ed. Crowe Frederick E. and Robert M. Doran, Collected Works of Bernard Lonergan (Toronto: University of Toronto Press, 1992), 384.
8. Ibid., 383.
9. Ibid., 384.
10. *Method in Theology* (London: Darton, Longman & Todd, 1972), 238–40.

with Suarez: "'Don't you see it?' 'No.' 'Well, have a better look. Do you see it now?'"[11]

Where then does this leave us in relation to being? For both authors the notion of being is fundamental and primitive. We cannot get to it through something else because being is already and everywhere present: "it underpins, penetrates, and goes beyond all other cognitional contents."[12] Still while Gilson would have us simply "have a better look" Lonergan at least provides some framework through his approach to being through questioning. His notion of being as a dynamic, conscious, intelligent and reasonable orientation within the subject provides something to hold on to and something verifiable in personal experience. On the other hand this approach is rejected by Gilson because it smacks of idealism. For Gilson to start with the subject is to remain locked within subjectivity.

If direct argument is not possible, is there another approach to the question of being? Here both Gilson and Lonergan turn to the history of philosophy, to a more dialectical method, as a testing ground for philosophical experiments on the notion of being.

The Philosophical Laboratory of History

Another major similarity between these two thinkers is that we must read the history of philosophy through the lens of a struggle to come to grips with the puzzling notion of being. Indeed Lonergan describes Gilson's work in *Being and Some Philosophers* as an "extraordinarily erudite application of the method Aristotle names 'dialectic'."[13] This is not a necessary dialectic in the Hegelian sense, but a historical and contingent unfolding of successes and failures (largely failures) to come to grips with being. Gilson's strategy is in some sense akin to the Sherlock Holmes methodology: consider all the alternatives; eliminate what does not work; and whatever is left must be right.[14] Gilson considers the range of philosophical offerings that arose from Plato onwards, highlighting the difficulties each position encounters, with the posi-

11. Gilson, *Being and Some Philosophers*, 104.
12. Lonergan, *Insight*, 384.
13. See "Review of Étienne Gilson, *Being and Some Philosophers*," in *Shorter Papers*, ed. Robert Croken, Robert M. Doran, and H. Daniel Monsour (Toronto: University of Torontw, 2007), 185.
14. The question is then whether the history of philosophy to date exhausts the possibilities. In his comments on Gilson's approach, Gerald McCool has something like this in mind when he notes, "Some day a better metaphysics might be invented but to date Thomism was still the most satisfactory philosophy, and the way to be a Thomist was to immerse oneself in the philosophy of the Angelic Doctor." Gerald A. McCool, "How Can There Be Such a Thing as a Christian Philosophy?," *Proceedings of the American Catholic Philosophical Association* 54 (1980): 126–34, at 131.

tion of Aquinas being the last man standing (again reminiscent of Mac-Intyre's notion of traditions of rationality in contest with one another). The failures of the various positions (in terms of unresolved problems) he details bring into sharp focus the difficulties that arise with the neglect of being. The purpose of the historical narrative is to assist the reader to "see" what Gilson "sees," the centrality of being. Nonetheless the force of the argument depends on precisely how much one ends up "seeing" what Gilson wants one to see.

Lonergan provides a similar, if somewhat more summary, dialectic account of the history of philosophy in his chapter on the notion of being.[15] Over a number of pages he spells out, from Parmenides through to Hegel, how different philosophers have formulated the notion of being and their dialectical relationship to his own account, covering many of the same figures as Gilson.[16] However, Lonergan's analysis is based not just on internal problems each philosopher is unable to deal with, but with their congruence or lack thereof in relation to the notion of being as the objective of intelligent inquiry and reasonable affirmation. Does the philosopher concerned attend to the difference between questions for intelligence (what is it?) and questions for judgment (is it so?)? Do they think of knowing as taking a look, or as assimilation of the known by the knower? As with Gilson a key question is whether being is treated as a conceptual content. Again it is the contribution of Aquinas that is decisive to the historical dialectic. He recognized the unrestrictedness of intellect, of the desire to know, as a *potens omnia fieri*, whose object is *ens*.[17] Still this is potency not act for an intellect fully in act must be an infinite act (God). Being is "per se and naturally known to us" through the light of intelligence that is "a created participation of the eternal and uncreated light."[18] What is important here is the correlation between questions of being and questions of intellect, so basic to Lonergan's program, which he draws from Aquinas. Thus it is not just a matter of neglecting being *per se* that

---

15. Lonergan, *Insight*, 388–98. It is not impossible that Lonergan is deliberately following Gilson's example here given his positive comments in the introduction to *Insight* in reference to Étienne Gilson, *The Unity of Philosophical Experience* (San Francisco, CA: Ignatius Press, 1999). See Lonergan, *Insight*, 15.

16. Plato, Aristotle, Scotus, Cajetan, Kant and Hegel are common to both authors.

17. For Lonergan this implied a natural desire to know God, so "by our nature we desire what by our nature we cannot achieve." Lonergan, *Insight*, 394. This is a position Lonergan will defend in various settings, for example, "The Natural Desire to see God," in *Collection*, ed. Frederick E. Crowe and Robert M. Doran, Collected Works of Bernard Lonergan (Toronto: Toronto University Press, 1988). It has ongoing significance in the debates around the *nouvelle théologie.*

18. *Insight*, 394. The language of participation here need not be read to imply any theological commitment; it is philosophical rather than theological.

Lonergan highlights, but also the ways in which being is misconstrued through a faulty understanding of the operations of intellect. In particular he focuses on the misconception of knowing as looking at or confrontation with its object, either an intellectual look as in Plato's idealism or a sensory look as in empiricism (Hume). In a way which echoes Gilson's view of the "experimental" nature of history in philosophy, Lonergan notes, "Five hundred years separate Hegel from Scotus. . . . that notable interval of time was largely devoted to working out in a variety of manners the possibilities of the assumption that knowing consists in taking a look. The ultimate conclusion was that it did not and could not."[19] In a later chapter entitled "The Method of Metaphysics" Lonergan extends this dialectic approach to consider a variety of philosophical positions—deductivism, universal doubt (Descartes), empiricism, commonsense eclecticism, Hegelian dialectic, and scientific method—measuring them each against the positions and counterpositions mentioned in our previous chapter.[20]

What emerges perhaps more clearly in Lonergan than Gilson is not just the question of the presence or absence of being in the dialectic unfolding of the history of philosophy, but the ways in which being can be misconstrued through a faulty cognitional analysis. This certainly provides a more precise account than that of Gilson because Lonergan can pinpoint the exact nature of the metaphysical problem by reference to a cognitional oversight or misunderstanding. But again this is a move Gilson would resist because of its idealist undercurrents. In this context, Lonergan's rejection of the method of universal doubt—"Universal doubt leads the philosopher to reject what he is not equipped to restore"—might come as some comfort.[21] However, it does lead us to the next major issue, the relationship between cognitional theory and metaphysics.

19. Ibid., 396–97.
20. Ibid., 410–55.
21. Ibid., 436. In fact Lonergan provides a thorough analysis and rejection of Descartes' program. As a counter proposal he often refers to John H. Newman's suggestion that it is better to believe everything and then remove error, than doubt everything and try to restore some semblance of knowledge. For example, Method, 223: "It was Newman who remarked, apropos of Descartes' methodic doubt, that it would be better to believe everything than to doubt everything. For universal doubt leaves one with no basis for advance, while universal belief may contain some truth that in time may gradually drive out the errors." Lonergan does not provide a source for this in Newman's work.

The Priority of Cognitional Theory over Metaphysics

In the question of the relationship between metaphysics and cognitional theory we have a clear divergence between our two authors. As Gilson makes it clear in his two works attacking the so-called "transcendental Thomists," any attempt to start with human subjectivity will not end with Thomistic realism, but in some form of idealism, an immanent subject locked into his or her own subjectivity.[22] "In other words, he who begins as an idealist ends as an idealist; one cannot safely make a concession or two to idealism here and there."[23] The starting point for any philosophy must therefore be "being," not "knowing." As he notes, "Nothing is more important for a philosopher than the choice he makes of his own philosophical principles"[24] and being is the most fundamental of all principles. As a primitive term it cannot be derived from anything else: "the truth about [being] cannot be proved, it can only be seen—or overlooked."[25] Any attempt to provide a "critical" basis for metaphysics necessitates philosophers "[devouring] their own feet without realizing it."[26] In more recent times this position has received some limited magisterial support in the encyclical *Fides et ratio* which expressed concern about the modern turn to the subject, fearing it leads to skepticism and relativism; while promoting a return to metaphysics as the core concern of philosophy.[27]

Still Gilson does acknowledge a relationship between knowing and being. He refers to the Thomistic axiom that "being is the first principle of human knowledge" in the initial pages of his work *Being and Some Philosophers*.[28] Further in the final chapter of that book he relates the distinctive component of the relationship to the act of judgment:

> The two prerequisites to the possibility of existential judgments are that reality should include an existential act over and above its essence, and that the human mind be naturally able to grasp it. . . . That the human mind is naturally able to grasp it is a fact, and if so many philosophers seem to doubt it, it is because they fail to grasp the cognitive power of judgment. Because it lies beyond essence, existence lies beyond abstract

---

22. Étienne Gilson, *Methodical Realism: A Handbook for Beginning Realist*, trans. Philip Trower (Front Royal VA: Christendom Press, 2011); *Thomist Realism and the Critique of Knowledge* (San Francisco: Ignatius Press, 2012).
23. Gilson, *Methodical Realism*, 21.
24. Gilson, *Being and Some Philosophers*, ix.
25. Ibid., x.
26. Gilson, *Methodical Realism*, 33.
27. *Fides et ratio*, n. 9.
28. Gilson, *Being and Some Philosophers*, 2.

representation, but not beyond the scope of intellectual knowledge; for judgment itself is the most perfect form of intellectual knowledge, and existence is its proper object.[29]

Judging is of course a *cognitional* activity, so there is some recognition here of a correlation between metaphysics and cognitional theory.[30] Still Gilson repudiates any attempt to ground metaphysics in cognitional theory. In his own terms his realism is "dogmatic," grounded in the assertion of being, something one either "sees" or doesn't "see."[31]

Lonergan however pushes the matter further. The question for our age is whether the dogmatic assertion of realism and a subsequent metaphysics is adequate. If there is some correlation between being and knowing, at least in terms of the activity of judging, why should we not examine knowing to further explicate our grasp of being? This is not to start with methodic doubt, as in Descartes, but to start with a particular instance of being, that of the being of knowing itself. And so the first part of *Insight* is entitled "Knowing as activity." This activity is a given instance of being, whose structures we can uncover, and in doing so we gain greater insight into being itself, precisely because the object of our knowing is being:

> the philosophy and metaphysics that result from insight into insight will be verifiable. . . . But if insight into insight is verifiable, then the consequent philosophy and metaphysics will be verifiable. In other words, just as every statement in theoretical science can be shown to imply statements regarding sensible fact, so every statement in philosophy and metaphysics can be shown to imply statements regarding cognitional fact.[32]

This "insight into insight" is a slow and painstaking development of self-knowledge, not gained through a withdrawal from the world or inward gaze, but by attending to the performance of knowing itself, and so "our first task will be to attain familiarity with what is meant by insight, and the only way to achieve this end is, it seems, to attend very closely to a series of instances all of which are rather remarkable for

29. Ibid., 202.
30. John Knasas, a strong defender of Gilson acknowledges that Gilson's account of judgment needs further filling out. See John F. X. Knasas, "A Heideggerian Critique of Aquinas and a Gilsonian Reply," *The Thomist* 58, no. 3 (1994): 415–39, at 436–47.
31. Gilson, *Being and Some Philosophers*, 104.
32. Lonergan, *Insight*, 5.

their banality."[33] In another setting Lonergan takes up more directly the challenge posed by Gilson:

> For example, on a view associated with the name of Étienne Gilson, one can claim that one can begin philosophy with metaphysics. There is no doubt that this view has a solid foundation in tradition. Metaphysics was discovered, I would say, simultaneously with a satisfactory psychology and epistemology, but it was much easier to express the metaphysics, and then to express the psychology and epistemology in terms of the metaphysics, than to express the psychology and epistemology in a way that was independent of metaphysics. For that reason, you have in Aristotle and in St Thomas the expression of psychology and similarly of epistemology, the treatment of epistemological questions such as existed at their time, on a metaphysical basis.[34]

What advantage does Lonergan find then in starting with cognitional theory? His aim is to be able to settle metaphysical disputes by reference to cognitional fact: "so every statement in philosophy and metaphysics can be shown to imply statements regarding cognitional fact."[35] Such statements are then personally verifiable through attending to the data of human consciousness.

We are perhaps now in a position to respond more fully to Gilson's charge of idealism in relation to the approach Lonergan has taken. We should begin by reaffirming that Lonergan does not begin with methodic doubt, but with the *fact* of knowing. This fact is itself an instance of being, not to be doubted. What the meaning of this knowing is, its structures and objects may be, are yet to be determined. And so Lonergan's starting point is "knowing as an activity," that is, as a given. How then does Lonergan deal with the problem of the "bridge"? Does his starting point in cognitional theory problematize the existence of the "external world"? Lonergan would view this anxiety as misplaced. Both the "internal" and "external" worlds are instances of being. The manner in which they are to be known is exactly the same, through intelligent grasp and reasonable affirmation. While our knowledge of the external world is known through the senses, our knowledge of the internal world is attained by attention to the data of consciousness. One attends to the data of consciousness not by withdrawal from

---

33. Ibid., 27.
34. Bernard J. F. Lonergan, "Mathematical Logic and Scholasticism," in *Phenomenology and Logic: The Boston College Lectures on Mathematical Logic and Existentialism*, ed. Philip J. McShane, Collected Works of Bernard Lonergan (Toronto: University of Toronto, 2002), 117.
35. Lonergan, *Insight*, 5.

the senses or by some inner look as with Descartes, but through a heightened attention to one's own performance as a knower.[36] Lonergan would then counter Gilson's claim to idealism with the suggestion that Gilson himself is not completely free from a counter-position that the real is to be found in the already-out-there-now of extroverted consciousness.[37] Indeed Gilson regularly references the real as "external." As a consequence Gilson shows little or no interest in exploring consciousness in its own terms rather than metaphysically.[38] He seems to posit the inner-outer disjunction as primordial and prioritizes the external as the really real. Starting with the inner world then creates the problem of the bridge. Lonergan on the other hand views the disjunction as not given in the data itself, but as known through intelligence and reason. Thus we can truly know as real both the inner and outer worlds. For Lonergan there is no need for a bridge; rather one learns to build a moat, to properly distinguish between these two realms of being.[39]

Finally, let me take up an objection to the turn to subjectivity from the writings of Alasdair MacIntyre, an objection with which I think Gilson might be sympathetic. As MacIntyre puts it, with characteristic incisiveness:

> Suppose, then, that someone aspired to adjudicate between Augustinian and Aristotelian claims by appealing away from their theoretical conceptualization to how things *in fact* are in the human *psyche*. Any such appeal would have to present empirical data. Yet at the level at which such data are characterizable in a way that makes them independent of and neutral

36. This was also realised by Augustine in Book 10 of *De Trinitate*. For Augustine the mind "should not start looking for itself as though it had drawn off from itself, but should draw off what it has added to itself. . . . Let the mind then recognise itself and not go looking for itself as if it were absent, but rather turn to itself the interest of its will [*intentionem voluntatis*]. (Book 10.11). Lonergan also cites Aristotle's claim that "intellect knows itself, not by a species of itself, but by a species of its object" in relation to the question of introspection. See Bernard J. F. Lonergan, *Verbum: Word and Idea in Aquinas*, ed. Frederick E. Crowe and Robert M. Doran, Collected Works of Bernard Lonergan (Toronto: University of Toronto Press, 1997), 5.

37. Lonergan, *Insight*, 413. One can identify the same sort of counter-positional stance in Gaven Kerr, "Aquinas, Lonergan, and the Isomorphism between Intellect and Reality," *International Philosophical Quarterly* 54, no. 1 (2014): 43-57. Kerr argues along Gilsonian lines that "any metaphysical position that recognises the structure of cognition, as opposed to that of reality, as methodologically basic is essentially an idealist position" (50). What is problematic here is the opposition of the "structure of cognition" to "reality" as if cognitional acts and their structures are themselves not real.

38. For example in the final chapter of Gilson, *Being and Some Philosophers*, he addresses the issue of knowing and being, but immediately diverts the discussion to one of proposition, without any real attempt to get to the "inside" of knowing.

39. Of course Gilson too rejects the metaphor of the bridge, but seems to argue that starting with knowing necessitates it as a difficulty. Lonergan resolves the problem, despite starting with knowing.

between schemes as conceptually rich and organized as the Aristotelian and the Augustinian . . . the data are too meagre and underdetermine any characterization at the required level. They are no more than matter still to be given form by characterization at a higher, more theoretical level. And if the data are themselves presented as more fully and richly characterized, in a way which makes them relevant to the disputes between Augustinians and Aristotelians, then some conclusion as to where the truth lies in those disputes will already have been presupposed by the way in which the data have been conceptualized.[40]

MacIntyre is correct to highlight the difficulties involved in the whole project of turning to human consciousness as a starting point. It cannot be achieved by some immediate and direct "inner look" to uncover the "facts" and inevitably draws on various and perhaps conflicting conceptualizations. On the other hand, the types of difficulty that MacIntyre is claiming here are no less than what Gilson has uncovered in his history of the neglect of the notion of being. Being too is elusive and difficult to characterize. It has given rise to unending philosophical conflicts with the conflicting parties each appealing to the "facts."

Lonergan himself acknowledges the difficulty in identifying the cognitional facts he is alluding to. He describes it as an "arduous explanatory journey"[41] and anyone who has read *Insight* is likely to agree. In some ways the characterizations Lonergan deploys have taken centuries to clarify. He finds antecedents to the turn to the subject in Aristotle, Aquinas, and Augustine:

Aquinas explicitly appealed to inner experience and, I submit, Aristotle's account of intelligence, of insight into phantasm, and of the fact that intellect knows itself, not by a species of itself, but by a species of its object, has too uncanny an accuracy to be possible without the greatest introspective skill. But if Aristotle and Aquinas used introspection and did so brilliantly, it remains that they did not thematize their use, did not elevate it into a reflectively elaborated technique, did not work out a proper method for psychology.[42]

That thematization has taken centuries to unfold. From Lonergan's perspective the modern turn to subjectivity initiated by Descartes was just a further step in the long process of that thematization, refining

---

40. MacIntyre, *Three Rival Versions*, 111–12.
41. Lonergan, *Insight*.
42. Lonergan, *Verbum*, 5–6. There is of course no need to locate antecedents in Augustine who was a master of interiority.

and clarifying the "meager" data of consciousness that MacIntyre alludes to.[43] In the end, however, Lonergan's position comes down to a very personal experiment, self-appropriation and one's self-affirmation as a knower, spelt out in chapter 11 of *Insight*.

As an experiment it may succeed or fail. The reader of *Insight* may or may not get the point and we would be left like Gilson in his frustration with Suarez on being. "'Don't you see it?' 'No.' 'Well, have a better look. Do you see it now?'" [44] The only additional philosophical weapon Lonergan adds to this process is a retortion argument, which identifies the incongruity between the cognitional performance of the subject and any alternate cognitional proposal they might like to hypothesize. The use of retortion however is a mixed blessing. As Lonergan scholar Robert Doran notes, "retortion arguments, however valid they may be, seem to convince only those who have already become convinced on other grounds, while only angering those who will not allow themselves to be convinced."[45] Doran concedes that the form of a retortion argument is valid, but it is not a deduction using some syllogistic form. To insist on such a form of deduction is to "presume that conceptualization is more basic than pragmatic engagement"[46], whereas the retortion argument pushes us towards the issue of pragmatic engagement. Still, to those schooled in the more conceptualist approach, retortion will appear as an *ad hominem* argument, a turning away from the object of the argument to focus on the arguing subject. It is little wonder that such a shift might provoke anger.[47]

In both cases, then, whether we start with metaphysics or with cognitional theory, there are similar if not parallel difficulties, largely because we are dealing with first principles. There is something irreducible about both starting points precisely because as Gilson notes, "*being* is the first principle of *human knowledge*."[48] Intelligence and being are linked principles, a position Lonergan fully exploits in his whole approach. In defending his starting point in *Insight*, Lonergan notes:

43. Here the work of Charles Taylor, *Sources of the Self: the Making of the Modern Identity* (Cambridge, MA: Harvard University Press, 1989), provides rich historical data on the modern turn to the subject.
44. Gilson, *Being and Some Philosophers*, 104.
45. Robert M. Doran, *What is Systematic Theology?* (Toronto: University of Toronto Press, 2006), 91.
46. Ibid.
47. Telling someone they are not intellectually converted is not going to win any argument!
48. Gilson, *Being and Some Philosophers*, 2.

The ontological and the cognitional are not incompatible alternatives, but interdependent procedures. If one is assigning ontological causes, one must begin from metaphysics; if one is assigning cognitional reasons, one must begin from knowledge. Nor can one assign ontological causes without having cognitional reasons; nor can there be cognitional reasons without corresponding ontological causes. . . . Aristotle affirmed matter and form as ontological causes; but Aristotle did not affirm these ontological causes without having cognitional reasons, namely, sense and insight into phantasm.[49]

Nonetheless Lonergan argues for the priority of the cognitional approach as what is first for us. "What began with Aristotle was, not form, but knowledge of form. What began with Aquinas was, not existence, but knowledge of existence."[50]

Two issues thus emerge from this. One would be the claim that Gilson's concerns about the starting point of knowing failing to lead us to the reality of the external world are based on a counterpositional stance (according to Lonergan) of the real as already out there now. Moving from this "persistent myth" lies at the heart of what Lonergan calls intellectual conversion. For Lonergan, reality is not given as inner or outer, but known as such through intelligent grasp and reasonable affirmation. The second is the question of the role of judgment in relation to being. To this issue we now turn.

On the Role of Judgment

Much of the preceding discussion is thus pointing us to the nature, role and significance of the cognitional act of judgment. Both Gilson and Lonergan identify judgment as playing a decisive role in relation to the question of being. As Gilson notes, "The two prerequisites to the possibility of existential judgments are that reality should include an existential act over and above its essence, and that the human mind be naturally able to grasp it. . . . That the human mind is naturally able to grasp it is a fact, and if so many philosophers seem to doubt it, it is *because they fail to grasp the cognitive power of judgment* . . . for judgment itself is the most perfect form of intellectual knowledge, and existence is its proper object."[51] I think it fair to say that Lonergan

49. Bernard J. F. Lonergan, "*Insight*: Preface to a Discussion," in *Collection*, ed. Frederick E. Crowe and Robert M. Doran, Collected Works of Bernard Lonergan (Toronto: University of Toronto Press, 1993), 144.
50. Ibid., 144.
51. Gilson, *Being and Some Philosophers*, 202. Emphasis added.

would agree with this summation completely. For Lonergan, the isomorphism of knowing and being implies that judging corresponds to the metaphysical principle of act, which grasps the being or reality of the object. Significantly Gilson posits various philosophers' failures not in their failure to attend to being but to their failure *"to grasp the cognitive power of judgment,"* again completely congruent with Lonergan's position. Gilson refers to judgment as "the most perfect form of intellectual knowledge," while Lonergan constantly repeats that until we judge we do not know in the full and proper sense. These are important similarities.

Where they differ, however, is in their account of the act itself. We have already noted in chapter 2 that Gilson, while noting the relationship between judgment and existence in *Being and Some Philosophers,* immediately shifts his attention to propositions, not to cognitional theory. While his analysis is no doubt sound and helpful, in the context it tells us nothing about how a judgment is made—nor, tellingly, where propositions come from in the first place. When he does turn his attention to this issue he appears to posit an immediate link between judging and sensory data. "What comes first is a sensible perception whose object is immediately known by our intellect as 'being.'"[52] Since being is known in judgment, one can infer that the sensible perception leads immediately to a cognitional judgment. "We directly know perceived data as beings, so that our direct knowledge of them includes an intuitive experience of their very acts of existing."[53] Gilson repeats similar statements in his other works. Thus, "One is led . . . to make the existence of the outside world a matter of evidence, but the direct and concrete evidence of a sensory intuition, *which translates itself abstractly and directly into a judgment."* [54] Further "This much is certain, then, from the beginning of this new inquiry: the apprehension of being by the intellect consists of directly seeing the concept of being in some sensible datum."[55]

However, there is a tension here. Initially Gilson speaks of judgment in relation to propositions: "Propositions are usually defined as enun-

52. Ibid.
53. Ibid., 206–7.
54. Gilson, *Methodical Realism*, 77–78, emphasis added. Also: "Thus, no matter in what manner nor with what profundity we may pose the question as to how we know that something exists, realism will always respond: by perceiving it." Gilson, *Thomist Realism and the Critique of Knowledge*, 186. Also: "As soon as it comes into touch with sensible experience, the human intellect elicits the immediate intuition of being: X is, or exists." Gilson, *The Unity of Philosophical Experience*, 252.
55. Gilson, *Thomist Realism and the Critique of Knowledge*, 197. Again some care is needed here because, as we have seen, Gilson also denies that we have a concept of being *per se.*

ciations which affirm or deny one concept of another concept."[56] Affirmations and denials are of course judgments, the yes or no by which we express our conclusions. These concepts, as Gilson notes from Aquinas, arise "when our intellect forms the quiddity of a thing" leading to the formation of a *conceptus*.[57] So such judgments presume acts of concept formation. Yet he also affirms an immediate step from sensory intuition to judgment without any intervening act of intellect.

> What the senses perceive exists, and existence is included in what the senses perceive, but the senses are only the bearers of a message which they are incapable of reading, for only the intellect can decipher it. However, the intellect alone cannot decipher it completely. What it is able to read in the sensible datum is the answer to the question: what is this?[58]

Here the question "what is it?," which provides the quiddity of a thing, appears to come after the judgment of being. So one may ask then, which comes first? Do we form concepts, which then become the object of judgments, or do we form judgments immediately upon a sensory "intuition" from which we are then able to develop concepts. Gilson scholar, John Knasas, while noting the significance of the place of judgment in Gilson's account of being, acknowledges that there is a "shortcoming" here: "Gilson at least gives the impression of equating the judgment with the proposition."[59] He goes on to note, "the task remains of explaining how judgment in the just described cognitional operation sense is a *respicit esse rei* [a grasp of the being of a thing] rather than simply the recomposition of an intelligible with some designated matter."[60] Gilson does not undertake this task. Metaphysically this problem is significant because unless this is clarified, Gilson's position would be Aristotelian, not Thomist, whereby the existing thing would be more like a composition of form and matter. Knasas proposes a deeper appreciation of Thomistic texts on knowledge of individual material being so that a "consideration of the individual body as possible permits judgment to recombine the abstracted intelligible with the individual in a fashion that leaves the recomposition of the individual

---

56. Gilson, *Being and Some Philosophers*, 190.
57. Ibid., 190.
58. Gilson, *Thomist Realism and the Critique of Knowledge*, 199.
59. Knasas, "A Heideggerian Critique of Aquinas and a Gilsonian Reply," 138. Apart from a reference to *Being and Some Philosophers*, he also cites Étienne Gilson, *The Christian Philosophy of St. Thomas Aquinas*, trans. I. T. Eschmann (New York: Random House, 1956), 41: "The formula in which this composition is expressed is precisely the proposition or judgment."
60. Knasas, "A Heideggerian Critique of Aquinas and a Gilsonian Reply," 139.

with its *esse* as a further distinct and crowning moment in judgment."[61]
Still Knasas's suggestions, helpful as they may be, do not elucidate the
relationship between the first and second acts of intellect, that is, conceptualization and judging, and Gilson's claim that judgment arises
from an immediate sensory intuition. What is clear, however, from
Knasas's argument is the point made by Lonergan that "The ontological and the cognitional are not incompatible alternatives, but interdependent procedures."[62]

Lonergan, on the other hand, presents a much clearer account of
the relationship between the different cognitional operations. Lonergan would not accept Gilson's account of a judgment of existence
immediately upon reception of the sensory data. Rather than a judgment the encounter with sensory data evokes a question: what is it?
This is not a *concept* of being but an *intending* of being in the question
itself. As an intending, it remains unfulfilled until questions are properly answered. But nonetheless it is an intending, which arises from
the notion of being, orienting the subject to intelligence and reason.
There is a focus of our attending onto a set of data, the emergence of a
question through wonder, but no judgment or intuition of being. This
inquiring status is the prelude to what Aquinas calls the first act of
intellect, what Lonergan calls insight or the act of understanding, leading to the formation of a concept. The formation of the concept fulfils
the intention of the question "what is it?" by giving us an answer, it is
X. However, it does not yet fulfil the intention of being. The answer to
the question "what is it?" remains purely hypothetical, a possibility not
a certainty, and so its final existential status is yet to be determined.
The intending of being moves from the question "what is it?" to the
question of judgment "is it so?" For Lonergan, the judgment of existence is doubly mediated by intelligence and reason, not immediate
as in Gilson. This is almost certainly the conclusion that Gilson sought
to avoid in his account of judgment as immediate precisely because it
pushes us deeper into subjectivity and so raises his fears of idealism.
However, it is more congruent with his other stance that relates judgment to propositions arising from concepts.

61. Ibid., 139. Significantly Knasas seeks a solution in a closer examination of texts rather than attending to the data of consciousness. Elsewhere Gilson distinguishes between the problems of individuation and individuality. "Though *esse* is not the principle of individuation, it is the first act of all
individuality." Étienne Gilson, *The Philosopher and Theology* (New York: Random House, 1962), 54.
It seems to the present author that the focus on an intuition of being in the senses is to blur this
distinction.
62. Lonergan, "*Insight*: Preface to a Discussion," 144.

The conflict then concerns a question of cognitional fact. How do the first and second acts of intellect relate to one another? How do concepts and judgments relate? How do the two types of questions, "what is it?" and "is it so?" relate within the human drive to know? To address this question is, as Lonergan avers, a matter of self-appropriation, of attending to one's own performance, through an engagement with a work such as *Insight*. Lonergan's strategy in the early chapters of that work is to focus on mathematical and scientific forms of knowing, not in order to make them paradigmatic, but to help delineate more clearly the different cognitional operations and their sequencing. I shall adopt the same approach with a very particular and recent scientific example, the discovery of the Higgs boson. The test I would propose is how these two authors would handle the question, "Is the Higgs boson real? Does it exist?"

Science, Insight, and Judgment[63]

To single out the Higgs boson is not an attempt to privilege the subatomic realm as somehow foundational for all reality or to confuse the physical with the metaphysical. It is to ask about the basis on which one would say that it is, or is not, real—that it exists, or does not exist. One could address the question to any supposed existent, but to pose it of the Higgs boson raises certain questions in more pointed fashion. The Higgs boson received much prominence in 2012 with the announcement that scientists had uncovered evidence for its existence using data from the Large Hadron Collider (LHC) at CERN. The LHC had been built at enormous cost (over $6 billion) largely for the purpose of testing the Standard Model in particle physics, which among other things predicted the existence of the Higgs boson.[64] The theory arose from identifying patterns or symmetries within known existing subatomic particles and the forces between them. These patterns were expressed in complex mathematical formulae which were then used to identify gaps in the symmetries, that is, particles that were needed to fill out the patterns found in the existing particles.[65] Three such possible particles were identified, two of which were discovered with rela-

---

63. At the time of writing this book an announcement has just been made on the first direct evidence for gravity waves, one of the consequences of Einstein's theory of general relativity. This is equally stunning as the discovery of the Higgs boson; and the argument of the present section could easily be transcribed into that completely different situation.

64. For an account of the standard model and its development see Robert Oerter, *The Theory of Almost Everything: The Standard Model, the Unsung Triumph of Modern Physics* (New York: Penguin Group US, 2006).

tive ease (the W and Z^0 bosons). The last, predicted by Peter Higgs, and henceforth known as the Higgs boson, was of such a mass that a much larger particle accelerator was needed to create the energies required to produce a possible Higgs boson.[66] After some initial hiccups, the LHC was fired up and data began to flow. Eventually the physicist had sufficient data to conclude that the hypothetically proposed particle actually exists. This was a remarkable confluence of theory and experiment. In fact the match between theory and experiment is stunning, as one physicist blogger, Adam Falkowski who was working at the CERN at the time, notes:

> One cannot help noticing that the data are indecently consistent with the simplest Higgs boson of the Standard Model. Overall, adding the [latest] data improved the consistency, eradicating some of the hints of non-standard behavior we had last year. It's been often stressed that the Higgs boson is the special one, a particle different from all the others, a type of matter never observed before. Yet it appears in front of us exactly as described in detail over the last 40 years. This is a great triumph of particle theory.[67]

We need to ask, however, what it is the physicists at CERN had that made them make this announcement with confidence. They did not have a collection of Higgs bosons in a jar to display to the world. These particles exist, if they exist, for fractions of a second, far shorter time than the blinking of an eye. There is no immediate sensory data that relates directly to the boson. They cannot directly be seen or heard, touched or tasted. What the physicists presented to the world was a graph with a tiny bump in it, called a resonance pattern. This bump was not direct evidence of the Higgs boson itself, but of the expected decay patterns the particle was predicted to produce (see Figure 1). This pattern had been reproduced through multiple experiments and was deemed to be statistically significant. Moreover, it fitted exactly into the pattern predicted by the Standard Model for the Higgs boson. This was not just sufficient scientific proof for the existence of the

---

65. We can identify a similar process at work when the periodic table in chemistry was first proposed. A pattern was identified, but there remained gaps in the table, elements that had not yet been discovered. The table allowed for properties of these undiscovered elements to be proposed leading eventually to their discovery.

66. This is a consequence of Einstein's famous equation, $E = mc^2$. The greater the mass (m) the larger the energy needed (E) to create the conditions under which the particle can be created.

67. See his blog entry for Monday, July 23, 2012, at http://resonaances.blogspot.com/.

Higgs boson, but more importantly an empirical verification for the Standard Model of particle physics. The two go hand in hand.

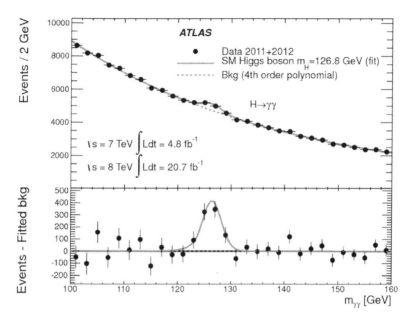

Figure 1: This graph, as provided by CERN, demonstrates a resonance 'bump' at around 126 GeV, as was predicted by the existence of the Higgs boson.

It is difficult to know where a Gilsonian approach would begin in addressing the question of the reality of the Higgs boson. There is no direct sensory data from which a judgment of existence can be made, nothing which translates itself abstractly and directly into a judgment. What the scientists produced was a graph, not of the particle, but of the consequence of its predicted decay patterns. More importantly, this presentation of data is thoroughly theory-laden, completely mediated by scientific intelligence. The machinery used to accelerate the subatomic particles in the LHC relies completely on theories of electromagnetism, electronics and special relativity for its correct operation; the instruments to read the outcome of the collisions similarly so. For the scientists who constructed the graph, the whole mathematical apparatus of the Standard Model sat in the background to focus their attention on a particular part of the graph where the data was expected to be present. Stripped of all these theories the bump on the graph would just be an oddity looking for an explanation, something which might not even be noticed. What it might signify would be a complete puzzle, an unknown needing possible explanation before any judgment about the existence of anything could be proclaimed. Here Gilson's own suggestion that "modern physics teaches us that years and years of mathematical speculation never become knowledge until, through art or chance, its results are confirmed by a sometimes almost instantaneous sense perception" appears simply naïve [68] While he appreciates the necessity of empirical verification, there is little by way of "instantaneous sense perception" involved in the highly theoretically mediated outcomes of the experiments performed at the LHC.

For Lonergan on the other hand, the whole process is confirmation of his understanding of science (and knowing) as based on empirical data, hypothesis formation, and verification. The Standard Model arose from the empirical data produced by scientists working in various particle accelerators around the world. Intelligible patterns were identified in the data, patterns based on possible symmetries between known existing particles and their interactions, symmetries which allowed for forms of theoretical mathematization. This type of theoretical construct provides an explanatory mathematical framework of things in relation to other things. The various subatomic particles are related to one another through sophisticated symmetry operations which specify both the particles and the interactions between them. In Lonergan's account this framework specifies the intelligible *form* of the particles and their interactions, or at least a hypothetical approximation to that form, which is only truly known when a fully explanatory science is available. For Lonergan a judgment of existence (the metaphysical element of *act*) of the Higgs boson only makes sense within the intelligible framework of the Standard Model. Without that framework we would not be able to make a judgment about anything in relation to the Higgs boson.

Lonergan would not be concerned that such a judgment remains theoretically mediated. Such a concern only arises where intelligence and judgment are thought of as unrelated to the real, where reality is conceived as already out there now. But where reality is grasped through intelligence and reason, the theoretical mediation of the results is entirely to be expected. Further, physicists are already aware of limitations within the Standard Model. For example, it does not predict that neutrinos have mass, though there is growing empirical evi-

68. Gilson, *Being and Some Philosophers*, 212.

dence that they do. Further the holy grail of modern physics of incorporating gravity into its account of the quantum world may produce new surprises. The Standard Model will be in need of future modifications and extensions. But the underlying symmetries which predicted the existence of the Higgs boson will need to be preserved in any supervening account. Any new theory will need to include the newly discovered particle within its account of things in relationship to other things at the subatomic level. Lonergan would be happy to accept the scientific conclusion about the existence and reality of the Higgs boson.

I think part of Gilson's difficulty lies in failing to distinguish between descriptive and explanatory understanding. His commitment to common sense knowing means he does not attend to the differences between commonsense knowing and scientific knowing, reducing science to just a refined form of common sense: "This is how science goes about things; *science is not a critique of common sense but of the successive approximations to reality made by common sense.*"[69] On the other hand Lonergan argues that commonsense knowing relates things to us, while scientific knowing relates things to other things. The first is descriptive, the second explanatory. This oversight in Gilson then creates distortions in his account of judgment. The world of common sense is a world of the familiar and habitual. As long as one operates within a commonsense realm of meaning, one can easily miss the intervening contributions of intelligence prior to making a judgment of existence, simply because the objects involved and the related commonsense insights have become part of the habitual furniture of one's mind. Once one moves into the realm of theoretic and explanatory knowledge, as found in scientific knowing, it becomes possible to more clearly delineate the role of intelligence prior to the act of judgment, as Lonergan does in the first chapters of *Insight*. Judgment is then a judgment that this hypothesis is in fact verified in the empirical data. Or in metaphysical terms, this act of existence is the act of existence of the form which informs this prime matter.

---

69. Gilson, *Methodical Realism*, 132–33. Emphasis added. This same commonsense approach is evident in his later work, Étienne Gilson, *From Aristotle to Darwin and Back Again: A Journey in Final Causality, Species, and Evolution* (San Francisco: Ignatius Press, 2009). There Gilson begins his account of an Aristotelian distinction between non-living and living beings on the basis of the distinction between homogeneity and heterogeneity. The issue of finality then arises because of the heterogeneity of living beings (2–4). However, the distinction between homogeneity and heterogeneity is a descriptive commonsense distinction which breaks down where we realize that scientifically heterogeneity extends all the way down to the subatomic level. As Lonergan notes the question of finality extends to all material being, not just living being—hence his notion of emergent probability to capture the finality of proportionate being. See Lonergan, *Insight*, 126–62; 470–76.

The Possibility of Christian Philosophy

At this stage one might wonder what all this has to do with the possibility of the Christian philosophy and questions of the relationship between faith and reason. Certainly as we argued in chapter 1, any debate on the question of faith and reason requires as a prerequisite at least a relatively elaborate and accurate account of reason itself. The debate above about cognition and the role of judgment is a case in point. Any account of reason in the contemporary setting must be able to provide a sound account of scientific knowing to be credible. One thing both our authors agree upon is the very "secular" nature of knowing. No strictly theological notions such as the Incarnation, the Trinity or divine illumination have been deployed or imported in their accounts. Similarly in relation to metaphysics, both present non-theological accounts of metaphysics, avoid the importing of strictly revealed theological content into their account of being, while arguing for the existence of God (natural theology) as a consequence of their metaphysical reflections. Whatever we might make of claims to the possibility of a Christian philosophy, it will not be found, for these authors, in eliminating the distinction between faith and reason, or between theology and philosophy.

On the other hand both authors are quite explicit about the ways in which revealed truths can impact fruitfully upon philosophical reflection. Gilson, for example, puts great store on the significance of Exodus 3:13–14, which he refers to as *haec sublimis veritas*, as providing an impetus in revelation for the distinction between essence and existence.[70] The text becomes a philosophical locus for Gilson, not because we could not know this distinction without divine revelation, but because the positive content of revelation spurs philosophical development which remains nonetheless purely philosophical. In a more deeply theological move Lonergan draws on the Chalcedonian definition of the Incarnation—one person in two natures—to claim that without the distinction between essence and existence one cannot make the needed dogmatic distinction, so central to Christological belief, between person and nature. Moreover, his detailed and profound account of knowing and its epistemological and metaphysical implications in *Insight* were preceded by corresponding historical studies in Aquinas, in the context of the Trinitarian procession, published as

---

70. See chapter 4 of Gilson, *Christian Philosophy of St. Thomas Aquinas*.

Verbum: Word and Idea in Aquinas.[71] In many ways Lonergan's Trinitarian theology and his cognitional and epistemological accounts form a unity, through the mechanism of the psychological analogy. Nonetheless the positions so elaborated remain strictly philosophical, as *Insight* itself demonstrates.

Both these authors maintain the taut "unity-in-difference" of theology and philosophy, the dance of faith and reason. Both remain open to the transformative impact on reason of divine revelation while maintaining the distinctive features of theology and philosophy. As Gilson notes, "neither Duns Scotus nor Thomas Aquinas founded their theology on any philosophy, not even Aristotle's. As theologians, they used philosophy in the light of faith, and thereby philosophy emerged transformed."[72] As both Gilson and Lonergan would concur, the proper distinction is not between reason and faith, but between reason illuminated by its own natural light, and reason illuminated by the light of faith.[73]

On the Distinction of Existence and Essence

As we have just noted both Gilson and Lonergan find a theological basis for maintaining the distinction between essence and existence. However, while this basis might provide a motivation for the distinction, both have philosophical grounds for it, which are independent of that motivation. Indeed both take their stand on the basis of the role of judgment. We have already noted the close link between existence and judgment for Gilson. The very "possibility of existential judgments are that reality should include an existential act over and above its essence." Philosophers who do not recognize this "fail to grasp the cognitive power of judgment." For Gilson "judgment itself is the most perfect form of intellectual knowledge, and existence is its proper object."[74] For Lonergan the distinction is grounded in the distinctive questions, "what is it?" and "is it so?" This is enough for Lonergan

71. Lonergan, *Verbum.* Even a critic of Lonergan's approach, Gaven Kerr, can acknowledge the Thomistic basis of Lonergan's epistemological work: "I am of the view that Lonergan's thought presents one of the most consistent and coherent presentations of Aquinas's somewhat latent epistemological thought." Kerr, "Aquinas, Lonergan, and the Isomorphism between Intellect and Reality," 57.
72. Étienne Gilson, *Medieval Essays*, trans. James G. Colbert (Eugene, OR: Cascade Books, 2011).
73. Gilson, *Christian Philosophy of St. Thomas Aquinas*, 18: "Faith in revelation does not destroy the rationality of our knowledge but rather permits it to develop more fully. Even as, indeed, grace does not destroy nature but heals and perfects it, so faith, through the influence it wields from above over reason as reason, permits the development of a far more true and fruitful rational activity."
74. Gilson, *Being and Some Philosophers*, 202.

because of the isomorphism of being and knowing, which isomorphism is to some extent implicit in this quote from Gilson.

For both our thinkers the distinction between essence and existence is fundamental to a proper grasp of the contingency of our universe. Within the realm of our experience there are no essences from which we can arrive at their necessary existence. In the realm of what Lonergan calls "proportionate being," that is, being proportionate to our knowing, metaphysical contingency is built into the very structure of our cognition. Each answer to the question "what is it?" is immediately followed by the next question, but "is it so?" This deep contingency of existence, which is to be distinguished from the contingency of chance in worldly events,[75] gives rise to the question, "why is there anything at all?" For both Gilson and Lonergan the distinction between essence and existence naturally leads one to the question of God. Is there a being that is not so conditioned by contingency, but is necessary and a necessary cause of being for everything else?

Still there are differences between Gilson and Lonergan—differences that arise from their divergent accounts of the act of judgment. As I have already argued above, Lonergan's account of judgment is more consistent and coherent both internally and in relation to the methods of modern science; Gilson's account of the immediacy of judgment lies in his failure to grasp the difference between explanatory and descriptive knowing, and in his misplaced concern with idealism. So while they are in verbal agreement on the distinction between essence and existence, their relative meanings of these terms are not simply coincident. Again I would argue that Lonergan's account is the more secure.

On the Existence of God

Here again our two thinkers are largely in agreement. Both uphold the possibility of proving the existence of God through the natural light of reason. Both identify the key insight in the five ways of Aquinas to be the incomplete intelligibility of reality without the positing of God's existence. There is a difference reflective of their divergent understandings of the relationship between metaphysics and cognitional theory, so that for Gilson God is "being itself" (*ipsum esse*) while Lonergan prefers the designation "understanding itself" (*ipsum intelligere*).

75. Lonergan also recognizes a type of contingency at the level of essence or form, to which there corresponds a type of statistical lawfulness. See Lonergan, *Insight*, 60–91. For a more recent account see Neil Ormerod and Cynthia S. W. Crysdale, *Creator God, Evolving World* (Minneapolis, MN: Fortress Press, 2013).

However, these two stances should not hide the fact that both are firmly within the tradition of classical theism that is so commonly attacked from various sides of contemporary thinking.[76] For both thinkers, God is pure act, distinct from all space and time, unchanging, all knowing, all loving and all powerful.

Where Lonergan may represent something of a development is his thematization of the problem of being in terms of the need for intellectual conversion. As we have noted above for Gilson the problem of being remains an unresolved puzzle, both what is most obvious, yet most neglected. Lonergan formulates this more precisely in terms of the need for an intellectual conversion, a conversion to being, that is required in order for any proof of the existence of God to gain traction. As Lonergan notes in a brief essay on natural theology, "One cannot prove the existence of God to a Kantian without first breaking his allegiance to Kant. One cannot prove the existence of God to a positivist without first converting him from positivism."[77] In theological terms one could argue that the natural light of reason is so dimmed by original sin that we need an intellectual healing (conversion) before we can fruitfully embark on the task of a natural theology. Indeed he refers to the "endlessly multiplied philosophies" as a component in the "reign of sin."[78] To arrive at this conversion to being may be the work of grace. However, Lonergan notes that while the argument may require grace to be convincing, nonetheless the knowledge so gained remains natural knowledge.[79] In later writings Lonergan will focus less on the question of proof and more on the very question of God, on what are the questions that God is meant to be an answer for:

> The question of God, then, lies within man's horizon. Man's transcendental subjectivity is mutilated or abolished, unless he is stretching forth towards the intelligible, the unconditioned, the good of value. The reach,

---

76. There are a number of challenges to classical theism, from process thought, those who would place suffering in God and so on. For a defence of classical theism from the perspective of modern science see Ormerod and Crysdale, *Creator God, Evolving World*.

77. Bernard J. F. Lonergan, "The General Character of the Natural Theology of *Insight*," in *Philosophical and Theological Papers 1965-1980*, ed. Robert M. Doran and Frederick E. Crowe, Collected Works of Bernard Lonergan (Toronto: University of Toronto Press, 2004), 6.

78. Lonergan, *Insight*, 714.

79. Lonergan, "Natural Knowledge of God," in *A Second Collection*, ed. William Ryan and Bernard Tyrrell (Philadelphia: Westminster Press, 1974), 117–33, at 133. While this may sound paradoxical it is not. Even knowledge in something like mathematics might be blocked cognitively for someone because of less than helpful encounters with teachers or peers who denigrated their faltering attempts to understand. This might require genuine healing to take place before such a person can advance in mathematical knowledge, yet such knowledge would remain purely natural in its object.

not of his attainment, but of his intending is unrestricted. There lies within his horizon a region for the divine, a shrine for ultimate holiness. It cannot be ignored. The atheist may pronounce it empty. The agnostic may urge that he finds his investigation has been inconclusive. The contemporary humanist will refuse to allow the question to arise. But their negations presuppose the spark in our clod, our native orientation to the divine.[80]

The more Lonergan moves into the realm of interiority the more Augustinian his thought becomes, not inasmuch as he adopts a Platonic or neo-Platonic stance evident in Augustine, but the more existential and religious his writings become. Increasingly Lonergan writes about the notion of religious experience. We are reminded that in the end Lonergan was a theologian for whom philosophy was more a means than an end in itself. Even his major work *Insight* was a preliminary study to his central concern for theological method.[81] In this regard Lonergan is closer to their common master, Thomas Aquinas, for Gilson's contribution remained in the discipline of philosophy and did not venture as much into theology properly so called.[82]

Faith and Reason

Finally we can turn to the question of the relationship between faith and reason. Again our thinkers are largely in agreement on this, for both hold to a taut unity-in-difference between faith and reason. Reason has its own "natural light" by which it can judge natural truths, whereas faith has as its proper object truths known through divine revelation. The "light of faith" illuminates our reason so that we may assent to the truths God reveals to us. Both our thinkers recognize the formal distinction between philosophy and theology, while maintaining an essential role for the former in the latter. If anything, Gilson states the case more forcefully, whereas for Lonergan it is almost taken for granted. This may well be because Lonergan deals with this broad concern under the banner of grace and nature in his theological writings.

However, Lonergan does open up the topic to a broader consideration and analysis. Whereas Gilson generally uses the terms "faith" and

---

80. Lonergan, *Method*, 103.
81. Ibid., 7n2.
82. There is some more overtly theological material touching on Trinitarian issues in his later work, Gilson, *The Philosopher and Theology*.

"belief" in a religious context, correlative to divine revelation, Lonergan develops a more thorough account of the act of believing and its important role as a principle of progress. If each of us were limited in our knowing to what we can immanently generate through our own experience, understanding and judgment, then there could be no cooperation and progress in knowing. We would all start with a blank sheet and have to reproduce for ourselves the achievements of the past. Believing occurs when we acknowledge the value in sharing our knowledge and make a judgment about the credibility of its source. Even science is then shot through with belief, for no scientist is the master of the whole of her field. This breaks down the dichotomy of faith and reason to the extent that Lonergan argues that individual reason itself is dependent on believing a range of matters that it has not generated itself but reasonably believes to be the case. This reasonable stance does not preclude the possibility of error, but accepts this possibility as a price for progress. Error is to be eliminated not by a refusal to believe, but by the constant scrutiny of false beliefs, including hunting down to the root causes for its adoption. What is distinctive about religious belief is not the fact that it involves believing *per se*, but the object of that belief which is what God has revealed through the testimony of God's witnesses. This observation on the common role of believing is particularly useful in light of some modern debates on the relationship between science and religion.

Conclusion

I began this work with a claim, restated at the beginning of this chapter, that Lonergan's position was "rationally superior" to that of Gilson as a development of the Thomistic tradition of rationality. While I do not expect everyone to agree, what I have demonstrated is that Lonergan's account of cognition is more precise than that offered by Gilson; that it clarifies more accurately the place of judgment in cognition; that it more closely coheres to the methodology present in science, afforded by Lonergan's distinction between descriptive and explanatory insights; and finally that it overcomes Gilson's concerns about idealism. This enables Lonergan to avoid an immediacy of knowing in either the inner or outer worlds, for both are equally mediated through intelligence and reason.

None of this is to slight Gilson's achievement, particularly his incorporation of the history of philosophy into the philosophical endeavor itself. Lonergan recognized in Gilson's efforts a massive and erudite exercise in Aristotelian dialectic, some of whose features he incorporated into his own stance in *Insight*. And as we have indicated above the two thinkers have much common ground. My task now is to bring them into a dialogue that goes beyond their own set of historical concerns to address some of the more pressing issues raised in our own era. While the ground may have shifted significantly, their insights can act as an important corrective to debates today.

5

———

Contemporary Debates on Faith and Reason

Both Gilson and Lonergan are proponents of the taut unity-in-difference of reason and faith. Yet, since the time of their writings in the twentieth century, new challenges have arisen, which would threaten that unity-in-difference so central to both their projects. The question that needs to be asked is whether insights from these two authors still have something to contribute to these contemporary debates. Today these debates are often waged not just in academic journals and publications, but in heated public arenas, on internet pages, in public meetings and the like. The late twentieth century witnessed a resurgence of interest in and reaction to the rise of religion in the public arena, particularly associated with the emergence of Islam as a global phenomenon, and often linked to acts of politically and religiously motivated violence. Some secular voices have argued passionately for the incompatibility of religious faith and secular society, on the grounds that religious faith is inherently irrational and hence prone to violence. On the other side of the fence there are religious thinkers who counter with claims as to the unfounded nature of secularity, which has its own forms of irrationality and violence, for which the only solution is religious faith. Then only religious faith is truly reasonable while other claims to reason are just masks for the will to power. If nothing else, this divergence is a good reminder that such debates are never closed off as historical options and continue to be raised as circumstances change and opportunities arise.

Now both Gilson and Lonergan believed in the inherent unity-in-difference of these two aspects of human living—faith and reason. Indeed Lonergan ends his magnum opus, *Insight*, with an appeal not to faith seeking understanding (*fides quaerens intellectum*), but to understanding seeking faith (*intellectus quaerens fidem*), based on the radical limitations of individual understanding—what Lonergan refers to an immanently generated knowledge—and the necessity of belief as a social and cultural cooperation in sharing knowledge.[1] In that context, belief as a general construct (not restricted to religious belief) is the principle of social and cultural progress. Specifically, religious belief then becomes an extension of that general construct into the realm of revealed knowing. An Enlightenment critique of belief is exposed not so much as a critique of belief *per se*, but of religious belief as inherently *untrue in its content*. Nowhere is this stance more pointed than in the critique offered by the new atheists that belief in God is ruled out by the advances of modern science. Here I have in mind authors such as Richard Dawkins and Lawrence Krauss, both eminent scientists in their respective fields.[2] This stance puts belief and reason into direct opposition, so that belief is viewed as inherently irrational and hence false. In many public debates this appears to be the default position of those who oppose religious belief.[3]

Another fault line between faith and reason is opened up by those who make an inherent link between religious belief and violence. Here we can identify contributions not only from the ranks of the new atheists, such as Christopher Hitchens and Sam Harris, but also sociological authors such as Mark Juergensmeyer who argue for such a link.[4] In this case there would appear to be some empirical data in support, with the regular linkage of Islam with acts of political violence and ter-

---

1. Bernard J. F. Lonergan, *Insight: A Study of Human Understanding*, ed. Crowe Frederick E. and Robert M. Doran, Collected Works of Bernard Lonergan (Toronto: University of Toronto Press, 1992), 725–40.
2. Richard Dawkins, *The Blind Watchmaker: Why the Evidence of Evolution Reveals a Universe without Design* (New York: Norton, 1996); *The Selfish Gene*, 30th anniversary ed. (Oxford; New York: Oxford University Press, 2006); *The God Delusion* (London: Bantam, 2006); Lawrence Krauss, *A Universe from Nothing: Why there is Something rather than Nothing* (New York: Free Press, 2012).
3. In atheist literature there are repeated references to "fairies at the bottom of the garden," "the invisible friend," and the "flying spaghetti monster" as ways of denigrating religious belief.
4. Christopher Hitchens, *God is not Great: How Religion Poisons Everything* (New York: Twelve, 2007); Sam Harris, *The End of Faith: Religion, Terror, and the Future of Reason* (New York: Norton, 2004); Mark Juergensmeyer, *Terror in the Mind of God: The Global Rise of Religious Violence* (Berkley: University of California Press, 2003).

rorism, and in the less recent past of Catholic-Protestant violence in Ireland.[5] There can be no doubt that communities with religious commitments have in fact regularly been involved in acts of violence, as have many non-religious communities as found in Communist states of USSR, China, and North Korea. Still there is something absolute about the claims of religious belief which can appear unreasonable and even violent to the non-believer. The end result is that, as with the irrationality of belief, the link between religions and violence has become yet another default position for many contemporary debates.[6]

As a counterweight to these defaults there has been an "Augustinian" resurgence among some Christian religious thinkers whose response to these positions has been one of rejecting the basic premise of the autonomy of reason. Drawing on religious doctrines such as original sin and the universal need for grace, they argue that claims for autonomous reason are the product of our fallen nature; sinfulness has darkened our reason and the only remedy for a fallen reason is the light of faith. The claims of the secularists and atheists to being the voice of reason in the face of religious irrationality are thus turned on their heads. Their claims to reason are a mask for hubris, while religious faith marks a position of humble trust in God and what God has revealed. As we noted in the opening chapter, such a position easily becomes one of "only a Christian philosophy is a true philosophy." Here the voices of the Radical Orthodoxy movement have been prominent, notably its leader John Milbank, as well as other post-foundationalist narrative theologians such as William Cavanaugh.[7] As with the new atheists, the debates here are not just epistemological and metaphysical but overtly political, raising serious questions about the nature of our secular social orders. Nonetheless there are inherent philosophical claims being made which also require a response.

And so these are the three areas where I intend to bring perspectives from Gilson and Lonergan to bear. I begin with the easiest of the three, that of the new atheism and its claims in relation to science, before moving on to those of increasing complexity, religion and violence, and the modern rise of Augustinianism. I shall then conclude with

---

5. Hitchens identifies religiously-linked violence with all the major religious traditions of the world.
6. At the level of news reporting, we often hear reports of "inter-religious violence" as if ethnic, cultural, economic and political factors were not important or even decisive in causing the conflict.
7. John Milbank, *Theology and Social Theory: Beyond Secular Reason* (Cambridge, Mass.: Blackwell, 1991); *The Word made Strange: Theology, Language, Culture* (Cambridge, MA: Blackwell Publishers, 1997); William T. Cavanaugh, *Torture and Eucharist: Theology, Politics, and the Body of Christ* (Oxford: Blackwell Publishers, 1998); *The Myth of Religious Violence: Secular Ideology and the Roots of Modern Conflict* (New York: Oxford University Press, 2009).

some comments about the overall question of the possibility of a Christian philosophy.

Science, Faith, and the New Atheism

Why would one think that the new atheists are the easiest to address? Largely because their own positions are so philosophically naive and inconsistent. The works of Dawkins and Krauss are polemic works, neither truly scientific in their approach nor philosophically sophisticated in their arguments. Nonetheless the narrative that they tell of science overcoming religious belief, one that has often been recycled since the Enlightenment, continues to have popular traction in many circles, to the extent that even some good religious believers begin to fall under its sway. Of course they do tend to target (particularly Dawkins) the more fundamentalist end of the religious spectrum, those who reject evolution and other science because of some perceived contradiction with biblical texts, and for this targeting one can share some sympathy. Some religious believers do no service to their religion by insisting on literalist readings of texts never meant to convey scientific information. They bring religion into dispute and perpetuate a false split between faith and reason. In a sense these two polemic camps, new atheists and religious fundamentalists, are locked into a *danse macabre*—a mutual dance of co-dependence between two intellectual dead-ends.

On the other hand, there is an underlying claim that religious belief and scientific method are inherently incompatible and given the success of science in explaining the world, the only reasonable option is to adopt science, not religion, as one's life guide. More recently Krauss has pushed the argument so far as to claim that not only does science explain how the world operates, but it can even explain—if not exactly now, then in the near future—why there is a universe at all. The whole universe would then be self-explanatory, without any need for God as an explanatory cause. This is the issue I shall focus upon.

Let's return to the summary account of the discovery of the Higgs boson in the previous chapter. Modern particle physics presents us with an amazing narrative of the scientific method in process. The initially discovered family of sub-atomic particles, protons, neutrons, and electrons, that constitute our normal matter, exploded into a veritable zoo of particles as physicists developed particle accelerators and examined high energy cosmic rays from space. As the number of "elementary" particles expanded, patterns or families of particles emerged, patterns which linked the particles through hypothetical symmetries; symmetries were connected to physical conservation laws; these were formulated into explanatory accounts of different families of particles: first in quantum electrodynamics, and then quantum chromodynamics. Each of these mathematical formulations or hypotheses needed empirical verification before they would be accepted. Out of these various theories a major unification of the various families of sub-atomic particles emerged, the so-called Standard Model. As with the theories that had preceded it, it not only fit the available data, it also made predictions of new phenomena that could be either verified or falsified. As we noted previously, one such prediction was that of the existence of the Higgs boson. Indeed its existence was vital to the theory because it provided an explanatory account of the mass of all the other particles in the model. Its discovery was not an added bonus, but essential to the explanatory power of the model.[8]

What can we identify in this account? Scientific method has three essential and interlocking components: gathering data; hypothesis or theory formulation; empirical verification of hypotheses through the data. The data gathering can be relatively blind, as with the early work by particle physicists and their accelerators, basically banging things together to see what would happen; or it can be quite deliberate and purposefully, as with the search for the Higgs boson. What distinguishes these is that the second approach is theory driven. The theory tells the researcher where to look, what data to seek, what is significant. Theory turns data into evidence. Without the theory of the Standard Model, the scientists at CERN would have found a bump in a graph, but its significance would have been unknown. With the Standard Model in place, that bump became conclusive evidence of the existence of the Higgs boson. Of course the data may not fit the evidence, in which case the theory will need to be revised. And so while the Standard Model did successfully predict the existence of the Higgs boson exactly as predicted, it fails to predict or fit other now known aspects of elementary particles, such as the mass of the different types of neutrinos. There is still more theoretical work to be done. Many would suggest the next step will be the incorporation of gravity into the model, but how this can be done is an open question. Whatever

---

8. For an account of the history read Robert Oerter, *The Theory of Almost Everything: The Standard Model, the Unsung Triumph of Modern Physics* (New York: Penguin Group US, 2006).

such developments might be, however, they will need to incorporate the existence of the Higgs boson as predicted by the Standard Model.

There are a number of things to note from this account. The first is how closely it follows Lonergan's structure of experience, understanding, and judgment. Experience is concerned with data; understanding with theory; judgment with empirical verification of our understanding. Scientific method is entirely congruent with Lonergan's cognitional theory, and so provides a happy point of verification for that theory not just based on appeals to interiority.

Secondly, in the method we find expression of the demand for complete intelligibility. No scientist would ever suggest that we just draw a line under its achievements, say of the Standard Model, and say no further, the rest is just mystery. The search is now on in earnest for the next theory, the one which incorporates the achievements of the Standard Model while overcoming its limitations.[9] At no point would a scientist suggest that there is simply no further intelligibility to be found. That would mean an abandonment of the very heart of science. Yet this quest for complete intelligibility is a premise for scientific method, one which is in fact metaphysical in nature. Complete intelligibility cannot be verified by scientific method *per se* because it is presupposed by that method. This highlights an important limitation to scientific method (and knowledge). It is based on something which while possibly true—the complete intelligibility of the data—actually lies outside the field of science altogether. Again we are reminded that both Gilson and Lonergan argue from the demand for complete intelligibility to the existence of God. Arguments for God's existence draw on the incomplete intelligibility made evident in the contingency of the universe to argue for the existence of a necessary, self-explanatory being.

Thirdly, this matter of contingency is most evident in the demand for empirical verification. No scientific theory is held to be self-verifying. The Standard Model was mathematically elegant and matched much of what was already known. But no one would have suggested foregoing the need for further verification. Without empirical verification the Model remained hypothetical, lacking something scientifically essential. In metaphysical terms this means that the phenomena that science deals with are not necessary but contingent. Things could be other than they are, the laws of physics could be different, and there is nothing in their formulation that makes them so elegant, so

9. Of course that search had begun long before the proof of the existence of the Higgs boson. But that is now a settled matter and any advance must incorporate this from the start.

convincing, that they *must* be true.[10] To make such a claim would be unscientific because it would completely bypass the need for empirical verification, a cornerstone of the scientific method.

Yet this is exactly the claim being made by those who want to argue that modern science has made belief in God redundant. This claim is spelt out by Krauss in his book, *A Universe from Nothing*, and supported by Richard Dawkins who compares it with Darwin's *Origin of Species*, doing for cosmology what Darwin's work did for biology in eliminating the need for God.[11] In place of a creator God who is the source of existence for the universe Krauss posits a multiverse, an infinite number of universes each with different physical laws coming into and out of existence.

> The possibility that our universe is one of a large, even possibly infinite set of distinct and causally separated universes, in each of which any number of fundamental aspects of physical reality may be different opens up a vast new possibility for understanding our existence.[12]

The multiverse eliminates the need for any causal explanation of the universe we experience.

> The question of what determined the laws of nature that allowed our universe to form and evolve now becomes less significant. If the laws of nature are themselves stochastic and random, then there is no prescribed "cause" for our universe.[13]

The question is: on what basis can we claim that the multiverse itself exists? As a proposed hypothesis, how can it be verified? As Krauss notes on three occasions, the various universes that constitute the multiverse are "causally disconnected."[14] In fact they have "always been and always will be causally disconnected from ours"[15] which implies that we can have no empirical knowledge of their existence

10. An interesting example here is that of Einstein's theory of general relativity. So intellectually compelling was this appeal to the pure intelligibility of physical laws, that when Einstein was asked what he would do if his theory was not verified in its first test by Eddington, he stated, "Then I would feel sorry for the dear Lord. The theory is correct anyway." Ilse Rosenthal-Schneider, *Reality and Scientific Truth: Discussions With Einstein, Von Laue, and Plank*, ed. T. Braun (Detroit: Wayne State University Press, 1980), 74.
11. Krauss, *A Universe from Nothing*, 191. It received similar endorsements from Sam Harris who declares it a "brilliant and disarming book" and A. C. Grayling who claims it is a "triumph of science over metaphysics, reason and enquiry over obfuscation and myth, made plain for all to see."
12. Ibid., 176.
13. Ibid., 177.
14. Ibid., 127, 130, 176.
15. Ibid., 127.

as any such empirical knowledge can only arise through a causal connection. They thus remain forever—"always have been and always will be"—empirically unverifiable. So in order to overcome the question of contingency and the need for a creator, Krauss and others who propose the multiverse as an alternative to belief in God are willing to ditch a fundamental aspect of scientific method, the demand for empirical verification.

A similar set of observations could be made about claims of a possible future "theory of everything" in which all physical constants are determined uniquely, so there can be only one possible universe, uniquely determined by "one big equation." Such a theory would unite the four forces of nature in one account of quantum gravity.[16] These two approaches intersect when the "one big equation" is used to generate not just this universe, but the whole multiverse. Either way, we run into the same problem that either such a theory needs to be empirically verified in which case the question of contingency returns; or it seeks to go beyond a fundamental aspect of scientific method of requiring empirical verification. This claim is thus no longer a scientific claim, but a metaphysical one, alleviating science from the need for empirical verification altogether.

Indeed Gilson might find in this project a modern scientific version of the essentialism he so thoroughly rejected within the various philosophical accounts presented in *Being and some Philosophers*.[17] Krauss and others promoting such a position are seeking to deduce existence from essence; act from form. They want to find in some finite intelligibility sufficient reason for existence. However, as both Gilson and Lonergan argue, the real distinction between essence and existence means no such move is possible. If essentialism were true, science would be so much easier because it could do without the need for empirical verification. But then it would not be science as we know it. Royal astronomer Martin Rees picks up this point when he notes, "Theorists may, some day, be able to write down fundamental equations governing physical reality. But physics can never explain what 'breathes fire' into the equations, and actualizes them in a real cosmos."[18] One can

16. The most common popularized proposal is "string theory" which seeks to unite all forces and particles in a ten- or eleven- dimensional model of space-time. See Brian Greene, *The Elegant Universe: Superstrings, Hidden Dimensions, and the Quest for the Ultimate Theory* (London: Jonathan Cape, 1999), for an account. Interestingly Krauss is critical of string theory because it has made no verifiable physical claims. See Krauss, *A Universe from Nothing*, 132.
17. Étienne Gilson, *Being and Some Philosophers*, 2d ed. (Toronto: Pontifical Institute of Mediaeval Studies, 1952).

know whether "fire" has been breathed into the equations through empirical verification, but such verification remains from a scientific perspective a contingent fact. Rees might be surprised to be told that the distinction he is drawing is nothing other than the metaphysical distinction between essence and existence, which distinction is central to the contingency of the universe.

What might inhibit Gilson in recognizing this, however, is his relatively underdeveloped account of science and its relationship to the metaphysical elements. Here Lonergan's account of the notion of "central form" as what is grasped in fully explanatory science is a real advance. This allows us to identify the theoretical constructs of science as prospective or approximate forms expressed mathematically. Much of the scholastic accounts of what they would term "substantial forms," as distinct from Lonergan's term central form, is hampered by a failure to distinguish descriptive commonsense knowing from explanatory knowing. The connection between the work of the scientist and the metaphysician is then not made clear.

We can push this argument further. Not only do advances in science fail to make God redundant, it becomes increasingly clear that science can never either verify or falsify the existence of God. Because scientific method is concerned with empirical verification of hypotheses, its field of knowing is only concerned with contingent being. God, if existing, exists not as contingent but as necessary being. This however does not preclude the existence of God from reasoned argument. The very same type of metaphysical reasoning that can justify scientific method through an appeal to the intelligibility of reality can be used to justify the existence of God. This is neatly captured by the physicist turned natural philosopher, Paul Davies:

> Science is founded on the notion of the rationality and logicality of nature. The universe is ordered in a meaningful way, and scientists seek reasons for why things are the way they are. If the universe as a whole is pointless, then it exists reasonlessly. In other words, it is ultimately arbitrary and absurd. We are then invited to contemplate a state of affairs in which all scientific chains of reasoning are grounded in absurdity. The order of the world would have no foundation and its breathtaking rationality would have to spring, miraculously, from absurdity. So Weinberg's dictum is neatly turned on its head: the more the universe seems pointless, the more it seems incomprehensible.[19]

18. Martin J. Rees, *Just Six Numbers: The Deep Forces that Shape the Universe* (New York: Basic Books, 2000), 131.

Of course Davies is not suggesting that the universe is absurd. He is suggesting that if the universe has no source in intelligence (God), then the success of science is incomprehensible. Davies is implying that this is somehow offensive to reason itself. Or as Albert Einstein noted "The most incomprehensible thing about the universe is that it is comprehensible."[20]

Overall natural theology of the type undertaken by both Gilson and Lonergan has a continuing role to play in the ongoing discussions about faith and reason. Arguments for the existence of God lie on the boundary of both faith and reason, often to be exiled by both sides: by atheists who dismiss God's existence on the basis of reason; by believers who find in natural theology an unnecessary and even misleading and idolatrous crutch to genuine religious belief.[21] While the ground has shifted from the more philosophical issues—for example Kant's rejection of natural theology—to those raised by the findings of modern science, it is important not to focus too much on the content of the science but on its underlying method. The method reveals the operations of intelligence and reason, which operations entail an implicit metaphysics. The real difficulty we face with the new atheists is not their belief in science and its method, but in the incongruity between the implicit metaphysics of that method and the materialist metaphysical assumptions so prevalent in their explicit and extra-scientific declarations that belief in God has been rendered redundant by science.[22]

The other point to make here is to raise the question, who actually knows, as immanently generated knowledge, that the Higgs boson exists? By the very nature of the project—the construction of the LHC, the distinctive contribution of theoreticians and practitioners, the cooperative nature of modern scientific research—what we have here is almost a distributed web of knowing, a mixture of immanently generated knowledge in the minds of individual scientists weaved together

19. Paul Davies, "Now is the reason for our discontent," *Sydney Morning Herald*, 1 January 2003. Weinberg's dictum is "The more the universe seems comprehensible the more it also seems pointless." Davies basically repeats his argument in *The Goldilocks Enigma: Why is the Universe Just Right for Life?* (London: Allen Lane, 2006), 17–18.
20. Albert Einstein, *Ideas and Opinions*, trans. Sonja Bargmann (New York: Bonanza, 1954), 292.
21. For example Karl Barth said of natural theology, "If one occupies oneself with real theology one can pass by so-called natural theology only as one would pass by an abyss into which it is inadvisable to step if one does not want to fall. All one can do is to turn one's back upon it as upon the great temptation and source of error, by having nothing to do with it and by making it clear to oneself and to others from time to time why one acts that way." Emil Brunner and Karl Barth, *Natural Theology* (London: Geoffrey Bles, 1946) 75, quoted in Andrew Moore, "Should Christians do Natural Theology?," *Scottish Journal of Theology* 63 (2010): 127–45, at 134n24.
22. For a fuller discussion of natural theology see Neil Ormerod, *A Public God: Natural Theology Reconsidered* (Minneapolis: Fortress, 2015).

with reasonably grounded belief in the contributions of one's fellow researchers and in the skills of those who actually constructed this massive device. It is probably impossible to separate out the different components of immanently generated knowledge and shared believing that constitutes the scientific judgment that the Higgs boson exists. It is highly unlikely that any particular scientist can honestly put up his or her hand and say they have personally verified every aspect and genuinely know that it all works, it all makes sense. From this perspective believing is an important aspect of the whole scientific method. Without the reasonable exercise of belief, we could not now say with confidence that the Higgs boson exists. There is no dichotomy between science and belief, no presumption of the irrationality of believing, on such an account. Religious belief differs from science not because it believes, but because of what it believes and why. The truths believed arise not from a purely human source, but from God who can neither deceive nor be deceived. While there are questions to be raised in relation to this stance, how these truths are witnessed throughout human history and so on, at least we can claim that reason is not opposed to believing in general, whatever issues it may raise in relation to specifically religious belief. Believing in itself may be a perfectly reasonable thing to do.

Myths of Religious Violence—Religion, Reason, and Violence[23]

If the arguments of the new atheism and its scientific proponents represent one fault line in the debate between faith and reason, the other major fault line lies in the persistent linking of religion and violence. While initially spurred in modern debates by so-called Islamic extremism and their acts of terrorism, it has grown to encompass examples of historical religious violence (the Crusades, the European "wars of religion" after the Reformation and so on), to more recent examples of inter-religious communal violence between Catholics and Protestants (Northern Ireland), Muslims and Hindus (India), Buddhists and Muslims (Myanmar) as well as various acts of religiously motivated violence by extremists (abortion clinic bombings, Aum sect sarin gas attack on the Tokyo subway). One need only read Christopher Hitchens's work, *God is not Great*, to feel the force of the moral complaint against religion.

23. For a more extended response to this question see Dominic Arcamone, *Religion and Violence: A Dialectical Engagement through the Insights of Bernard Lonergan* (Eugene OR: Wipf & Stock, 2015).

One important response to this litany of evil perpetrated in the name of religious faith is to attempt to draw a distinction between religion as a normative phenomenon and the various ways it is actually lived out in practice, ways which fall away from that norm to varying degrees. The fact that people claim a particular religious motivation for their violent actions may in fact have nothing to do with that religion viewed normatively. The issue for many religious traditions is who determines what that norm is. Is an evangelical televangelist as valid an expression of Christian faith as the pope in Rome? If ISIS is not actually representative of what it means to be Muslim, then who speaks for what Islam should be? Finally, is a bad Christian, Muslim or Buddhist still a Christian, Muslim or Buddhist, and if so in what sense? In fact for many people, their religious belief can be very childish and immature, more a form of tribalism and a talisman for warding off bad life experiences, than a genuine participation in their own religious tradition. At worst, some religious groups seem to be little more than a shared psychosis, with little connection to any reality at all. Such stances should not be defended in any attempt to counter claims of a link between religion and violence. This is not religion at its best if it can properly be called religion at all.

A second level of response is to argue the difficulty in separating out religious motivations from the complex web of economic, political and cultural factors involved in much of the communal and terrorist related acts of violence. Often the religious identity of actors within these dramas is inseparable from ethnic and cultural identities, and bound with a variety of historical, economic and political injustices, some going back centuries. Focusing on religious belief is then little more than a cipher for a much more complex picture of group identity, one which is exploited both by those seeking to further their own political ends and by those who wish to tar all religions with the brush of violence.[24]

However, we also need to acknowledge that at the heart of the very nature of religious belief—not just in its various distortions and immature forms—is a sense of an absolute claim being made on the believer. For believers their religious life is all-important, the thing around which the rest of their life revolves. The demands of faith can be absolute, an act of complete obedience or trust in God (I speak

24. For example one often finds the media reporting instances of "religious violence" when what is really at stake are long-standing ethnic disputes and injustices, of which religion is one component. In this way the media feed into the myth of religious violence.

here for simplicity of theistic beliefs such as Christianity, Judaism, and Islam). If God reveals, a believer has no place to stand except to believe. This absolute dimension of faith seems to sideline or even exclude reason, which exclusion is a real concern. Does my belief in God and my adherence to the divine will require or even demand that I overturn my reason? The case is not helped by those who would suggest exactly this. For example Martin Luther proclaimed,

> There is on earth among all dangers no more dangerous thing than a richly endowed and adroit reason, especially if she enters into spiritual matters which concern the soul and God. . . . Reason must be . . . blinded, and destroyed. Faith must trample underfoot all reason, sense, and understanding, and whatever it sees it must put out of sight. . . . Whoever wants to be a Christian should tear the eyes out of his reason."[25]

In a similar vein and more recently Karl Barth argued that "Faith takes reason by the throat and strangles the beast."[26] Of course all such statements have a particular context and intention, but at face value they present us with exactly the types of concerns raised by those who link religion with violence. If reason is eliminated then God can demand anything, even frightful acts of violence.[27] Ironically the quote from Luther above is regularly referred to on the web—particularly on atheist websites—and can even be purchased emblazoned on a tee-shirt from such sites.

Now there are many situations where religions are linked with violence, some fairly, some unjustly, where religion is just one of a complex web of motivations for a particular act. In order to focus on instances of religious violence where the religious motivation is in the foreground, I would like to concentrate on those acts which can be associated with religious conversion, where violence is used to coerce such conversion. We can find this concern raised by Pope Benedict XVI in his famous Regensburg Address.[28] While it was controversial at the time because of its apparent linking of Islam with violence, the underlying point Benedict was attempting to make was the importance of maintaining the taut unity-in-difference of faith and reason.

25. Quoted in Walter Kaufmann, *The Faith of a Heretic* (Garden City, NY: Doubleday, 1963), 75.
26. Karl Barth, *The Epistle to the Romans*, trans. Edwyn Clement Hoskyns (London: Oxford University Press, 1933), 143.
27. Such a situation often arises in the Biblical witness. See Phyllis Trible, *Texts of Terror: Literary-Feminist Readings of Biblical Narratives* (Philadelphia: Fortress Press, 1984).
28. Benedict XVI, "Faith, Reason and the University: Memories and Reflections," http://w2.vatican.va/content/benedict-xvi/en/speeches/2006/september/documents/hf_ben-xvi_spe_200609 12_university-regensburg.html. All quotes below taken from this site.

Where faith separates itself from reason then violence can easily follow. Benedict refers to a historical encounter between an "erudite Byzantine emperor Manuel II Paleologus and an educated Persian on the subject of Christianity and Islam" around the topic of faith, reason, and violence. The point the emperor is arguing in the debate is the theme, "why spreading the faith through violence is something unreasonable." As Benedict notes, "the decisive statement in this argument against violent conversion is this: not to act in accordance with reason is contrary to God's nature." What is important here for Benedict is the maintenance of the close connection between our conception of God and reason. If this is not kept in focus God's will "is not bound up with any of our categories, even that of rationality" resulting in a voluntarism and "a capricious God, who is not even bound to truth and goodness." Against this he proposes, "God does not become more divine when we push him away from us in a sheer, impenetrable voluntarism; rather, the truly divine God is the God who has revealed himself as *logos* [reason]."

For Benedict reason plays an indispensable role in the purification of faith. Without a strong link between faith and reason, faith quickly goes off the rails, and in doing so it betrays itself. For this reason he finds in the early encounter between Biblical revelation and Greek philosophy the hand of divine providence. "The encounter between the Biblical message and Greek thought did not happen by chance." Indeed this "inner rapprochement between Biblical faith and Greek philosophical inquiry was an event of decisive importance not only from the standpoint of the history of religions, but also from that of world history." It led to a mutual enrichment of faith and reason, a theme evident in the encyclical *Fides et ratio* written by Pope John Paul II. Benedict is aware that there are those who would sunder this unity of faith and reason in the name of the self-sufficiency of the Gospel, through a program of dehellenization. On the other side there are those who invoke scientific reason to likewise sunder this unity, where we are faced with a "reduction of the radius of science and reason, one which needs to be questioned." Not only does reason help purify faith, faith can liberate reason from a truncated self-understanding that would reduce reason to calculative and scientific reasoning.

Here again the natural theology of Gilson and Lonergan can be of great assistance. For both thinkers God is the intelligent source of being, the one whose existence is "understanding itself" (*ipsum intelligere*) and "being itself" (*ipsum esse*). This position is the product of reason, not simply of religious faith, but it is a reason that has undergone a "conversion" to being, what Lonergan refers to as intellectual conversion. This conversion opens reason up fully to its proper object, being, as intelligently grasped and reasonably affirmed. While such a conversion may arise in a religious context—for Gilson it was the impact of Exodus 3:14; for Lonergan it was the church's early Christological and Trinitarian doctrines—it can arise independently of this context, and as we have already argued, is fully congruent with the implicit metaphysics of the scientific method. Any attempt to separate God from reason or to claim that God's "will is not bound up with any of our categories, even that of rationality" is rejected because outside of being there is only nothing, nothing at all. What is irrational simply lacks the requisites of existence, to be intelligently grasped and reasonably affirmed. This stance achieves the outcome sought by Benedict: "not to act in accordance with reason is contrary to God's nature." Natural theology can in this way perform an important role in purifying our religious convictions, particularly an anthropomorphizing and tribalizing of God that would reduce God to a larger, more powerful version of ourselves, a God who is "on our side." Both Gilson and Lonergan can maintain the otherness of God while holding firmly to the *analogia entis*, the analogical relationship between divine being and the rest of creation.

Thus the debate over the link between religious faith and violence does in fact demand the ongoing purification of all religious belief through the type of engagement with philosophical reasoning exemplified by Gilson and Lonergan (and more broadly the Thomist tradition). While one can appreciate the critique of the myth of religious violence offered by, for example, William Cavanaugh, which highlights the often unrestrained violence perpetrated in the name of secular reason, it cannot stand alone without an ongoing commitment to the purification of religious traditions through the continual struggle to bring faith and reason into fruitful dialogue.

Supernaturalizing the Natural, Radical Orthodoxy, and a New Augustinianism

Perhaps in a development that neither Gilson nor Lonergan would have anticipated, the late twentieth and early twenty-first centuries have witnessed a resurgence of the neo-Platonic Augustinian option that both thinkers had soundly rejected. While it is true that in many ways

Lonergan's thought became more Augustinian in some of its aspects during his later writings, this was more a matter of a greater attention to the existential and religious dimension within his thought and never an adoption of the platonizing elements in Augustine. However, through the influence of Joseph Ratzinger (later Pope Benedict XVI), Hans Urs von Balthasar, Henri de Lubac and others, Augustine's stance has enjoyed a resurgence. One group that took up this resurgence is Radical Orthodoxy with its intellectual driving force, John Milbank.[29] Rather than attempt to overview the whole range of literature available in relation to this shift to a more Augustinian stance, I shall focus on some of the common themes, which I shall illustrate in reference to the work of Milbank. I shall then respond to this movement from the perspective of Gilson and Lonergan. Here, significantly Gilson takes the leading role. For Gilson this particular approach is one of a failed historical experiment he identifies as "theologism."[30]

A neat phrase to express the intentionality of the movement is that of "supernaturalizing the natural."[31] Driven by a religious sentiment that "all is grace," it then seeks to eliminate any particular reference point that might stand as distinct from grace; the natural order, so carefully delineated in the work of Aquinas, is overwhelmed (or eliminated) through its incorporation into the supernatural order. Any reference to some posited natural order is viewed as an assertion of human autonomy, a work of human hubris and driven by our original alienation from God, original sin. No longer does grace complete and perfect a natural order distinct from grace; rather the natural order is itself always and everywhere disordered needing to be completely reshaped through the obedience of faith and in the light of divine grace. It was the work of de Lubac who reminded Catholic scholars that the early Church Fathers, largely of neo-Platonic orientation, had no need of the later grace-nature distinction. This later development was due to the impact of Aristotelian philosophy, and if the Church had lived without the distinction for over one thousand years, it could not be considered essential to our understanding of the faith.[32] The Platonic solution to a Christian world view was based on a distinction

29. As Paul J. DeHart, *Aquinas and Radical Orthodoxy: A Critical Inquiry* (New York: Routledge, 2012), 34, notes, it often appears as if the term "radical Orthodoxy" is just a coded reference for Milbank. Still there are others in the movement, and they are not uniform in their opinions. I shall focus, however, on Milbank's contribution for the purposes of this discussion.

30. Étienne Gilson, *The Unity of Philosophical Experience* (San Francisco, CA: Ignatius Press, 1999), particularly 25–48.

31. Milbank uses the phrase at Milbank, *Theology and Social Theory*, 207, and repeatedly throughout his chapter 8, "Founding the Supernatural."

between the fixed and eternal world of Truth, known to the mind of God, and the mutable and temporal world of our existence, tenuously held in existence by God as a shadow world, a distorted reflection of the divine order. Rather than a grace-nature distinction, at the heart of this understanding is a grace-sin dialectic. A realm of grace, faith, and truth stands in opposition to a realm of sin, infidelity, and falsehood.

There are a couple of important consequences of this neo-Platonic stance. One is that our world suffers from an ontological instability. Ours is a world of change, of mutability, so there can be no certainty about its ordering. For Augustine, human nature was not a metaphysical constant. Rather there was human nature prior to the Fall, after the Fall, and as redeemed by Christ. Milbank pushes the matter even further. Even this relatively stable formulation of Augustine is too solid; rather the world is one of Heraclitian flux, a linguistic world in which truth is made, unmade, and remade constantly, to such an extent that in the end there is no more truth and falsehood. "If for Christianity, 'philosophy' is finished and surpassed, then there can be no more 'truth and falsity.'"[33] There can be no metaphysics—philosophy is "finished"—for Milbank, because there are no stable substances or forms from which one can hold onto a metaphysical truth. In a provocatively entitled essay, "Only Theology can overcome Metaphysics" Milbank argues that:

> This means that the domain of metaphysics is not only subordinated to, but completely *evacuated* by theology, for metaphysics refers its subject matter—Being—wholesale to its first principle, God, which is the subject of another higher science, namely God's own, only accessible to us via revelation.[34]

This is a far more radical and post-modern conclusion, beyond what Augustine would have envisaged, but not entirely incongruent with some of his stated positions.

Another consequence follows from the ontological instability of the world. Given the impermanence of truth in itself and our own participation in the instability of the world, our only access to the truth can be through a participation in or illumination by the divine mind. Certainly Augustine held to such an illuminationist account of knowing,

---

32. Of course the encyclical *Humani Generis* of Pope Pius XII argued that the distinction was essential to Catholic thought.

33. Milbank, *Theology and Social Theory*, 430.

34. Milbank, *Word Made Strange*, 44.

whose logic derived from his neo-Platonic sources. Placed in a Christian and religious context however this teaching takes on a different significance. As Gilson notes in relation to the great Augustinian figure of the Middle Ages, Bonaventure, who held to such an illuminationist account:

> Granted that we cannot know truth without some additional influx of divine light, how are we to conceive the nature of that divine illumination? If we take it as a particular instance of the general action by which God creates and runs the world, it is but the natural light of reason, that is the human intellect itself, which can therefore know truth without any further illumination from God. If on the contrary, we see that intellectual light as a further gift, superadded by God to the natural light of man, we make it to be supernatural. It then becomes a grace, with the result that not a single instance of our true knowledge can be considered natural.[35]

As Gilson rightly points out, the danger here is that outside of the realm of grace, there can be no true knowledge. As we have already noted in Chapter 1, this was a conclusion that Augustine was later to regret. "I do not approve having said in the prayer, O God, Who dost wish the sinless alone to know the truth; for it may be answered that many who are not sinless know many truths."[36] The illuminationist account threatens to break down the distinction between natural and supernatural truth, the natural light of reason and the light of faith.

Again this is where Milbank pushes the matter into a more extreme direction. For him these distinctions do in fact break down. Just as theology evacuates metaphysics, revealed truth is our only true source of knowledge of the world, significantly a position he attributes to Aquinas: "The distinction between 'revealed' and 'natural' knowledge is really located by Aquinas in a much more fundamental framework of the participation of all human rationality in divine reason. (So *all* knowledge implies faith in God for Aquinas.)"[37] Given all we have already said in relation to Aquinas and his careful delineation of the orders of grace and nature, faith and reason, this is a startling claim on Milbank's part. One is entitled to ask on what basis such a claim can be made. In a footnote Milbank references three texts in Aquinas, *In Boeth. De Trin* q.3 a1. resp. and *STh* I q1 a5, ad2, and a6. The first of these relates to the question, "Whether God Is the First Object Known by the

35. Gilson, *The Unity of Philosophical Experience*, 44–45.
36. Augustine, *Retractations*, i, 4 quoted in *STh* I–II q109 a1, sed contra.
37. Milbank, *Theology and Social Theory*, 248.

Mind." Given Milbank provides no direct quote from this material it is not clear to what he is referring. However, we do find the following text pertinent to Milbank's concerns:

> Moreover, in the attempt to arrive at some knowledge of God, the human mind is greatly assisted when its natural light is fortified by a new illumination: namely, the light of faith and that of the gifts of wisdom and of understanding, by which the mind is elevated above itself in contemplation, inasmuch as it knows God to be above anything which it naturally apprehends.[38]

Here as one would expect we have a carefully delineated account of the distinction between the natural light of reason and the "new illumination" provided by the light of faith. There is nothing else in the text referenced by Milbank that this reader could find which would provide the least support for his claim that "*all* knowledge implies faith in God for Aquinas." If we turn to the two texts from the *Summa Theologiae* we find similar difficulties. No direct evidence can be found in support of his claim. Rather we find, as we would expect, the same clear distinctions being drawn between the power of the natural light of reason and the added illumination received through divine revelation. While the superiority of the latter is stated, it in no way undermines or replaces the role of the former.[39] Finally, we can refer to the already cited text of Aquinas in chapter 1 *STh* I–II q109 a1:

> We must therefore say that, if a man is to know any truth whatsoever, he needs divine help in order that his intellect may be moved to its act by God. But he does not need a new light added to his natural light in order to know the truth in all things, but only in such things as transcend his natural knowledge.

To which Aquinas adds in *STh* I–II q109 a1 ad2, "Hence the natural light bestowed upon the soul is God's enlightenment, whereby we are enlightened to see what pertains to natural knowledge; and for this there is required no further knowledge, but only for such things as surpass natural knowledge." Again all of which presupposes the distinction between the natural light of reason and the added light of faith.

---

38. *De Trin* q.3 a1. resp, available at http://www.dhspriory.org/thomas/BoethiusDeTr.htm#13.
39. This is not the only time that Milbank plays fast and loose with texts from Aquinas. See DeHart, *Aquinas and Radical Orthodoxy*; also Neil Ormerod, "'It is Easy to See': The Footnotes of John Milbank," *Philosophy and Theology* 11, no. 2 (1999): 257–64.

On the basis of his own chosen texts, Milbank's claim in relation to Aquinas is not substantiated.

As Gilson rightly predicted, the stance of theologism we find in Milbank ends in mysticism. On his detailed analysis of Milbank's work on Aquinas, DeHart argues that according to Milbank's account of Aquinas, "the human mind can only make a true judgment about any created thing if such judgment is conjoined with some kind of apprehension of that thing's participatory relationship to God as its creative exemplar, and that this apprehension in turn depends upon an intuitive grasp of God's being (amounting to an anticipation in this life of the beatific vision of God's very essence)."[40] As Gilson wryly concludes, "the philosopher, as such, has nothing against mysticism; what he does not like is a mysticism that presupposes as its necessary condition the destruction of philosophy."[41] Theology may be the queen of the sciences, but on this account the queen is absorbing her handmaid, philosophy, into herself, leaving the handmaid with no independent existence to herself. The philosopher has become absorbed into the mystic.

We can find how far Milbank is willing to take his illuminationist account of knowing when we assess his claim that unless all intellectual disciplines are "explicitly ordered to theology (assuming this means participation in God's self-knowledge, as in the Augustinian tradition) they are objectively and demonstrably null and void, altogether lacking in truth."[42] It is interesting to know where this leaves mathematics and modern science. Is there a distinctive Christian mathematics and physics? Do Christians do these activities differently? Or are these disciplines "objectively and demonstrably null and void"? And indeed what is the account of objectivity being used here? That Milbank is willing to go this far is evident in his account of the natural sciences in his programmatic work, *Theology and Social Theory*. In a chapter entitled, "Science, Power and Reality," he takes his argument beyond the question of social theory and into the realm of the so-called "natural sciences." There he boldly states that, "it will also be contended that natural science itself possesses no privileged access to truth and cannot, purely on its own account, build up a realist ontology. Its 'truth' is merely that of instrumental control, and therefore, in the case of human interactions, is bounded by the peculiar fractiousness

40. DeHart, *Aquinas and Radical Orthodoxy*, 130–31.
41. Gilson, *The Unity of Philosophical Experience*, 28.
42. John Milbank, *The Future of Love: Essays in Political Theology* (London: SCM Press, 2009), 306.

and innovative capacity of human behavior."[43] Indeed modern science is simply an extension of the type of "secular" reason that Milbank is seeking to refute: "I shall show that understanding as well as explanation, humanism as well as science, is an aspect of modernist secular reason, which I am trying to isolate and refuse."[44] Like capitalism, science is only concerned with power.[45] Congruent with his linguistic approach to the world, "scientific theories and experiments are themselves repeatable narratives"[46] with no real explanatory power of the world.

This is again a remarkable claim. We live in an age of astounding scientific discovery: the absolutely remarkable accuracy of the theoretical calculation of the fine structure constant through quantum electrodynamics; the theoretical prediction and experimental discovery of the Higgs boson; the most recent experimental discovery of direct evidence for Einstein's long predicted gravitational waves. All this is to be assigned into the category of narratives, stories we tell ourselves about the world, with no basis in the real or the true. In fact Milbank's account of science reads like someone with no firsthand experience of the subject; rather it is mediated through the lens of philosophers who themselves have varying degrees of familiarity with the actual operation of science. None of this should be read as attempting to give scientific knowing some privileged place in epistemology or metaphysics. Nor do I seek to countenance scientists who speak beyond their expertise to make pronouncements about philosophical or theological topics. But to deny them any place at all in the realm of truth is to invite skepticism to say the least. More modestly with Augustine we can note, "it may be answered that many who are not sinless know many truths."[47] And there are many with no faith at all who still fruitfully contribute to our cultural heritage of knowledge.

Gilson had basically analyzed the type of development that Milbank represents in his account of what he terms "theologism," where philosophy "is handled by theologians, according to theological methods, for a theological end."[48] He notes that for these people it is "quite

43. Milbank, *Theology and Social Theory*, 259.
44. Ibid., 263.
45. Ibid., 274.
46. Ibid., 270.
47. Augustine, *Retractations*, i, 4, quoted in *STh* I–II q109 a1, sed contra. This is not even to raise the question of the status of mathematics in Milbank's claim that all intellectual disciplines need to be ordered to theology. What this might mean in relation to the brilliant work of Andrew Wiles on Fermat's Last Theorem is anyone's guess.
48. Gilson, *The Unity of Philosophical Experience*, 31.

useless to worry about the real nature and order of things, because things have indeed neither nature nor order."[49] Such a world is unfit for scientific knowledge because there are no laws inscribed in the very essence of things.[50] This absolves them from studying how things actually are, replacing it with how things should be, according to a predetermined theological end. In a striking parallel between Milbank and Bonaventure in his book, *On Reducing the Arts to Theology*, Gilson notes of Bonaventure's position:

> The ultimate meaning of our arts and techniques, of our various sciences and of philosophy itself, is to symbolize on a lower plane of perfection the perfection of the divine art and of the divine knowledge. That is what they are, but left to themselves, they do not know it. It is the proper function of theology to bring them to a complete awareness of their proper function, which is not to know things but to know God through things . . . the human arts should be reduced to theology and thereby to God.[51]

Rather than view this type of stance as a grand conclusion to be celebrated, for Gilson it is more a *reductio ad absurdum*, an end point so off center as to defy common sense and logic, another failed philosophical experiment in the history of philosophy. "I sometimes wonder how many similar experiments will be necessary before men acquire some philosophical experience."[52] Gilson wrote this about theologism in the 1930s. He would not have been happy to see this position yet again revived, though perhaps not surprised: "were it not for the natural forgetfulness of man, it would never have been revived."[53]

Lonergan did not provide such an insightful analysis of the position of theologism as did Gilson, though he would have had little time for it. For Lonergan the distinctions between grace and nature, faith and reason, are fundamental to the Catholic theological project; moreover his major work, *Insight,* is clearly a non-theological work in that it prescinds from revealed data, while drawing heavily on mathematics and

49. Ibid., 33.
50. Ibid., 38.
51. Ibid., 40. Lonergan rarely mentions Bonaventure (a number of times in Bernard J. F. Lonergan, *Grace and Freedom: Operative Grace in the Thought of St. Thomas Aquinas*, ed. Frederick E. Crowe and Robert M. Doran, Collected Works of Bernard Lonergan [Toronto: University of Toronto Press, 2000], as part of the historical context), but there is one mention where he basically concurs with Gilson's assessment on him. See Bernard J. F. Lonergan, "Time and Meaning," in *Philosophical and Theological Papers 1958-1964*, ed. Robert C. Croken, Frederick E. Crowe, and Robert M. Doran, Collected Works of Bernard Lonergan (Toronto: University of Toronto Press, 1996), 119. Lonergan is drawing on the work of Yves Congar.
52. Gilson, *The Unity of Philosophical Experience*, 47.
53. Ibid.

the sciences in its opening chapters. There is however one element in Lonergan's work that I do think sheds light on Milbank's position. Lonergan's grappling with modern mathematics and science taught him clearly the distinction between description and explanation. While recognizing the starting point of our knowing in description, there is in the desire to know a more systematic exigence for explanatory knowing, whereby things are understood in relation to other things.[54] Lonergan identified such a development in the creation of the grace-nature distinction, however unthematized the development was. In modern science this development reaches new heights with correlative explanatory power. It provides science and mathematics with an unprecedented control of meaning of their basic terms and relations. Lonergan does not then use this as a way of denigrating other forms of knowing—such as commonsense, literary, and historical knowing—or to provide science with some privileged epistemological status. But he does grasp the significance of the breakthrough that modern science represents. Lonergan concurs with the judgment of the historian of science, Herbert Butterfield, that the emergence of modern science "outshines everything since the rise of Christianity and reduces the Renaissance and the Reformation to mere episodes, mere internal displacements, within the system of medieval Christendom."[55] I would respectfully suggest that this significance eludes Milbank.

Rather for Milbank the starting points are twofold: truth is linguistically mediated; and all language is metaphorical. These two very (post)modern positions mark out his more radical stance from the medieval thinkers Gilson was arguing with. While I do not accept the first (basically Lonergan would argue that insights are pre-linguistic), it is the second I shall focus on: the claim that all language is metaphorical. This claim fails to adequately account for explanatory meanings. Let us take the word, "field." Clearly it can be used in various metaphorical senses with quite different connotations. However, when a physicist speaks of a field she has a precise meaning in mind, a designation of a value to a point in space-time. That value may be a scalar, a vector or a tensor; the field might be a classical field or a quantum field. But its meaning will be clear to any physicist undertaking this area of study. In mathematics, a field has a different meaning: a

54. This systematic exigence is evident in the Socratic search for universal definitions, a first approximation for explanatory knowing over descriptive knowing.

55. Bernard J. F. Lonergan, "Theology in its New Context," in *A Second Collection*, ed. William Ryan and Bernard Tyrrell (Philadelphia: Westminster, 1974), 55–67, at 56. Lonergan is referring to Herbert Butterfield, *The Origins of Modern Science, 1300–1800*, 2nd ed. (New York: Free Press, 1966).

set of numbers with two commutative operations, addition and multiplication, which interact in specified ways. Again, any mathematician will mean exactly the same thing by a field, allowing for rapid and common understanding across languages and cultures. Whatever other connotations the word might have, these are just a distraction from understanding either the physical or mathematical concerns present at hand.

Let us push the matter further. How might we establish the statement that all language is metaphorical? Clearly if the statement is true, it cannot be proved. All such attempts at a proof would be linguistically and metaphorically constrained. Meanings would be fluid and conclusions unstable. The best one could hope to achieve would be a rhetorical conviction, a persuasive narrative that might convince the listener, until such a time as an alternative and more persuasive position is presented. On the other hand to genuinely prove such a stance one would need to move beyond metaphorical meaning and move into a genuinely explanatory account of the meaning of meaning, where precision, reasoning and logic can take proper command of the situation and come to a definitive conclusion.[56] In the former case the basic appeal is to the authority of the presenter, in the latter case we have transcended the very limitations we are seeking to prove. We are in a performative contradiction. None of this is to suggest that metaphorical meanings are unimportant in human affairs, that language and metaphor dominate much of our world of meaning, and that our world would be all the poorer stripped of such meanings. It is, however, to suggest that this is an artificial constraint to place upon meaning, a constraint evidently transcended in mathematics and science. Unless we have an account of meaning that can also take into account these genuine human achievements, our account is inadequate. The only alternative is to denigrate these genuine achievements as somehow distortions and falsehoods.

In his fine study of the theologies of Joseph Ratzinger and John Milbank, Peter Samuel Kucer traces Milbank's intellectual genealogy to the figure of Giambattista Vico.[57] Writing at the end of one intellectual era and the emergence of the Renaissance, Vico turned away from the world of stable and knowable essences as found in Aristotle

---

56. See for example Bernard J. F. Lonergan, *Method in Theology* (London: Darton, Longman & Todd, 1972), chapter 3.
57. Peter Samuel Kucer, *Truth and Politics: A Theological Comparison of Joseph Ratzinger and John Milbank* (Minneapolis: Fortress Press, 2014).

to a more Platonic and less stable world of ever-changing flux. He rejected the scientific turn of Descartes to embrace the world of literature, history and culture, claiming that "historical knowledge is surer than knowledge gained through scientific observation since we can only truly know what we make."[58] Whereas Descartes tried to recreate all knowledge on the basis of mathematical knowing—a stance Gilson rightly attacks[59]—Vico equally attempted to recreate all knowledge on the basis of history and language. As Kucer notes, "Vico maintains that the study of language and not nature is the highest standard of truth for humanity."[60] The point is, of course, that both these areas are valid sources of knowledge, and neither is privileged over the other; while philosophy itself is an intellectual discipline distinct from both. With Gilson we can say that both the natural world and the human world of meanings and values are instances of being; and with Lonergan we can claim that both disciplines provide us with instances of human knowing from which we can enter into an analysis of cognition. Unless our metaphysics and our cognitional theory are adequate to both areas they cannot demand our allegiance.

There are many other concerns we could raise about the project that Milbank promotes. Given his dismissal of an independent notion of reason, with its own natural light, his position falls foul of exactly the concerns raised by Benedict in the previous section. Reason can no longer play a purifying role in relation to religious faith, which freed from the constraints of reason falls prey to a voluntaristic conception of divine action. Milbank may rhetorically orate an ontological priority of peace over violence, but history teaches us that a conception of God untethered from reason easily provides an excuse for violence. This was the weight of Benedict's concern in his Regensburg address. Also in a religiously plural environment, Milbank's insistence on the privileged position of the Christian narrative threatens to shut down any interreligious dialogue or cooperation even before it starts. Incommensurable narratives can find little common ground once natural reason has been eliminated. All this is to simply suggest that if one were looking for a candidate for a contemporary approach to the questions of faith and reason, and the possibility of a Christian philosophy, this might not be the best place to start.

---

58. Ibid., 7.
59. Gilson, *The Unity of Philosophical Experience*, 99–120.
60. Kucer, *Truth and Politics*, 15.

A Christian Philosophy—What's in a Name?

The question we can now return to, raised in chapter 1 of the present study, is that of the possibility of a Christian philosophy. Gilson was a strong proponent of the term, but meant it in a way which maintained the taut unity-in-difference between faith and reason. Christian belief, through the impact of divine revelation, had shaped the actual practice of philosophy by raising questions and posing possibilities that demanded the expansion of our philosophical resources and pushing developments that otherwise would have been overlooked or considered of minor significance. For Gilson the paradigmatic example was the essence-existence distinction which he drew from Exodus 3:14, the revelation of the divine name, "I am who is." Still whatever revelation might suggest or promote within philosophy, for Gilson it needed to stand on its own two feet philosophically. Faith did not replace reason, nor reason faith. But their mutual interaction was historically fruitful. In terms MacIntyre would use, there arose within the Christian tradition a particular tradition of rationality that drew upon and was sustained by revelation, while still adhering to the demands of the natural light of reason.

I have argued herein that in many ways Lonergan's work exemplifies the type of stance Gilson meant by a Christian philosophy. Lonergan drew on deeper and more substantial elements of Christian belief—Christology, Trinity, and grace—to further develop his metaphysical and cognitional approaches. For Lonergan it was not the text of Exodus that suggested the essence-existence distinction, but the doctrine of Chalcedon on one person and two natures. With Augustine and Aquinas, attempts to understand the doctrine of the Trinity drove Lonergan to ever more precise accounts of human cognitional activity and its epistemological implications. Further, his work on grace and freedom for his doctoral studies placed the distinction of grace and nature as the bedrock of everything he did. Lonergan went on to develop a robust metaphysics, transposing the traditional Thomistic account into a more explanatory stance, made possible by his attentiveness to modern science. And from that metaphysics emerges an equally robust natural theology, again with strong parallels to the modern traditional accounts. These are all the elements one would expect to find in Gilson's understanding of a Christian philosophy.

Nonetheless this is not the epitaph Lonergan chose for his self-understanding. In his comments on Gilson's term, he prefers to refer to his work under the heading of Christian realism. Lonergan refers explicitly to the debate initiated by Gilson and Bréhier in the 1930s on the question of a Christian philosophy, a debate which he briefly reviews. He then introduces his notion of Christian realism, claiming that "the question of Christian philosophy is not the same as my question of Christian realism, but it does provide something of an antecedent for it."[61] Lonergan gives no reason for this claim or why he is not happy with the terms of the earlier debate. And his own account of Christian realism highlights the ways in which Trinitarian and Christological dogmatic development drove Christian thinkers to consider philosophical issues and move, with some degree of intellectual necessity, towards a realist position. This has parallels, as I have already suggested, with Gilson's claims.

Of course one might ask, what's in a name? Certainly the term, Christian philosophy, is prone to misunderstanding. Even Gilson was accused of smuggling in Christian theological *content* into his philosophy, something he was at pains to avoid.[62] Indeed many might think the term automatically implies such a smuggling, such as we find in the work of John Milbank. For many Christians, Milbank's project might appear as the epitome of what a Christian philosophy should do, even if it were to notionally maintain the distinction between faith and reason. Surely a Christian philosophy would want to incorporate specifically Christian doctrinal commitments, in some form or another?[63] Particularly in a more post-modern setting where increasingly anything goes, why not incorporate such commitments? One set of commitments are as good a starting point as any other, after all.

Yet this is precisely why Gilson, Lonergan, and Benedict hold on to the importance of a notion of reason independent of faith. In the end, "anything goes" is an invitation to the irrational which can rapidly terminate in violence. On the other hand, for a faith perspective to embrace an autonomous understanding of reason is an expression of an enormous sense of self-confidence in one's faith. It is a statement

61. Bernard J. F. Lonergan, "The Origins of Christian Realism," in *Philosophical and Theological Papers: 1985-1964*, ed. Robert C. Croken, Frederick E. Crowe, and Robert M. Doran, Collected Works of Bernard Lonergan (Toronto: University of Toronto Press, 1996), 82. This paper appears to be a preliminary piece leading up to the identically named Bernard J. F. Lonergan, "The Origins of Christian Realism," in *A Second Collection*, ed. William F. Ryan and Bernard Tyrrell (Philadelphia: Westminster, 1974). This latter paper, however, makes no reference to the Gilson-Bréhier debate.
62. John F. X. Knasas, "A Heideggerian Critique of Aquinas and a Gilsonian Reply," *The Thomist* 58, no. 3 (1994): 415–39, at 137.
63. This is particularly evident among those who would claim to develop a "Trinitarian ontology." This is a not uncommon claim among certain approaches to Trinitarian theology.

that faith has nothing to fear from exposing itself to the full rigors of reasoning. And further that such an exposure can have a purifying effect on religious belief, rooting out anthropomorphisms, naïve accounts of divinity, childish perceptions and expectations in relation to God, and so on. An unwillingness to do so, far from being an exaltation of faith over reason, looks more like an act of moral cowardice, a fear than one's religious beliefs might prove irrational and hence untenable. Far from honoring God they do God a disservice. As Gilson notes in relation to theologism, "In theology, as in any other science, the main question is not to be pious, but to be right. For there is nothing pious in being wrong about God."[64]

There is a further issue and it relates to the continued "tension" between Augustinian and Thomistic approaches. Here I am not referring to a Platonic versus Aristotelian divide, but to the relative degree of abstraction and concreteness between the two approaches. The Augustinian approach starts with our concrete situation, our existential and religious subjectivity, torn between sin and grace. The Aristotelian approach takes a step back and seeks to abstract an intelligibility from the data, something that will persist regardless of the concrete circumstances. If I may give yet another scientific example, consider the discovery of the periodic table. Concretely those early chemists were faced with empirical data reflective of the atomic weight of the various known elements. There really is no obvious pattern in this data. The atomic masses are all over the place. It takes quite a creative leap to suggest that underlying these masses is a simple pattern, which orders them not by atomic weight, but by atomic number, especially when all this was done prior to our knowledge of the atomic constitution of the nucleus of elements. But once this suggestion was made, it transformed chemistry into a rigorous and systematic science. Now we simply take the periodic table for granted, and fail often to attend to the real breakthrough it represents.

There are two difficulties we face in this tension between the concrete and the abstract. The first is how we view the process of abstraction itself. Do we view the abstraction as a sort of washed out alternative view to the concrete, something that removes all the particularity, the color of the real world? Or do we view it as an enrichment of the data, like a schematic we overlay over the data which provides some order and patterning, without blocking our view of the totality we

---

64. Gilson, *The Unity of Philosophical Experience*, 42.

encounter? Often we treat intellectual constructs as more real than the world they represent. They become ideological constraints on our thinking rather than doorways into a richer perception. Here Lonergan speaks of abstraction as enriching,[65] and I think it is the more helpful way to understand what the more abstract position adds to the situation.

The second problem relates to the difference between the data of the natural sciences and that of the human sciences.[66] While the data of the natural sciences have a "natural" intelligibility, the data of our human world is a mix of both the intelligible (intelligent) and the unintelligible (unintelligent), the reasonable and the unreasonable, the true and the false. The gap between the abstract intelligibility and the real situation is not just one of a statistical variation around an ideal norm, it is a dialectic shift from an abstract intelligibility seeking to enrich the data of life to the radically unintelligible we encounter in the problem of evil. Our existential situation is in fact one of an ongoing drama between good and evil, between grace and sin. In the encounter with evil all our expectations of intelligibility and reasonableness begin to break down.[67] No matter how hard we try to understand evil, it remains an enigma beyond our comprehension. In the face of the problem of evil, reason comes up against its very real limits.

Does this mean we should abandon the more abstract approach wherein reason seeks the intelligibility within our human world? Certainly it makes the task more difficult as we must deal not only with truth but falsehood, not only with honesty but also mendacity. Discerning the intelligible ordering within human affairs is rendered much more difficult. More importantly, if we were to abandon the more abstract approach we would have no independent benchmark from which to recognize evil itself. While we might turn to our religious faith to tell us what is right and wrong, many of these teachings require the sort of purification by reason that Benedict and *Fides et ratio* spoke of as the essential contribution of reason to the life of faith. The very incomprehensibility of evil, its deficit in intelligibility and rea-

65. Lonergan, *Insight*, 112.
66. For a fuller account of the human sciences and their relationship to theology see Neil Ormerod, "A Dialectic Engagement with the Social Sciences in an Ecclesiological Context," *Theological Studies* 66 (2005): 815–40; *Re-Visioning the Church: An Experiment in Systematic-Historical Ecclesiology* (Minneapolis: Fortress, 2014), especially chapter 2.
67. Lonergan is very clear on the problem of evil as a problem of a deficit in intelligibility. See Lonergan, *Insight*, chapter 20. Gilson similarly notes that "whatever is contrary to reason is evil." Étienne Gilson, *The Christian Philosophy of St. Thomas Aquinas*, trans. I. T. Eschmann (New York: Random House, 1956), 260.

sonableness, then acts as an independent warning sign that something is seriously out of kilter here. Even people of no faith or no religious perspective can recognize horrendous evil through the natural light of reason when they encounter it.

On the other hand, this is also a situation where religious faith can be of great assistance to the life of reason. In our encounter with a mixture of the intelligible and the unintelligible, the reasonable and the unreasonable, the true and the false, it is very easy for reason itself to become confused. It can abandon the search for intelligibility, reasonableness and truth as thoroughly misguided, leading to nihilism. Or in complete confusion, it can mistake the intelligible for the unintelligible, the reasonable for the unreasonable, and the true for the false, leading to rationalizations of evil itself. Here faith can remind us that an intelligent, reasonable, and loving God is the source of all that is, that we must not abandon reason because of the difficulties we face in discerning truth, and that faith can provide some guidance in living the moral life. In the end, reason needs faith to maintain faith in reason itself.

And so whether we use the term Christian philosophy, or adopt Lonergan's term of Christian realism, the ongoing dance of faith and reason, this ever present struggle to maintain the taut unity-in-difference between the natural light of reason and the light of faith, remains a necessary element for both the life of faith and the life of reason. To abandon either is to leave the other wounded, perhaps fatally. Gilson and Lonergan exemplify how to hold these two aspects in creative tension. Theirs is an example we can continue to learn from and appreciate.

Bibliography

Amour, Paul St. "Lonergan and Gilson on the Problem of Critical Realism." *Thomist* 69 (2005): 557–92.

Arcamone, Dominic. *Religion and Violence: A Dialectical Engagement through the Insights of Bernard Lonergan.* Eugene, OR: Wipf & Stock, 2015.

Augustine. *The City of God.* Translated by Marcus Dods. Available at http://www.newadvent.org/fathers/120110.htm.

———. *The Confessions.* Translated by Maria Boulding. New York: Vintage Books, 1998.

Barth, Karl. *The Epistle to the Romans.* Translated by Edwyn Clement Hoskyns. London: Oxford University Press, 1933.

Baum, Gregory. *Essays in Critical Theology.* Kansas City, MO: Sheed & Ward, 1994.

Behr, John. *The Way to Nicaea.* The Formation of Christian Theology; V. 1. Crestwood, NY: St. Vladimir's Seminary Press, 2001.

Benedict XVI. "Faith, Reason and the University: Memories and Reflections." http://w2.vatican.va/content/benedict-xvi/en/speeches/2006/september/documents/hf_ben-xvi_spe_20060912_university-regensburg.html.

Berger, Peter L., and Thomas Luckmann. *The Social Construction of Reality: A Treatise in the Sociology of Knowledge.* New York: Anchor Books, 1990.

Blondel, Maurice. "Does Christian Philosophy Exist as Philosophy?" Translated by Gregory B. Sadler. In *Reason Fulillled by Revelation: The 1930s Christian Philosophy Debate in France,* edited by Gregory B. Sadler. 139–49. Washington, DC: CUA Press, 2011.

Burrell, David. *Faith and Freedom: An Interfaith Perspective.* Malden, MA: Wiley, 2008.

Butterfield, Herbert. *The Origins of Modern Science, 1300-1800.* 2nd ed. New York: Free Press, 1966.

Cavanaugh, William T. *The Myth of Religious Violence: Secular Ideology and the Roots of Modern Conflict.* New York: Oxford University Press, 2009.

_____. *Torture and Eucharist: Theology, Politics, and the Body of Christ*. Oxford: Blackwell Publishers, 1998.

Chenu, Marie-Dominique. *Aquinas and His Role in Theology*. Collegeville, MN: Liturgical Press, 2002.

Crowe, Frederick E. *Developing the Lonergan Legacy: Historical, Theoretical and Existential Themes*. Edited by Michael Vertin Toronto: University of Toronto Press, 2004.

_____. *Lonergan*. Outstanding Christian Thinkers. Collegeville, MN: Liturgical Press, 1992.

Davies, Paul. *The Goldilocks Enigma: Why Is the Universe Just Right for Life?* London: Allen Lane, 2006.

_____. "Now Is the Reason for Our Discontent." *Sydney Morning Herald*, 1 January 2003.

Dawkins, Richard. *The Blind Watchmaker: Why the Evidence of Evolution Reveals a Universe without Design*. New York: Norton, 1996.

_____. *The God Delusion*. London: Bantam, 2006.

_____. *The Selfish Gene*. 30th anniversary ed. Oxford; New York: Oxford University Press, 2006.

DeHart, Paul J. *Aquinas and Radical Orthodoxy: A Critical Inquiry*. New York: Routledge, 2012.

Dobell, Brian. *Augustine's Intellectual Conversion: The Journey from Platonism to Christianity*. Cambridge: Cambridge University Press, 2009.

Doran, Robert. "Ignatian Themes in the Thought of Bernard Lonergan." *Toronto Journal of Theology* 22, no. 1 (2006): 39–54.

Doran, Robert M. *Theology and the Dialectics of History*. Toronto: University of Toronto Press, 1990.

_____. *What Is Systematic Theology?* Toronto: University of Toronto Press, 2006.

Duffy, Stephen. *The Graced Horizon: Nature and Grace in Modern Catholic Thought*. Collegeville, MN: Liturgical Press, 1992.

Einstein, Albert. *Ideas and Opinions*. Translated by Sonja Bargmann. New York: Bonanza, 1954.

Fafara, Richard. "Gilson and Gouhier: Framing 'Christian Philosophy'." *Heythrop Journal* 49, no. 6 (2008): 995–1014.

Feingold, Lawrence. *The Natural Desire to See God According to St. Thomas Aquinas and His Interpreters*. Naples, FL: Sapientia Press of Ave Maria University, 2010.

Gilson, Étienne. *Being and Some Philosophers*. 2nd ed. Toronto: Pontifical Institute of Mediaeval Studies, 1952.

_____. *The Christian Philosophy of St. Thomas Aquinas*. Translated by I. T. Eschmann. New York: Random House, 1956.

_____. *Christianity and Philosophy*. Translated by Ralph MacDonald. London; New York: Sheed & Ward, 1939.

_____. *Elements of Christian Philosophy*. Garden City, NY: Doubleday, 1960.

_____. *From Aristotle to Darwin and Back Again: A Journey in Final Causality, Species, and Evolution*. San Francisco: Ignatius Press, 2009.

_____. *God and Philosophy*. 2nd ed. New Haven, CT: Yale University Press, 2002.

_____. *Medieval Essays*. Translated by James G. Colbert. Eugene, OR: Cascade Books, 2011.

_____. *Methodical Realism: A Handbook for Beginning Realist*. Translated by Philip Trower. Front Royal, VA: Christendom Press, 2011.

_____. "The Notion of Christian Philosophy." Translated by Gregory B. Sadler. In *Reason Fulfilled by Revelation: The 1930s Christian Philosophy Debates in France*, edited by Gregory B. Sadler. 128–40. Washington DC: CUA Press, 2011.

_____. *The Philosopher and Theology*. New York: Random House, 1962.

_____. *The Spirit of Mediaeval Philosophy*. Translated by A. H. C. Downes. Notre Dame: University of Notre Dame Press, 1991.

_____. *Thomist Realism and the Critique of Knowledge*. San Francisco: Ignatius Press, 2012.

_____. *The Unity of Philosophical Experience*. San Francisco: Ignatius Press, 1999.

Greene, Brian. *The Elegant Universe: Superstrings, Hidden Dimensions, and the Quest for the Ultimate Theory*. London: Jonathan Cape, 1999.

Hall, Douglas C. *The Trinity: An Analysis of St. Thomas Aquinas' "Expositio" of the "De Trinitate" of Boethius*. Leiden: Brill, 1992.

Hankey, Wayne John. "From Metaphysics to History, from Exodus to Neoplatonism, from Scholasticism to Pluralism: The Fate of Gilsonian Thomism in English-Speaking North America." *Dionysius* 16 (1998): 157–88.

Harris, Sam. *The End of Faith: Religion, Terror, and the Future of Reason*. New York: Norton, 2004.

Heidegger, Martin. *Being and Time*. Translated by Joan Stambaugh. New York: State University of New York, 1996.

Himes, Brian. "Lonergan's Position on the Natural Desire to See God and Aquinas' Metaphysical Theology of Creation and Participation." *Heythrop Journal* 54, no. 5 (2013): 767–83.

Hitchens, Christopher. *God Is Not Great: How Religion Poisons Everything*. 1st ed. New York: Twelve, 2007.

Hyatt, J. Philip. *Exodus*. Grand Rapids, MI: Eerdmanns, 1980.

Jacobs-Vandegeer, Christiaan. "The Hermeneutics of Interiority: Transpositions in the Third Stage of Meaning." In *Meaning and History in Systematic*

Theology: Essays in Honor of Robert Doran, Sj, edited by John Dadosky. 191–215. Milwaukee, WI: Marquette University Press, 2009.

Jordan, Mark D. "Truth in Aquinas by John Milbank, Catherine Pickstock." *The Journal of Religion* 83, no. 2 (2003): 304–5.

Juergensmeyer, Mark. *Terror in the Mind of God: The Global Rise of Religious Violence*. Berkley: University of California Press, 2003.

Kenny, Anthony. *Aquinas on Mind*. Routledge, 2013.

Kerr, Gaven. "Aquinas, Lonergan, and the Isomorphism between Intellect and Reality." *International Philosophical Quarterly* 54, no. 1 (2014): 43–57.

Knasas, John F. X. "A Heideggerian Critique of Aquinas and a Gilsonian Reply." *The Thomist* 58, no. 3 (1994): 415–39.

Krauss, Lawrence. *A Universe from Nothing: Why There Is Something Rather Than Nothing*. New York: Free Press, 2012.

Kucer, Peter Samuel. *Truth and Politics: A Theological Comparison of Joseph Ratzinger and John Milbank*. Minneapolis: Fortress Press, 2014.

Lauer, J. Quentin. "Comment on 'An Interpretation'." *Modern Schoolman* 25 (1947–1948): 251–59.

Liddy, Richard M. *Transforming Light: Intellectual Conversion in the Early Lonergan*. Collegeville, MN: Liturgical Press, 1993.

Lonergan, Bernard J. F. *Collection*. Collected Works of Bernard Lonergan. Edited by Frederick E. Crowe and Robert M. Doran, 2nd ed. Toronto: Toronto University Press, 1988.

_____. *For a New Political Economy*. Collected Works of Bernard Lonergan. Edited by Philip McShane. Toronto: University of Toronto Press, 1998.

_____. "The General Character of the Natural Theology of *Insight*." In *Philosophical and Theological Papers 1965-1980*, edited by Robert M. Doran and Frederick E. Crowe. Collected Works of Bernard Lonergan, 3–9. Toronto: University of Toronto Press, 2004.

_____. *Grace and Freedom: Operative Grace in the Thought of St. Thomas Aquinas*. London: Darton, Longman & Todd, 1971.

_____. *Grace and Freedom: Operative Grace in the Thought of St. Thomas Aquinas*. Collected Works of Bernard Lonergan. Edited by Frederick E. Crowe and Robert M. Doran. Toronto: University of Toronto Press, 2000.

_____. *Insight: A Study of Human Understanding*. Collected Works of Bernard Lonergan. Edited by Crowe Frederick E. and Robert M. Doran. Toronto: University of Toronto Press, 1992.

_____. *Insight: A Study of Human Understanding*. London: Darton, Longman & Todd, 1958.

_____. "*Insight*: Preface to a Discussion." In *Collection*, edited by Frederick E. Crowe and Robert M. Doran. Collected Works of Bernard Lonergan, 142–52. Toronto: University of Toronto Press, 1993.

_____. *Macroeconomic Dynamics: An Essay in Circulation Analysis*. Collected Works of Bernard Lonergan. edited by Frederick G. Lawrence, Patrick Hugh Byrne and Charles C. Hefling Toronto: University of Toronto Press, 1999.

_____. "Mathematical Logic and Scholasticism." In *Phenomenology and Logic: The Boston College Lectures on Mathematical Logic and Existentialism*, edited by Philip J. McShane. Collected Works of Bernard Lonergan, 115–40. Toronto: University of Toronto, 2002.

_____. "Metaphysics as Horizon." In *Collection*, edited by Frederick E. Crowe and Robert M. Doran. Collected Works of Bernard Lonergan, 188–204. Toronto: University of Toronto, 1988.

_____. *Method in Theology*. London: Darton, Longman & Todd, 1972.

_____. "The Natural Desire to See God." In *Collection*, edited by Frederick E. Crowe and Robert M. Doran. Collected Works of Bernard Lonergan, 81–91. Toronto: Toronto University Press, 1988.

_____. "Natural Knowledge of God." In *A Second Collection*, edited by William Ryan and Bernard Tyrrell. 117–33. Philadelphia: Westminster Press, 1974.

_____. *The Ontological and Psychological Constitution of Christ*. Translated by Michael G. Shields, in Collected Works of Bernard Lonergan. Edited by Frederick E. Crowe and Robert M. Doran. Toronto: University of Toronto Press, 2002.

_____. "The Origins of Christian Realism." In *A Second Collection*, edited by William F. Ryan and Bernard Tyrrell. 239–62. Philadelphia: Westminster, 1974.

_____. "The Origins of Christian Realism." In *Philosophical and Theological Papers: 1985-1964*, edited by Robert C. Croken, Frederick E. Crowe and Robert M. Doran. Collected Works of Bernard Lonergan, 80–93. Toronto: University of Toronto Press, 1996.

_____. "Review of Étienne Gilson, *Being and Some Philosophers*." In *Shorter Papers*, edited by Robert Croken, Robert M. Doran and H. Daniel Monsour. Collected Works of Bernard Lonergan, 185–88. Toronto: University of Toronto Press, 2007.

_____. *A Second Collection*. Edited by William F. Ryan and Bernard Tyrrell. Philadelphia: Westminster, 1974.

_____. "The Subject." In *A Second Collection*, edited by William Ryan and Bernard Tyrrell. 69–86. Philadelphia: Westminster, 1974.

_____. "Theology in Its New Context." In *A Second Collection*, edited by William Ryan and Bernard Tyrrell. 55–68. Philadelphia: Westminster, 1974.

_____. *A Third Collection*. edited by Frederick E. Crowe New York: Paulist Press, 1985.

_____. "Time and Meaning." In *Philosophical and Theological Papers 1958-1964*, edited by Robert C. Croken, Frederick E. Crowe and Robert M. Doran. Collected Works of Bernard Lonergan, 94–121. Toronoto: University of Toronto Press, 1996.

_____. "The Transition from a Classicist World-View to Historical Mindedness." In *A Second Collection*, edited by William F. Ryan and Bernard Tyrrell. 1–9. Philadelphia: Westminster, 1974.

_____. *The Triune God: Doctrines*. Translated by Michael Shields. Collected Works of Bernard Lonergan. Edited by Robert M. Doran and H. Daniel Monsour. Toronto: University of Toronto Press, 2009.

_____. *The Triune God: Systematics*. Translated by Michael Shields. Collected Works of Bernard Lonergan. Edited by Robert M. Doran and H. Daniel Monsour. Toronto: Toronto University Press, 2007.

_____. *Verbum: Word and Idea in Aquinas*. Collected Works of Bernard Lonergan. Edited by Frederick E. Crowe and Robert M. Doran. Toronto: University of Toronto Press, 1997.

_____. *Verbum: Word and Idea in Aquinas*. Notre Dame, IN: University of Notre Dame Press, 1967.

_____. *The Way to Nicea: The Dialectical Development of Trinitarian Theology*. Translated by Conn O'Donovan. London: Darton, Longman & Todd, 1976.

_____, P. Lambert, C. Tansey, and C. M. Going. *Caring About Meaning: Patterns in the Life of Bernard Lonergan*. Montreal: Thomas More Institute, 1982.

Long, Steven. *Natura Pura: On the Recovery of Nature in the Doctrine of Grace*. Bronx, NY: Fordham University Press, 2010.

MacIntyre, Alasdair. *After Virtue: A Study in Moral Theory*. 2nd ed. Notre Dame, IN: University of Notre Dame Press, 1984.

_____. *Three Rival Versions of Moral Enquiry: Encyclopaedia, Genealogy, and Tradition*. Notre Dame, IN: University of Notre Dame Press, 1990.

_____. *Whose Justice? Which Rationality?* Notre Dame, IN: University of Notre Dame Press, 1988.

Mango, Peter. "Macintyre's Gilsonian Preference." *Studia Gilsoniana* 2 (2013): 21–32.

Marshall, Bruce. "Truth in Aquinas." *Thomist* 66, no. 4 (2002): 632–37.

Mascall, Eric. *The Openness of Being: Natural Theology Today*. London: Darton, Longman and Todd, 1971.

Mathews, William A. *Lonergan's Quest: A Study of Desire in the Authoring of Insight.* Toronto: University of Toronto Press, 2005.

McCool, Gerald A. "How Can There Be Such a Thing as a Christian Philosophy?". *Proceedings of the American Catholic Philosophical Association* 54 (1980): 126–34.

Milbank, John. *The Future of Love: Essays in Political Theology.* London: SCM Press, 2009.

_____. *The Suspended Middle: Henri De Lubac and the Debate Concerning the Supernatural.* William B. Eerdmans, 2005.

_____. *Theology and Social Theory: Beyond Secular Reason.* Cambridge, MA: Blackwell, 1991.

_____. *The Word Made Strange: Theology, Language, Culture.* Cambridge, MA: Blackwell Publishers, 1997.

_____, and Catherine Pickstock. *Truth in Aquinas.* New York: Routledge, 2001.

Moore, Andrew. "Should Christians Do Natural Theology?" *Scottish Journal of Theology* 63 (2010): 127–45.

Morelli, Mark. "Lonergan's Debt to Hegel and the Appropriation of Critical Realism." In *Meaning and History in Systematic Theology: Essays in Honor of Robert Doran, Sj,* edited by John Dadosky. 405–21. Marquette, MI: Marquette University Press, 2009.

Muck, Otto. *The Transcendental Method.* New York: Herder and Herder, 1968.

Newman, John Henry. *An Essay in Aid of a Grammar of Assent.* London: Burns, Oates and Co., 1874.

Nichols, Aidan. *Discovering Aquinas: An Introduction to His Life, Work, and Influence.* Grand Rapids, MI: Eerdmans, 2003.

O'Connell, Matthew J. "St Thomas and the Verbum: An Interpretation." *Modern Schoolman* 24 (1946–47): 224–34.

Oerter, Robert. *The Theory of Almost Everything: The Standard Model, the Unsung Triumph of Modern Physics.* New York: Penguin Group US, 2006.

Olkovich, Nick. "Conceptualism, Classicism and Bernard Lonergan's Retrieval of Aquinas." *Pacifica* 26, no. 1 (2013): 37–58.

Ormerod, Neil. "Bernard Lonergan and the Recovery of a Metaphysical Frame." *Theological Studies* 74 (2013): 960–82.

_____. "Chance and Necessity, Providence and God." *Irish Theological Quarterly* 70 (2005): 263–78.

_____. "A Dialectic Engagement with the Social Sciences in an Ecclesiological Context." *Theological Studies* 66 (2005): 815–40.

_____. "Faith and Reason: Perspectives from Macintyre and Lonergan." *Heythrop Journal* 46 (2005): 11–22.

_____. "'It Is Easy to See': The Footnotes of John Milbank." *Philosophy and Theology* 11, no. 2 (1999): 257–64.

_____. "The Psychological Analogy for the Trinity – at Odds with Modernity." *Pacifica* 14 (2001): 281–94.

_____. *A Public God: Natural Theology Reconsidered.* Minneapolis: Fortress, 2015.

_____. *Re-Visioning the Church: An Experiment in Systematic-Historical Ecclesiology.* Minneapolis: Fortress, 2014.

_____, and Cynthia S. W. Crysdale. *Creator God, Evolving World.* Minneapolis: Fortress Press, 2013.

Rahner, Karl. *Foundations of Christian Faith: An Introduction to the Idea of Christianity.* New York: Crossroad, 1982.

_____. *Spirit in the World.* New York: Bloomsbury, 1994.

_____. *Reason Fulfilled by Revelation: The 1930s Christian Philosophy Debates in France.* Translated and edited by Gregory B. Sadler. Washington, DC: Catholic University of America, 2011.

Rees, Martin J. *Just Six Numbers: The Deep Forces That Shape the Universe.* New York: Basic Books, 2000.

Rosenthal-Schneider, Ilse. *Reality and Scientific Truth: Discussions with Einstein, Von Laue, and Plank.* edited by T. Braun. Detroit: Wayne State University Press, 1980.

Stebbins, J. Michael. *The Divine Initiative: Grace, World-Order, and Human Freedom in the Early Writings of Bernard Lonergan.* Toronto: University of Toronto Press, 1995.

Tanner, Kathryn. *God and Creation in Christian Theology: Tyranny and Empowerment?* Minneapolis, MN: Fortress, 2004.

Taylor, Charles. *A Secular Age.* Cambridge, MA: Belknap Press, 2007.

_____. *Sources of the Self: The Making of the Modern Identity.* Cambridge, MA: Harvard University Press, 1989.

Tracy, David. *The Achievement of Bernard Lonergan.* Herder and Herder, 1970.

Trible, Phyllis. *Texts of Terror: Literary-Feminist Readings of Biblical Narratives.* Philadelphia: Fortress Press, 1984.

Tyrrell, Bernard. *Bernard Lonergan's Philosophy of God.* Notre Dame, Ind.: University of Notre Dame Press, 1974.

van Riet, G. *L'épistémologie Thomiste. Recherches Sur Le Problème De La Connaissance Dans L'école Thomiste Contemporaine.* 1946.

Voegelin, Eric. *The New Science of Politics: An Introduction.* Chicago: University of Chicago Press, 1952.

Williams, Hugh. "The Continuing Relevance of Etienne Gilson's Christian Philosophy: A Review of Etienne Gilson's, *Three Quests in Philosophy*." *Science et Esprit* 63, no. 1 (2011): 85–100.

Permissions Granted

185

Index

abstraction, 174–76

Aeterni Patris (Leo XIII), 23; Thomas
    Aquinas and, 15–21

affectivity, 101

analogia entis, 161

analytical philosophy, 5n6

animal extroversion, 94

animal knowing, 94, 96

Anschauung (Kant), 116

Anselm of Bec, 58, 60; ontological
    argument of, 65

Aquinas, Thomas. *See* Thomas
    Aquinas

Aristotle: Aquinas and, 11–15,
    52n88; metaphysics, 47–48

Athanasius, 113

atheism: new, 7, 29–30; old, 29n71

Augustine of Hippo, 8, 47, 59 60, 61;
    Confessions, The, 8–10; *De Libero
    Arbitrio* (On Free Will), 10; *De
    Trinitate* (On the Trinity), 10–11,
    82; on grace, 78; human interi-
    ority and, 26; on human nature,
    78; intellectual conversion, 8–9;
    Platonism and, 8–11; on truth, 9

Augustinianism, 161–71; Thomism
    and, 174

Averroes, 48

Banez, Domingo, 77n12

Banezian school of Thomism, 77, 80

Barth, Karl, 28n66; on faith and rea-
    son, 159; on natural theology,
    156n21

being, 53; causes of, 80; essence
    and, 13–14, 48–55, 64–65,
    110–11, 141–42, 154–55; intellect
    and, 42–45, 130–31; intellectual
    conversion and, 46–47; judg-
    ment and, 125–26, 131–32;
    knowing and, 50, 53–56, 92–93,
    106–7, 125–31; nature and, 12;
    notion of, 47, 120–24; propor-
    tionate, 92–93, 96–98; question-
    ing and, 117; realism and, 45;
    science and, 155; the senses and,
    117; substance and, 47–48,
    52–53; transcendent, 93, 96–98;
    understanding and, 160–61. *See
    also* existence

Being and Some Philosophers (Gilson),
    45, 53, 115–16

belief. *See* faith

believing, 107–10

Benedict XVI, Pope: Regensburg
    Address, 30–32, 159–60. *See also*
    Ratzinger, Joseph

biases, 96
Blondel, Maurice, 22, 60–62
Bonaventure, 164, 168
Bréhier, Emile, 59
Burrell, David, 81
Butterfield, Herbert, 107n123, 169

Calvin, John, 80n25
causality, 97
Cavanaugh, William, 27
"central form," 155
Christ, 3, 5
Christian philosophy: after Gilson,
    71–73; Gilson and, 35–73; misun-
    derstandings of, 173–74; objec-
    tive and subjective aspects,
    24–25; possibility of, 5–15,
    21–23, 56–62, 140–45, 172–76;
    term, 24; Thomism and, 21–23.
    See also Christian realism
Christian Philosophy of Thomas
    Aquinas, The (Gilson), 62–67
Christian realism, 110–14, 173
Christology, 110–11
"Cogito ergo sum" (Descartes), 40
cognition, 14; Augustine on, 9–11;
    being and, 106–7; interiority
    and, 101. See also knowing
cognitional activity/theory, 88–92
Collected Works (Lonergan), 75
commonsense knowing, 139
conception (of concepts), 54–56;
    judgment and, 133–35
concrete vs. abstract approaches,
    174–76
Confessions, The (Augustine of
    Hippo), 8–10
consciousness, 88–89, 95; nature of,
    40

contingency, 142; general relativity
    and, 153n10; science and,
    152–54
conversion: intellectual, 84, 105,
    114, 121–22, 143–44, 161; moral,
    114; religious, 114, 159
Coreth, Emerich, 116–17
Corinthians, first letter to the, 3
creation and metaphysics, 52
critical history, 17–18
culture: belief and, 148; religion
    and, 158; types, 69n156

Darwin, Charles: Origin of Species,
    153
Davies, Paul, 155–56
Dawkins, Richard, 148, 150, 153
De Ente Supernaturalis (Lonergan),
    103
De Esse et Essentia (Aquinas), 13–14
DeHart, Paul J., 85n43; on Milbank,
    166
Dei Filius (Vatican I), 23
De Libero Arbitrio (Augustine), 10
de Lubac, Henri, 28, 162
demonic, the, 30
Descartes, René, 38–39, 49, 87n48,
    95, 171; "Cogito ergo sum," 40;
    turn to the subject, 19
descriptive vs. explanatory under-
    standing, 79, 139, 155, 169
desire, 102–4
De Trinitate (Augustine), 10–11, 82
divine illumination, 9–11
divine transcendence, 79–80
divine will, 80
divine Wisdom, 5
Dogmatic Constitution on the Catholic
    Faith (Vatican I), 63n134

dogmatic realism, 38, 53, 116–17, 126

dogmatic teaching and philosophy, 113–14

Dominican (Banezian) school of Thomism, 77

Doran, Robert, 130

Eckhart, Meister, 47

Einstein, Albert, 156; general relativity, 153n10

Elements of Christian Philosophy (Gilson), 58

emanatio intelligibilis (intelligible emanation), 83–84

empiricism, 7

Enlightenment and belief, 148

epistemology. *See* knowing; knowledge; known, the

essence and being, 13–14, 48–55, 64–65, 110–11, 141–42, 154–55

essentialism, 51, 154–55

evil. *See* sin

existence: contingency of, 142; essence and, 13–14, 48–55, 64–65, 110–11, 141–42, 154–55; of God, 142–44; judgment and, 120. *See also* being

existential, the, 100–101

existentialism, 51

existential judgments, 44–45

Exodus, book of, 14, 64; metaphysics and, 70–71

experience, 88–89, 91–92; scientific method and, 152

explanatory vs. descriptive understanding, 79, 139, 155, 169

"external" vs. "internal" worlds, 127–28

extroversion, animal, 94

faith: Enlightenment and, 148; Justin Martyr and, 4; knowledge and, 166–68; nature of, 5–6; new atheism, and, 150–57; priority of, 10–11; revelation and, 9; science and, 150–57; stages toward, 108; violence and, 29–30; wisdom and, 3

faith and reason, 4–9, 30–32, 63, 72, 105–10, 144–45; in concert, 24, 27, 81, 159–60, 176; in opposition, 29–30, 158–59; Thomas Aquinas and, 51

Falkowski, Adam, 136

Farara, Richard, 57–58

fideism, 22, 31, 59

Fides et ratio (John Paul II), 35n1, 60, 63, 125, 160; human subjectivity and, 25–26; metaphysics and, 23–27; Thomism and, 27

fields, 169–70

"five proofs" of Aquinas, 66–67

forms, 155

freedom: divine, 80n23; grace and, 12–13, 77–81; human, 80–81

fundamentalism, religious, 150

general relativity and contingency, 153n10

Gilson, Étienne, 8, 18, 21–22; achievements, 35–36, 72; on being, 120–24; on being and knowing, 125–31; *Being and Some Philosophers*, 45, 53, 115–16; Christian philosophy and, 35–73, 140–45, 172; *Christian Philosophy of Thomas Aquinas, The*, 62–64; critiques of, 67–72; development of thought, 36; *Elements of Christian Philosophy*, 58; on existence of God, 142–44; on faith and reason, 144–45; Higgs boson and, 137–38; on history of philosophy, 122–24; on judgment, 131–35; on Leuven Thomists, 37–45; on Lonergan, 37; Lonergan and, 32–33, 72–73, 145–46; Lonergan on, 32n80, 35n2, 115–17; *Methodical Realism*, 37; "Notion of Christian Philosophy, The," 59; *On Reducing the Arts to Theology*, 168; *Thomist Realism and the Critique of Knowledge*, 37, 116; transcendental Thomism and, 20–21, 32; *Unity of Philosophical Experience, The*, 45

God: desire to see God, 102–4; existence of, 66, 96–98, 142–44; human freedom and, 80–81; illumination by, 9–11; intelligibility and, 155–56; knowing and, 9–11; natural knowledge of, 104–6; need for, 150; reality and, 104–5; reason and, 3, 30, 160, 171; science and, 155–56; sin and, 10, 79–80; transcendence of, 79–80; will of, 80; wisdom of, 5

God Is Not Great (Hitchens), 157

Gospel of John, 4

grace, 143, 162–63; freedom and, 12–13, 77–81; knowledge and, 9–11, 164–66; nature and, 12–13, 72, 78–79, 162–63; sin and, 162–63, 175; truth and, 12–13, 163–66

Grace and Freedom (Lonergan), 77–81, 88

grace-nature debate, 78–79, 162–63

grace-sin dialectic, 163

Grammar of Assent (Newman), 91

Grayling, A. C., 153n11

Hall, Douglas, 84

Hankey, Wayne John, 67–70

Harris, Sam, 148–49, 153n11

Hegel, G. W. F., 50–51

Higgs boson, 135–39, 150–52

Hilbert, David, 88

history: critical, 17–18; as experiment, 115; philosophy and, 45–56

Hitchens, Christopher, 148–49; *God Is Not Great*, 157

homoousios, 113

human consciousness. *See* interiority; turn to the subject

Humani Generis (Pius XII), 163n32

human nature, 12, 78–79, 163; being and, 12; grace and, 12–13, 72, 78–79, 162–63; person and, 113–14

human sciences and natural sciences, 175

Hume, David, 50

idealism, 7, 37–38, 40, 42, 50–51; realism and, 93

illuminationist account of knowing, 9–11, 163–66

individuality and individuation, 48

inner/outer disjunction, 127–28, 131

inner word, 83–84

insight: activity, 87, 91; judgment and, 135–39; knowledge, 91; science and, 135–39

Insight (Lonergan), 20, 75, 85–100, 104

insights: descriptive/explanatory, 88; vulnerable/invulnerable, 90–91

intellect, 105–6; being and, 42–45; sense and, 117; will and, 31

intellectual conversion, 84, 114, 121–22, 143–44, 161; being and, 46–47; reality and, 94–96; understanding and, 105

intelligence: being and, 130–31; intelligibility and, 84

intelligibility: God and, 155–56; science and, 152

intelligible emanation, 83–84

interiority, 82; Augustine and, 26; cognition and, 101

"internal"/"external" worlds, 127–28

intuition, 116

Isaiah, book of the prophet, 10

James, William: definition of "philosophy," 45–46

Jesuit (Molinist) school of Thomism, 77

Jesus, 3, 5

John, Gospel of, 4

John Paul II, Pope. *See Fides et ratio* (John Paul II)

judgment/s, 44–45, 54–56, 84, 88–91, 115–16, 131–35, 139; being and, 125–26, 131–32; concepts and, 133–35; existence and, 120; insight and, 135–39; knowing, and, 125–26; science and, 135–39, 152

Juergensmeyer, Mark, 148–49

Justin Martyr, 4

Kant, Immanuel, 49–50; *Anschauung*, 116; Lonergan and, 105; turn to the subject, 19

Kenny, Anthony, 84

Kerr, Gaven, 84n41

Kierkegaard, Søren, 51

Knasas, John, 133–34

knowing, 14, 116; activity, 91; animal/human, 94, 96; Augustine on, 9–11; being and, 50, 53–56, 92–93, 106–7, 125–31; believing and, 108–10; commonsense knowing, 139; illuminationist account, 9–11, 163–66; judgment, and, 125–26; reasoning and, 26–27; scientific, 139; sin and, 10; Trinitarian theology and, 111–12. *See also* grace; truth

knowledge: faith and, 166–68; grace and, 164–66; metaphysics and, 39–41; natural human, 13; natural knowledge of God, 104–6; philosophy and, 171; transcendental, 96–99. *See also* revelation

known, the: knowing, being, and, 92–93

Krauss, Lawrence, 148, 150; *A Universe from Nothing*, 153

Kucer, Peter Samuel, 170–71

language and metaphor, 169–70

Lauer, J. Quentin, 85n42

Leo XIII, Pope: *Aeterni Patris*, 15–16, 23; *Rerum Novarum*, 15

Leuven Thomists, 37–45

liberty. *See* freedom

Liddy, Richard: *Transforming Light*, 110–11

Lindbeck, George, 68 69

logos, 4

Logos and the Word, 9

Lonergan, Bernard, 8, 20–21; Aquinas and, 107; on being, 120–24; Christian philosopher, 102–14; Christian philosophy and, 140–45, 172–73; cognitional theory, 152; *Collected Works*, 75; *De Ente Supernaturalis*, 103; on existence of God, 142–44; on faith and reason, 144–45; on Gilson, 32n80, 35n2, 115–17; Gilson and, 32–33, 72–73, 145–46; Gilson on, 37; *Grace and Freedom*, 77–81, 88; Higgs boson and, 138–39; on history and philosophy, 46n55, 122–24; inner word, 83–84; *Insight*, 20, 75, 85–100, 104; on judgment, 131–35; Kant and, 105; on knowing and being, 125–31; "Metaphysics as Horizon," 116–17; *Method in Theology*, 20, 75; "On the Natural Desire to See God," 103; "Origins of Christian Realism, The," 113–14; positivism and, 105; on questioning, 103–4; science and, 100; on sin, 80; on theological method, 77–78; "theorem of the supernatural," 78–79; turn to the subject and, 72–73; *Verbum*, 81–85, 101, 111–12

Lonergan's Quest (Mathew), 110–11

Luther, Martin, 159

MacIntyre, Alasdair, 18, 68; traditions of rationality, 60, 119; on turn to the subject, 128–29

Mandonnet, Pierre, 21

Marcel, Gabriel, 23

Maréchal, Joseph, 37, 41–42; turn to the subject and, 19

Maritain, Jacques, 18

Mascall, Eric, 21n53

Mathew, William; *Lonergan's Quest*, 110–11

matter, 51–52

Mercier, Cardinal Désiré-Joseph, 37

metaphor and language, 169–70

metaphysical and transcendental critiques, 41–42

metaphysics: Aristotelian, 47–48; cognitional theory and, 92–93; creation and, 52; in Exodus, 70–71; *Fides et ratio* and, 23–27; knowledge and, 39–41; science and, 29, 31, 155–56; theology and, 163

"Metaphysics as Horizon" (Lonergan), 116–17

Methodical Realism (Gilson), 37

Method in Theology (Lonergan), 20, 75

Milbank, John, 11, 85, 162, 173; on natural sciences, 166–67; "Only Theology Can Overcome Metaphysics," 163; *Theology and Social Theory*, 28, 166–67

modernism, 17–18

Modern Schoolman, The, 84–85

Molina, Luis du, 77n11

Molinist school of Thomism, 77, 79–80

moral conversion, 114

multiverse, 153–54

mysticism and philosophy, 47, 166

mythology, 30

"narratives" of reason, 27–28

natural: meaning of term, 103

natural sciences, 166–67: human
    sciences and, 175
natural theology, 65–67, 156,
    160–61
nature, human. *See* human nature
Neoplatonism, 47; Thomas Aquinas
    and, 68–69
Neo-Thomism, 16–17, 23; Christian
    philosophy and, 21
"new atheism/atheists," 7, 29–30,
    106; faith, science, and, 150–57
Newman, John Henry, 91
Noel, Fr L., 37
"Notion of Christian Philosophy,
    The" (Gilson), 59
notions, 93
nouvelle théologie movement, 22n59

objectivity, 95–96, 116
object/subject split, 95
O'Connell, Matthew, 84–85
old atheism, 29n71
"One, the," 47
"one big equation," 154
"Only Theology Can Overcome
    Metaphysics" (Milbank), 163
On Reducing the Arts to Theology
    (Gilson), 168
"On the Natural Desire to See God"
    (Lonergan), 103
ontological argument (Anselm), 65
Origen, 5, 113
Origin of Species (Darwin), 153
"Origins of Christian Realism, The"
    (Lonergan), 113–14
outer/inner disjunction, 127–28,
    131

particle physics, 150–52
Pegis, Anton, 67–68

Pendio, M. T.-L., 82
periodic table, 174
person and nature, 4, 113–14
Philip the Chancellor (of Paris),
    11–12, 78
philosophy: analytical, 5n6; defini-
    tion, 5n6, 45–46; dogmatic
    teaching and, 113–14; founda-
    tion of, 37; history and, 45–56,
    122–24; knowledge and, 171;
    method in, 37; mysticism and,
    47, 166; process philosophy,
    52n87; the Reformers on, 31;
    revelation and, 25, 31, 53, 56–58,
    112, 160; science and, 167; theol-
    ogy and, 59–60, 63–64, 140–41;
    way of life, 5. *See also* Christian
    philosophy
physics, 150–52
Pius XII, Pope, 163n32
Plato, 47
Platonism: *logos* in, 4; Thomas
    Aquinas and, 14
Plotinus, 10n18
positivism, 31; Lonergan and, 105
precepts, transcendental, 101
processions, divine, 82–84
process philosophy, 52n87
proportionate being and transcen-
    dent being, 92–93, 96–98
propositions, 54, 132–33

questioning, 117; being and, 117;
    desire and, 103–4
quoad nos and *quoad se*, 106

Radical Orthodoxy, 23n62, 27–28,
    56n105, 161–71; Aquinas and, 28
Rahner, Karl, 19–20
rationalism, 22, 31, 59

rationality: revelation and, 114; traditions of, 119
Ratzinger, Joseph, 162. *See also* Benedict XVI, Pope
realism, 7, 55–56; being and, 45; Christian, 110–14, 173; critical, 38, 42; dogmatic, 38, 53, 116–17, 126; idealism and, 93; mediate, 39, 43
reality (the real), 94–95; God and, 104–5; intellectual conversion and, 94–96
reason, 6–7, 149; belief and, 148, 156–57; evil and, 175–76; God and, 3, 30, 160, 171; "narratives" of, 27–28; operation of, 7; religion, violence, and, 157–61; revelation and, 60; science and, 7; subordination of, 10–11; tradition and, 6. *See also* faith and reason
reasonableness, 6
reasoning and knowing, 26
Rees, Martin, 154–55
Reformers, the, 31
Regensburg Address (Benedict XVI), 30–32, 159–60
relationships and believing, 109–10
relativism, 24
religion: normative vs. lived, 158; reason and, 157–61; violence and, 147–49, 157–61
religious conversion, 114; violence and, 159–60
religious fundamentalism, 150
religious violence, 157–61
Rerum Novarum (Leo XIII), 15
retortion arguments, 92, 130
revelabilia, the, 63

revelation, 6, 13, 63–64; faith and, 9; philosophy and, 25, 31, 53, 56–58, 112, 160; rationality and, 114; reason and, 60; scope of, 62; truth and, 164–66
revelatum, the, 63
Romans, letter to the, 3, 114

science: being and, 155; contingency and, 152–54; faith and, 150–57; God and, 155–56; insight and, 135–39; intelligibility and, 152; judgment and, 135–39; Lonergan and, 100; metaphysics and, 155–56; new atheism and, 150–57; philosophy and, 167
scientific knowledge, 67n148, 139
scientific method, 53n90, 86–88; components, 151; essentialism and, 154–55; experience and, 152; faith and, 150, 156–57; judgment and, 152; limitations, 152; metaphysics and, 29, 31–32; reason and, 7; understanding and, 152
Scotus, Duns, 31n78, 48
secularism, 27–28, 56n105
self-knowledge, 76, 88–89, 95
senses, the, 55–56, 95, 117
Siger of Brabant, 48
sin, 99, 143; God and, 10, 79–80, 80; grace and, 162–63, 175; knowing and, 10; Lonergan on, 80; reason and, 3, 175–76
sociology, 28
soul, the, 82
Spirit, Holy, 82, 84, 112
Spirit in the World (Rahner), 19
Standard Model in particle physics, 151–52

Stoicism, 4
"string theory," 153n16
Suarez, Francisco, 48, 49, 120
subject, the, 82, 95. *See also* turn to
the subject
subjectivity, 51; *Fides et ratio* and,
25–26
subject/object split, 95
sublation, 89
subordinationism, 4
substance (*substantia*), 4; being and,
47–48, 52–53
"substantial forms," 155
Summa Contra Gentiles (Aquinas), 14
Summa Theologiae (Aquinas), 11, 12
"supernaturalizing the natural,"
162

Tanner, Kathryn, 80n23
Taylor, Charles, 29–30
Tertullian, 4, 113
theological method, 77–78
Theological Studies, 76, 82
theologism, 59, 162–63, 167–68, 174
theology: metaphysics and, 163;
method in, 77–78; natural,
65–67, 156, 160–61; orders of, 12;
philosophy and, 59–60, 63–64,
140–41; Trinitarian, 4
Theology and Social Theory (Milbank),
28, 166–67
"theorem of the supernatural"
(Lonergan), 78–79
"theory of everything," 154
Thomas Aquinas, 8, 61, 164–66;
Aeterni Patris and, 15–21; Aristotle and, 11–15, 52n88; Catholic
thought and, 26; Christian philosophy and, 15; *De Esse et Essentia*, 13–14; faith and reason in,

51; "five proofs" of, 98; Loner-
gan and, 107; metaphysics, 51;
Neoplatonism in, 68–69; Platon-
ism and, 14; Radical Orthodoxy
and, 28; *Summa Contra Gentiles*,
14; *Summa Theologiae*, 11, 12
Thomism: Augustinianism and, 174;
Cartesian Thomists, 38–41;
Dominican (Banezian) school,
77; *Fides et ratio* and, 27; historical, 17–19, 21–23; Jesuit (Molinist) school, 77; Kantian
Thomists, 41–42; Leuven
Thomists, 37–45. *See also* Neo-
Thomism; transcendental
Thomism
*Thomist Realism and the Critique of
Knowledge* (Gilson), 37, 116
thought, modes of, 23
Tracy, David, 89n59
tradition and reason, 6
transcendence, 79–80
transcendental and metaphysical
critiques, 41–42
transcendental knowledge, 96–99
transcendental precepts, 101
transcendental Thomism, 19–21, 23;
Christian philosophy and,
22–23; Gilson and, 20–21, 32;
movement, 37
transcendent being and proportionate being, 92–93, 96–98
Transforming Light (Liddy), 110–11
Trinitarian processions, 111–12
Trinitarian theology, 4; epistemology and, 111–12
truth: confidence in, 24; grace and,
12–13, 163–66; revelation and,
164–66

turn to the subject, 19, 25–26, 78, 107, 118, 128–30. *See also* interiority

understanding, 88–89, 91–92; being and, 160–61; descriptive vs. explanatory, 79; intellectual conversion and, 105; scientific method and, 152; understanding of, 86
"understanding seeking faith" (Lonergan), 100, 148
Unity of Philosophical Experience, The (Gilson), 45
Universe from Nothing, A (Krauss), 153

van Riet, Georges, 14
van Steenberghen, Fernand, 21

Vatican I: *Dei Filius*, 23; *Dogmatic Constitution on the Catholic Faith*, 63n134
Verbum (Lonergan), 81–85, 101, 111–12
Vico, Giambattista, 170–71
violence: faith and, 29–30; reason and, 157–61; religion and, 147–49, 157–61; religious conversion and, 159–60
von Balthasar, Hans Urs, 162
von Harnack, Adolf, 31

will and intellect, 30, 31n78
Williams, Hugh, 57
wisdom: divine, 5; faith and, 3; Jesus and, 3
Wolff, Christian, 50
word, inner, 83–84
Word, the: Logos and, 9; procession of, 82–84, 111–12